Gender, Globalization, and Postsocialism

Gender, Globalization, and Postsocialism

The Czech Republic After Communism

Jacqui True

COLUMBIA UNIVERSITY PRESS   NEW YORK

COLUMBIA UNIVERSITY PRESS
Publishers Since 1893
New York   Chichester, West Sussex
Copyright © 2003 Columbia University Press
All rights Reserved

Library of Congress Cataloging-in-Publication Data

True, Jacqui.
    Gender, globalization, and postsocialism : the Czech Republic after
        communism / Jacqui True.
        p. cm.
    Includes bibliographical references and index.
    ISBN 0–231–12714–6 (cl. : alk. paper) — ISBN 0–231–12715–4
        (pa. : alk. paper)
    1. Sex role — Czech Republic. 2. Man-woman relationships — Czech
    Republic. 3. Sexual division of labor — Czech Republic. 4. Women — Czech
    Republic — Social conditions. 5. Social structure — Czech Republic.
    6. Globalization. 7. Feminist economics. I. Title.

    HQ 1075.5.C94T78 2003
    305.3'094371 — dc21   2003043483

c 10 9 8 7 6 5 4 3 2 1
p 10 9 8 7 6 5 4 3 2 1

For my grandparents Joyce and Arthur

Contents

Preface

This book is a study of the linkages between globalization and gender dynamics in the postsocialist context. All books have a history; it goes without saying that this book would not have been conceivable without the changes that have taken place in Central and Eastern Europe in the 1990s. The idea for this book was planted in the summer of 1994 when I attended the New School for Social Research's Democracy and Diversity Institute in Krakow, Poland. My roommate at the Institute was a Czech, Petra Jedličková, who was working at that time in the Prague Gender Studies Center. Since it was not much more than a year after the separation of Czechoslovakia our room was filled practically every night with Czechs and Slovaks discussing their history and future. I became increasingly curious about Czechoslovakia and when Petra offered to show me around Prague I eagerly accepted the opportunity. No doubt like many New Zealanders who visit Prague, I was impressed by the visible presence of so much history in that city; the kind of "old-world" history that my own homeland lacks.

With the Czech Republic on my mind, the following year at Petra's invitation I returned to Prague to live for some months and immerse myself in Czech culture. The Republic's fast, uneven pace of change struck me as fascinating but also troubling. Everything seemed to be in flux and yet, as my friends reminded me, much remained the same. I recall being shocked by the juxtaposition of the old and the new at that time; by middle-aged women at the supermarket with plastic shopping bags depicting naked women astride motorcycles. I found it difficult, if not perplexing to interpret

Czech gender relations. When I entered the doctoral program in Political Science at York University in Canada in the fall of 1995 I already had a sense of what I wanted to study for my dissertation work.

Since then, there have been many people in the Czech Republic, Canada, and the United States who have taken an interest in this book project and who have facilitated my research and writing. I want to thank all of those who have been of assistance to me along the way, although I can only mention some here. First of all, I wish to express my gratitude to Petr Jedlická, Petra Jedličková, and Pavel Tychtl in whose homes I stayed during my successive research visits to Prague between 1995 and 1999. Their hospitality and generosity made my research possible; they also introduced me to Prague and to all things Czech. For this, I am greatly indebted. In the Czech Republic, I wish also to thank those Czechs who graciously agreed to talk with me about their work, their lives, and their country in transformation. Where possible, I have acknowledged these conversations as personal interviews but even where not cited, the Czechs I met, and their conceptualizations and experiences of living through the transition, have influenced my work.

At York University I wish to thank the Faculty of Graduate Studies for awarding me the President's Dissertation Scholarship and the Centre for International and Security Studies for their generous support of my research in the Czech Republic. I would especially like to thank Heather Chestnut and David Dewitt at the Centre for International and Security Studies, and the Graduate Programme in Political Science. For her intellectual example and encouragement with this book, I am grateful to Sandra Whitworth. My attempt to bridge critical international political economy and gender analysis has been inspired by Sandra's own synthetic work. My thinking has also been shaped by the work of Emeritus Professor Robert Cox of York University. Although I had no formal relationship with Professor Cox while at York, I have greatly benefited from his creative and critical approach to international relations in the seminars I attended at York and in ongoing interactions with him.

Scholars from universities other than York have also helped to influence my work. I want to thank especially Professor Andreas Pickel of Trent University for his careful reading of my manuscript, and his genuine openness to engaging with and learning from scholarly approaches other than his own. I want to thank to Alena Heitlinger, also of Trent University, for her help with my work as a Czech émigré and feminist scholar, and for including me in the Émigré Feminisms project in Canada. I am deeply indebted to the late H. Gordon Skilling, Emeritus Professor at the University of Toronto for passing on to me his impressive knowledge of Czech history and politics and to the members of East European studies seminar held in Professor Skilling's home, which I attended for several years between 1995 and 1998. From that group I would like to thank Marci Shore, in particular, for her intellectual insights and camaraderie both in Toronto and in Prague. For their helpful comments, I also want to thank those who attended seminars on my work at the Watson Institute for International Studies, Brown University, at Michigan State University, at the Maxwell School for Citizenship Studies at Syracuse University, Trent University(Ontario), and the University of Minnesota.

I began the revisions to this book in earnest while I was a post-doctoral fellow in the Center for International Studies at the University of Southern California in 2000–2001. During that time I greatly benefited from the intellectual guidance and encouragement of the Director, Ann Tickner, and her engagement with my work. Thanks to Ann, and to Brooke Ackerly (my fellow postdoctoral "fellow"), the Center was a wonderfully stimulating place to talk and write about gender and international relations. While in Los Angeles I was very fortunate to meet Jane Jaquette (Occidental College). I wish to thank her here for her close, thoughtful reading of my manuscript. It is a much better book for her excellent advice and input.

Finally, I wish to acknowledge my family. For the gift of education, I thank my parents. For their example, I thank my grandparents, to whom this book is dedicated. As third and fourth generation New Zealanders, they have shown me, like my friends in the Czech Republic, that it is possible to live a rich life in a small and relatively insignificant place. To my partner, Michael Mintrom, I am also grateful. He has always been supportive, believing in me and in this book. I have learnt a lot about scholarship, and about writing from Michael. Our conversations have inspired many of the arguments developed here and his careful editing of my work has helped me convey those arguments with greater clarity. Of course, despite these intellectual and personal debts, I take full responsibility for the work presented here.

Jacqui True
Auckland
January 2003

1   Gender, Globalization, and Postsocialism

In 1989 and 1990, all over Central and Eastern Europe communist regimes fell. The revolutions against communism raised the "Iron Curtain" and rolled out the carpet of liberty for the citizens of the former Soviet Bloc. From now on, it seemed, all roads would lead to the West rather than to Moscow. This story is a favorite with the western media and foreign policy establishment. It suggests the triumph of democracy and capitalism over a failed experiment. But how did people in the region influence and interpret these events? How far and in what ways have women and men's lives been shaped by processes of liberalization and globalization since 1989? Have they been agents or victims of these processes? Against the relief of their former socialist regimes, postsocialist countries present a telescoped view of the transformation of social relations in a period of rapid and unprecedented change.

For all their merits, the dominant scholarly approaches to postsocialist transformation do not shed much light on how people have *lived* the transitions from communism. Rather than changes in identities and everyday life, the focus has been on changes in institutions and political-economic settings. In particular, the macro-orientation of these approaches and their emphasis on economic and social aggregates lead them to ignore local complexity. Thus, we know little about how much things have changed and how much they have stayed the same for most people after communism.

Here, I develop a synthetic, gendered approach to understanding postsocialist transitions. The approach highlights how local people and organizations negotiate the global spread of capitalist markets and political democracy. It shows that people can be simultaneously empowered and exploited by the impact of global forces, and that what distinguishes one from the other can be fully understood and theorized only by scholars who are prepared to engage in the close study of local practices. In my view, the transitions in Central and Eastern Europe have involved transformations in masculine and feminine gender identities that have been accelerated by globalization and mediated by local norms. (Those local norms are themselves the result of past social and political practices.) Consequently, gender relations between men and women shape the way that global forces impact former socialist societies. But these global forces in turn, reshape gender relations.

To explore these matters, this book focuses on the case of the postsocialist Czech Republic. The study is motivated by two questions: First, how are changing gender relations shaping and being shaped by marketization and liberalization? And second, do these new forms of economic and cultural globalization open spaces for women's empowerment and feminist politics? The transition in the Czech Republic offers rich opportunities for exploring these questions. In the Czech case, the interplay between postsocialist transformations and global processes is not straightforward. Nor from a perspective attentive to gender are these processes wholly negative. Indeed, the transition from socialism to capitalism has provided spaces for the expression of new identities, including feminist identities. In their desire to "return to Europe" in 1989 and 1990, Czech citizens did not identify with an undifferentiated "West." Rather, they identified specifically with a set of western masculinities and femininities. Their selective adoption of these gendered identities has brought both new opportunities and forms of empowerment as well as widespread new inequalities and insecurities.

Mainstreaming Gender in International Relations

Beyond providing a deeper understanding of the gendered processes of postsocialist transformations, this book does two other things. First, it demonstrates the inextricability of gender and global transformations. Second, by analyzing gendered social relations in a specific historical, cultural, and global context it seeks both to advance a second-generation feminist perspective on international relations, and to contribute to the broader task of understanding globalization and its constitution.

Over the past decade or so feminist scholars have sought to challenge the conventional study of international relations. Initial efforts of this kind were undertaken so as to critique realist conceptions of international relations. But because this critique was developed primarily at the meta-theoretical level, the question remained open as to just what a feminist perspective on world politics would look like substantively, and how distinctive it would be from the perspectives that feminist scholars were opposing. Undoubtedly, previous efforts to establish a feminist approach to international relations have cleared space for new thinking. But too often that thinking has gone on at the margins of the discipline and, has not engaged the mainstream. Consequently, this important and path-breaking work has tended to be misunderstood or ignored by many who could benefit from its insights.[1]

Recently, a second generation of feminist international relations scholarship has emerged that seeks to build on earlier feminist theoretical contributions by studying aspects of global politics *as if* gender mattered. Scholars such as Sandra Whitworth (1994), Katherine Moon (1997) and Christine Chin (1999) have developed empirical cases where gender dynamics can be seen to be working simultaneously at local, national, and global levels and with important political consequences.[2] Clearly a need continues to exist for more of these studies of international relations and global political economy that empirically and theoretically integrate gender. This book is designed to make such a contribution. Here I address a central issue in contemporary international relations and international political economy — that is, the nature of the global integration process in Eastern Europe — doing so in a manner that pays close attention to gender dynamics. As such, I see this study as a contribution to a new wave of feminist international relations. One of the distinguishing features of this and other recent studies is a contextualized and empirically grounded exploration of *gender* relations and their interactions with processes of globalization.[3]

Czechoslovakia: The Path From Communism

In 1989 a nonviolent, "velvet" revolution removed the communist regime in Czechoslovakia. The estimated one million people who crowded Prague's Wenceslas Square in November of that year wanted to get rid of state socialism and everything associated with it. They called for "free elections" and proclaimed, "We are Europeans." Eager to quell their memories of the Soviet past, Czechs looked West. Yet twenty years earlier Czechs had believed in the prospect of their own unique version of socialism "with a human face" just as earlier still, at the end of the 1940s, they had thought liberation from poverty and fascism would come through a national socialist revolution. Before that, Czechs had struggled for independence from the shackles of the Austro-Hungarian Empire. They had high hopes for the Czechoslovak multinational democratic state established after World War I. These successive experiments in the Czech lands each came tantalizingly close to implementing ideals of freedom and equality for all citizens. But in each case they were violently crushed by foreign powers. Time and again, Czechs have made history but not on their own terms nor in conditions of their own choosing. In 1989, however, they thought things would be different. This was their chance for a truly emancipatory revolution.

Here, I provide a sketch of the various experiences Czechs have had of communism and democratization from the origin of Czechoslovakia in the interwar period to the federal state's breakup and the transition from communism in the 1990s. In a following section, I review the major scholarly approaches to postsocialist transformation and their interpretations of this history. That theoretical discussion serves to highlight the uniqueness of the gendered approach I take in the subsequent chapters of this book.

Fragile Democracy

The First Czechoslovak Democratic Republic was formed after World War One out of the ruins of the Austro-Hungarian Empire. At that time, Czechoslovakia was the tenth most industrialized country in the world. From its birth in 1918 through the interwar period it was unique in Central and Eastern Europe for retaining a democratic system. However, in 1938 Czechoslovakia's democracy and independence were sacrificed by the European powers in a peace treaty made with Hitler at Munich. In 1939 the Third Reich occupied Czechoslovakia. Bohemia and Moravia became a German Protectorate, Slovakia an independent state, and the *Sudety* region was incorporated into the Reich. Six years later, in 1945, the Soviet Red Army liberated most of Czechoslovakia. Following World War II, free elections were once again held in Czechoslovakia. After the experience of fascism, the reform program proffered by the Communist Party was widely popular and the party took close to 40 percent of the votes in elections held in 1946. In the democratic government, the communists gradually strengthened their hold on power. Pressured by the Soviets and the opposition parties, the Communist Party *legally* took power in February 1948, in what was effectively a "bloodless revolution" that ended the western-style system of multiparty democracy.

Socialist Revolution

Between 1948 and 1953 Czechoslovakia was transformed into a Stalinist-type totalitarian society. During the first five-year plan (*pětiletka*), private property was nationalized and national industry was reconstructed. This instituted a major social transformation in the class structure. Gender relations were also altered in the nationalization process as Czechoslovak women were integrated into the paid industrial labor force *en masse*. A new type of worker and a new type of man and woman were being molded. While communism adapted some of Henry Ford's approaches to mass industrialization and social engineering, the emphasis on bourgeois gender respectability and consumerism in the West ran contrary to developments in the postwar Soviet sphere. The socialist Eastern bloc, including Czechoslovakia, broke with the capitalist system and the past by radically nationalizing property and attempting to equalize the roles of men and woman in the labor force.

In the early 1950s a bloody purge of communist enemies, resembling that in the Soviet Union in the 1930s, was conducted both outside the Party and within its own ranks. Dr. Mílada Horáková, one of the most prominent Czech feminists in the interwar period[4] and chairperson of the Czechoslovak Women's Union after 1945, was among the first to be executed for treason in 1950 (Igger 1996; Shore 1998). The Women's Union that had become the women's section of the Communist Party after 1948 was abolished in 1952. Between 1952 and 1966, there was no Czechoslovak organization that directly represented the interests of women. With the nationalization of property, the regime assumed that the so-called "woman question" had been resolved, and a separate women's organization was considered to be bourgeois. Trade unions were thought to represent female as well as male workers, while "economically inactive" women (e.g. housewives, retirees) could participate in the local subcommittees of the Communist Party's national committee (Heitlinger 1978: 65–68).[5]

Czechoslovakia was one of the last of the communist "people's democracies" in Eastern Europe to react to Khrushchev's 1956 speech at the Twentieth Party Congress denouncing Stalinism. Although this speech, which marked the end of the "personality cult" and a gradual lessening of the Party's dictatorship role, sent shockwaves through Eastern Europe, the regime in Czechoslovakia remained relatively intransigent through the early 1960s.[6] De-Stalinization under the leadership of Antonín Novotný was largely internal to the Party and symbolic, consisting mainly of name changes. In the intellectual and cultural wings of the Party however, criticism of this rigid rule began to emerge. Moreover, the near collapse of the Czechoslovak economy in the third *pĕtiletka* (1961–65) prompted calls for policy changes. After an internal power struggle with conservatives at the Communist Party Congress in late 1967, Alexander Dubček, a reformer, became First Secretary in January 1968. The election of Dubček ushered in the beginning of a period of unprecedented democratization and liberalization that would become known as "the Prague Spring."

Socialism With a Human Face

The "Prague Spring" era saw the thawing of the Czechoslovak communist regime and the breakthrough of attempts at reforming the socialist system. The official program of reform during the Prague Spring, laid out in the *action program* passed by the Central Committee in April 1968,[7] drew on critical Marxist concepts and humanist reasoning first explored in the philosophical and cultural realms.[8] It incorporated reforms across political, economic, and cultural systems.

Beginning in January 1968, democratic procedures were introduced into the Communist Party, and new independent interest organizations were allowed to form. A proposal for a new mass women's organization that would increase women's participation in socialist political, economic, and cultural life had already been approved at the Thirteenth Party Congress in July 1967. But the political reforms in 1968 revived the independent Czechoslovak women's movement, which now began to challenge the gap between official declarations of women's *emancipation* and the reality of women's oppression by state policies. Autonomous of the Party structure, the Czechoslovak Women's Union became a member of the *National Front*, to which all non-Party groups were affiliated.[9] At its inception, the new political system was intended to facilitate the expression of public opinion and to draw upon the input of different societal groups and interests for the collective resolution of social and economic problems. However, the required unity of socialist society and the state prevented the formation of political parties and thus of multiparty democracy.

In the new economy, market coordination was introduced to inject more flexibility and consumer choice into the centralized system of planning. Designed by economist Ota Šik, the reform program mixed plan and market, seeking to rehabilitate only those positive features of the market for the benefit of society. For example, the price mechanism was used to shift the economy away from a model of extensive growth through heavy industry and ravenous use of resources toward one of intensive growth, generated by consumer-oriented light industries (Williams 1999: 22). In the cultural sphere, the censorship of the press was halted and an end was brought to all party interference in civic and cultural life. As a consequence, there was a spontaneous explosion of information and creativity unknown in any existing socialist regime. People used the independent media to criticize the glaring faults of the social system, to raise a whole range of new issues, and to express themselves artistically (see Šimečka 1984). Women's complaints about the unfulfilled promises of socialist emancipation were integral to this social ferment, and the Women's Union magazine *Vlasta*, which had wide circulation in the country at the time, doubled its length to accommodate reader's letters and concerns.

During the Prague Spring, Czechoslovak reformers and citizens self-consciously saw their country as a model for a "third way" marrying socialism and democracy (Skilling 1976: 849–50). Documents from that era reveal an outpouring of support for genuine pluralism and democratic evolution within the frame of socialism. Moscow saw these developments in Czechoslovakia as lurching inexorably toward the western sphere of liberal democracy. In contrast, American intelligence construed the developments as a series of power struggles inside the Czechoslovak Communist Party. Both assessments were wrong. To conclude otherwise would be to deny the experience of many men and women who believed they were building a system uniquely Czech (see Hruby 1980). But however we interpret the efforts by reform communists to give socialism "a human face," they were brutally ended in August 1968 by the Warsaw Pact invasion of Czechoslovakia.

Warsaw Pact Invasion

In the early hours of the 21st of August 1968, to the amazement and horror of Czechoslovak citizens, Soviet tanks rolled into Prague. Soviet Secretary Leonard Brezhnev ordered the Soviet move. There was no mass or armed resistance to the invasion, although there were many casualties. Ordinary people sought peacefully to convince the young Warsaw Pact soldiers of their misguidedness and to subvert the invasion effort by changing and removing signs (*all roads do not lead to Prague*). But their efforts did not succeed in expelling the foreign powers. First Secretary Dubček and his fellow reformers in the Central Committee of the Czechoslovak Communist Party were arrested and taken to the Ukraine. They eventually returned at the bequest of the President, General Ludvík Svoboda but were forced to gradually reverse the liberal reforms and agree to a Moscow-written accord. Among other things, the accord provided for the "temporary" stationing of Soviet troops on Czechoslovak soil.[10] Believing that he could make a compromise with the Soviets, Dubček sought to salvage some of the reforms by extracting voluntary concessions from the Czechoslovak population. During the Party Congress in December 1968 a debate took place between pro-Soviet conservatives and reformers. At this Congress, several members of the Central Committee of the Communist Party resigned. For now, a greatly chastised Dubček remained in power.

Soviet Normalization

The Soviet occupation instigated a policy of "normalization" to restore the communist regime to its status prior to 1968 (Šimečka 1984). In April 1969, Gustav Husák replaced Dubček as First Secretary.[11] After Dubček was removed, the pressure from the Soviets and Brezhnev's supporters inside the Czechoslovak government to repudiate the Prague Spring reforms greatly increased.[12] Starting in September 1969, autonomous organizations were brought back under the command and control of the Communist Party. Expulsions from the Party were vigorous and systematic, involving all levels from local committees upwards.[13] Much of Czech culture was stifled by the reinstitution of a highly repressive censorship system, while the intellectual sphere was purged of thoughtful and critical minds. The newly installed regime dismissed or demoted those writers, artists, social scientists, journalists, reform communists and humanists it considered to be responsible for the liberalization. The entire normalization process removed an estimated half a million people from official structures. Hundreds of thousands of people emigrated from Czechoslovakia. In the post-invasion society, the playwright Václav Havel (1991: 73) wrote, "all activity was so completely organized and so completely deadened." So it was, until the founding of *Charta 77*.

Charta 77 and Human Rights Resistance

With the suppression of the Prague Spring, the stark realization emerged that the reform of communism was no longer an option. The repression of the 1970s caused most people to withdraw from public life. But dark days once more gave rise to an alternative political discourse, this time outside of the Communist Party within the Czech cultural underground, in unofficial clandestine publishing (*samizdat*) and various independent civic initiatives (Skilling 1989). In 1977, after several years of enduring one of the most rigid, sterile, and stagnant types of communism, a loose association of dissident citizens concerned with ethical life and respect for human rights and united in their opposition to the state, founded *Charta 77*. The group was named after its manifesto; a series of documents signed initially by 242 people, dated January 1, 1977.

The men and women who signed the Charter and became its members expressed their opposition to communism through creative actions. For example, they made use of international human rights norms to call attention to the regime's illegitimacy. Taking the Husák government at its word, they demanded that it practice the fundamental human rights which it had proclaimed to the international community by ratifying the 1975 Helsinki agreement.[14] In this way, the dissidents carried on the *praxis* philosophy associated with the Prague Spring, defending "concrete human beings in the here and now" rather than "abstract political visions of the future" (Havel 1991: 148). But whereas the reformers in 1968 had sought to bring state and society closer together, the members of *Charta 77* formed a parallel society to oppose the Party state and its domination. Imprisoned for his activism between 1979–1982, Havel was one of the key leaders and theoretician's of the movement. His essays, most notably, "The Power of the Powerless," articulated the Chartists' philosophy. For Havel and his peers, the primary goal was to address and mobilize the hidden spheres of civil society rather than confront the regime on the level of actual power. Whether it wanted to or not, they maintained, the power structure would have to react to the "pressure created by free thought, alternative values and behaviors, and by independent self-realization" (Havel 1991: 198).

Velvet Revolution

In the spring of 1987, the Soviet communist leader Mikhail Gorbachev visited Prague. Asked about his wide-ranging reforms in the Soviet Union, he told his Czechoslovak audience that the only difference between *perestroika* and the Prague Spring was twenty years. Just two years later, in November 1989, Czechoslovakia had its Velvet Revolution that brought down the communist regime. Soviet *perestroika* and *glasnost* undoubtedly helped facilitate this negotiated change of regime in Czechoslovakia and across Central and Eastern Europe. Any internal enemies of these changes, this time, had little support abroad. For his part, Gorbachev did not seem likely to intervene to defend communist regimes, as Brezhnev had threatened to do in Poland in 1981, and had done in Czechoslovakia in 1968.[15]

It did not take much to topple the Czechoslovak communist regime; a reflection of its powerlessness in the end. Prague students set the events in motion when they marched on Wenceslas Square on November 17, 1989 to commemorate the Czech student killed by Nazis during World War II. The students marching in 1989 were brutally suppressed by security police. When other Czechs learned of this police action, they rallied to support the students. Inspired by earlier events in Poland and Hungary, *Charta 77* and other Czech dissidents rapidly formed a coalition — *Občanské Fórum* — a Civic Forum that assumed leadership of the revolution. In Slovakia, the Public Against Violence was formed to coordinate the opposition. In the Magic Lantern Theatre in Prague, the Forum drafted a program and set of demands to take to the government, foremost of them being the end of the dictatorship of the Communist Party, and the return to Europe — that is, to the normal stable conditions of a western European democracy (Garton-Ash 1990). A wave of protests occurred across the country opposing the communist government and supporting the Forum. A two-hour general strike was called, enough time to show the majority of workers' support for the revolution without jeopardizing the economy. People in the streets chanted, "Long Live the Forum" and "Havel to the Castle." Václav Havel was indeed at the center of things. He was the charismatic leader able to cement the various groups and factions within the Forum, and the major strategist vis à vis "the powers that be" (Garton-Ash 1990: 89–90).

With thousands of Czechs calling for their resignation in Wenceslas Square, the communists were forced to negotiate with the Civic Forum. They finally acceded to the Forum's demands. An interim government was formed on December 10, 1989 composed of Civic Forum Members and reformist members of the former communist government. Dubček was elected Chairman of the Federal Assembly on December 28, and the following day Václav Havel was elected the new President of Czechoslovakia by the Assembly. Six months later, in free elections under the slogan "Return to Europe," the Civic Forum became the first postsocialist democratic government in Czechoslovakia. The Forum won by a landslide. Many former dissidents chose to enter the government, but women dissidents were notable for their absence. Most of them chose instead to continue the pre-1989 work of building civil society outside of official politics and institutions.

Transition to Capitalist Democracy

Czechoslovakia, which had little previous experience with market reform within a planning context,was in a situation different from that in Hungary and Yugoslavia in 1989. Czechoslovakia also differed from Poland, in that it had not experienced the mobilization of a sizeable, self-regulating civil society. In 1989 Czechoslovakia had the greatest proportion of capital-goods exports to the West, and did not suffer either from high inflation or a foreign debt crisis as did its Central European neighbors. Given these propitious starting conditions for economic reform, the Czechoslovak government viewed itself as exceptional among postsocialist countries. It also had a cadre of energetic and competent reformers (Šiklová 1990), whose political organization and persuasive arguments won public support for radical reform. For these Czechoslovak reformers, getting the market rules right was seen as the fount from which all other transformations would occur. Social policy and domestic structural change were designed to support the imperative of macroeconomic adjustment (Potůček 1993). In this postsocialist context, questions of equality — for instance between the new rich and poor, or between men and women — were discredited and could only be addressed in the language of capitalism and freedom.

In December 1989 the Czechoslovak currency was devalued against a basket of convertible currencies. By May 1990, one month before free elections, the Civic Forum had agreed to institute an anti-inflationary economic program of financial stabilization, price liberalization, and privatization.

This restructuring program was launched in January 1991. The program looked much like that successfully adopted in other parts of the world, such as Latin America, and it was strongly supported by western governments and international institutions, most importantly the Group of Seven, World Bank and the International Monetary Fund (Kirk Laux 2000).[16]

But there was more to the Czech transition from communism than macroeconomic adjustment (Orenstein 2001). Between 1990 and 1992 a package of social policies was crafted to cushion the worst consequences of the liberalization of the economy and to ensure public support for reform. During these first years of transition the state played a key role in the design and delivery of social welfare measures that included short-term compensation payments, a guaranteed "living minimum" wage, and the maintenance of universal housing subsidies, as well as health and welfare benefits. A new labor market policy also aimed to reduce the workforce by offering incentives for women and older workers to leave, and to keep unemployment low by instituting a wage freeze. These policies reversed the socialist commitment to full employment, social equality, and emancipation through labor.

Such a mixed approach to reform, combining neoliberal macroeconomic policies with compensatory social policies was a political compromise brokered between former dissidents with social liberal values (many of whom had been reform communists in 1968) and those radical neoliberal reformers (typically economists) who participated in the Civic Forum government. However, this compromise came under increasing strain. The Forum was split between those advocates of radical market reform who wanted to form a western-style neoliberal political party, and those preferring gradual "social market" reform who wanted to keep the diverse, movement-type Forum. Economist Václav Klaus and his entrepreneurial cohort struck out on their own to form a right of center political party, the Civic Democratic Party (ODS).

As in other transitions to democracy, the new social movement that brought about the change of regime in Czechoslovakia was displaced in the second democratic elections in mid-1992 by savvy, organized political parties.[17] Klaus and the ODS proved themselves adept at electoral politics, severely defeating the Forum and its former dissident leaders. The consolidation of liberal democracy, and the elimination of quotas that accompanied it, saw a dramatic fall in women's share of parliamentary seats and the virtual male dominance of the executive branch of government. The Czechoslovak Velvet Revolution, which was in many respects a popular revolution — of civil society against the state — had become a revolution led by economists and other experts (Klaus 1991a).

Following the election of the coalition government led by the Civic Democratic Party (ODS) in 1992, Czechoslovakia began carrying out the most extensive privatization program in Central and Eastern Europe. It was the first country to attempt this denationalization through the popular method of voucher (share) sales to citizens (Young 1998). In addition, the Restitution Act returned property including residences and small and medium business enterprises that were nationalized in or after 1948 to their former Czech and Slovak owners. Nine percent of state property was privatized in this way. The service sector boomed as a result.[18] Initially, the public strongly supported privatization and after an extensive marketing campaign 80 percent of Czechs and Slovaks bought vouchers to directly participate in privatization. As well as positive incentives, Klaus and his ODS-led government used negative sanctions to ensure the political success of their reform program. They manipulated the anticommunist sentiments to neutralize any political opposition to privatization and economic restructuring (see Holý 1996). This anti-communist rhetoric effectively disabled many individuals and groups from participating in the political process, most importantly labor unions, former dissidents, and women.

Czechoslovak Divorce

By 1992 the national consensus behind market reform had begun to fracture. Slovak political elites led by the Slovak Premier Vladimír Mečiar, argued that the fast-paced liberalization and privatization was a Czech invention, designed and implemented by Czechs in Prague, effectively privileging the Czech Republic (Appel and Gould 2000). Mečiar and other Slovak politicians advocated a different reform path, one that preserved Slovak economic sovereignty, and was oriented toward the goal of a social market economy. The emergence of this alternative reform program supported by an explicitly nationalist ideology in Slovakia threatened to derail Klaus's neoliberal reform program. As Daniel Bůtorá (1998: 73) has noted, "the Slovak vision of a slower, 'softer' method allegedly stood in the way of [Czech] . . . reforms" (also Elster et al 1997: 278–82). This conflict between two different concepts of reform came to a head in 1992 and brought about a major turning point in the Czechoslovak transition from communism. The

Czech élite gave an ultimatum to the Slovak élite; either accept joint economic reform and a joint currency or leave the federation. This ultimatum gave Slovakia the political momentum to secede once Klaus and Mečiar came to a suitable agreement. The peaceful separation of Czechoslovakia allowed Slovak nationalists to pursue their own path of reform. Indeed, once independent in 1993, the Czech Republic proceeded with the second round of voucher privatization and asset sales while Slovakia put off the round, finally canceling it in 1994.

Disillusionment

In the first few years of transition the Czech government was hailed as a showcase for its neoliberal reform program. At that time it had retained a state social safety net. However, in 1994 the government began to address budget deficits by introducing austerity measures and reforming social policy along neoliberal lines favored by the World Bank and the IMF (Potůček and Radičová 1997). This shift in policy lost the Klaus government crucial public support. Klaus only narrowly prevailed in the mid-1996 national election. Things got much worse in 1997. A slew of bank failures and publicity scandals about the Civic Democratic party's finances and government's corruption precipitated a balance of payments and currency crisis (Orenstein 1998: 48). This resulted in the forced devaluation of the Czech currency. Klaus was forced to resign as Prime Minister and President Havel appointed a nine-month, expert caretaker government that was replaced in the mid-1998 national elections by the Social Democratic party (CSSD) (see Saxonberg 1999).

By the end of 1997, Czech confidence in the economic transition had dropped to an all time low. The Central and Eastern Eurobarometer reported the most dramatic decline in public support for the creation of a market economy since the first survey of 1,000 households in 1990.[19] Austerity measures failed to contain unemployment, which reached eight percent in 1998. The budget deficit increased. The privatization program did not have its intended effects. In fact, privatization produced corruption, asset-stripping, and "get rich quick" deals, reminiscent of the practice of "stealing from the state" in communist times. The most viable assets and firms had been "tunneled" out by aggressive investment funds in alliance with state banks and insider-informants, leaving only industrial liabilities and low-value stock in the hands of Czech shareholders.[20] One in seven Czechs are estimated to have lost their contributions to investment funds as a result ("Bohemia's Fading Rhapsody" 1997). The upshot of this crude market behavior is that structural reforms were postponed in the Czech Republic and a large, prosperous middle class failed to crystallize (Vrba 1997; Hellman 1998).

The Social Democrats promised a shift in policy that would put greater emphasis on the social welfare of people. Under their proposals, the state would play a stronger role in overseeing economic restructuring and regulating the marketplace. But they entered into an "opposition agreement" with the remnants of Klaus's ODS in the fall of 1998. The main effect of this agreement was to cause Czechs to lose much of their faith in their democratic institutions. In 2001 25 percent of Czechs thought the communist system was better than the current system, and 21 percent were of the opinion that there was no difference between the two systems.[21] Moreover, public support for regional integration was also consistently under or at 50 percent in the late 1990s as the Czech Republic prepared to join the European Union.

Between 1999 and 2001, two demonstrations took place rivaling in size the demonstrations that precipitated the Velvet Revolution in November 1989. In December 1999 tens of thousands of Czechs filled the main squares of more than twenty cities. Chanting the same pro-democratic slogans as in 1989, they protested against the opposition agreement and demanded the removal of the Prime Minister, Miloš Zeman, and the leader of the opposition, Klaus. The demonstrators argued that the indifference of these politicians to the interests of ordinary people was responsible for the economic and political crisis in the country. Citizens called for the renewal of civic values and democracy.[22] The second major public protest regarding democratic rights occurred one year later, in December 2000. This time a crowd of allegedly one million gathered to support the strike of journalists at Czech Television over the politically-motivated parliamentary appointment of Jiří Hodač, a close associate of the ODS party, as Director.[23] In this protest, as in the previous one, people demanded that their freedom of speech and the independence of the press be upheld. They called for greater democratic accountability of elected officials. In both events, many Czech citizens expressed their dissatisfaction with their decade-long economic transition and demanded meaningful democratic representation.

Interpreting Postsocialist Transformations in a Global Context

How can we understand the historical events and transformations that have taken place in what we now call the Czech Republic? Specifically, how do we make sense of the breathtaking Czechoslovak exit from communism and the subsequent political and economic transitions that have given rise to radical reforms in the contemporary Czech Republic? In a speech to the United States Congress in 1990 Václav Havel, then President of post-communist Czechoslovakia, remarked: "We playwrights, who have to cram a whole human life or an entire historical era into a two hour play, can scarcely understand this rapidity [of change] ourselves. And if it gives us trouble, think of the trouble it must give political scientists, who have less experience with the realm of the improbable." Indeed, there is a wide range of scholarly interpretations of the changing domestic and international politics since 1989. Conventional accounts of political and economic transformations in Eastern and Central Europe however, have relied either on neoliberal theories or institutionalist and neo-Marxist theories. Broadly speaking, neoliberal accounts have emphasized the freedom that comes with global liberalization and marketization. Meanwhile, alternative accounts have been much more pessimistic about the local implications of radical reform. I find both sorts of account inadequate and in this book I will show why that is. But first let us review these interpretations of postsocialist transformations.

Neoliberalism

Neoliberals are the most optimistic and enthusiastic advocates of free trade and integrated global markets. To them, the expansion of markets and democracy promotes greater efficiency and prosperity in Eastern and Central Europe, as well as political freedom and security. There are two faces of neoliberalism as seen in the region; the economic and the political. Economic neoliberalism focuses on the market fundamentals that need to be put in place to transform state socialist systems, and further integrate them with the global economy. The political variant of neoliberalism is concerned with the development of civil society and liberal values, which support the establishment of market capitalism in postsocialist Europe. Whether they argue that private property and the capitalist "free" market are preconditions for our democratic freedoms or vice versa, neoliberals hold that capitalism and democracy should go together.[24]

Economic neoliberals attribute the collapse of socialist regimes in Eastern Europe to the failings of planned economies. After 1989, in report after report proponents argued that the falling rate of productivity, foreign indebtedness, inflationary pressures, and the poor quality of goods and services gave no alternative to the rapid adoption of a market system. No sooner had the walls come down than radical reform programs were designed for making the transition to a market economy. In 1990, Václav Klaus's carefully crafted radical reform program for the Czechoslovak economy won out over Valtr Komárek's, gradualist approach.[25] Klaus became the real translator of neoliberal prescriptions in the Czech postsocialist context, writing his own guide to market reform like Friedrich Von Hayek and Milton Friedman before him.[26]

Neoliberal economists have consistently argued that speed and sequencing of adoption are the key to the success of these reforms in Eastern and Central Europe.[27] This is the line Klaus took in 1990. According to their prescriptions, market reformers take over the state and implement the reform program (see Murrell 1995). Meanwhile, they keep anti-reform opposition at bay and maintain popular legitimacy for reform. This much happened in the Czechoslovak transition. Foreign capital is then assumed to flow in and the "emerging market" economy is progressively integrated into the world market. Gradually social and economic living standards are predicted to improve for the majority of the population and a "middle class" is expected to emerge to sustain the reforms. In a second stage of transition, the framework for the market economy is completed by institutional reforms in the legal and banking systems and in the social security system. Market capitalism is now successfully established. From this perspective, the transformation from communism is fundamentally over once macroeconomic adjustment is achieved — as indicated by designated inflation and debt levels, GDP growth, and degrees of liberalization and privatization.[28] According to the World Bank, a new order takes root where:

> [Q]ueuing gives way to markets, the shortage economy gives way to an economy of vast choice. . . . Property rights are formally established and distributed and large amounts of wealth cease to be state-owned and controlled. Old institutions and organizations evolve, or are replaced, requiring new skills and attitudes. And the relationship be-

tween citizens and the state changes fundamentally with greater freedom of choice (World Bank 1996: 4).

On this account and that of Prime Minister Klaus (1997), the transformation was over in the Czech Republic by 1994.

If economic neoliberals focus singularly on abstract market mechanisms, then political neoliberals point to the central role played by civil society in the collapse of authoritarian regimes and the transition to capitalist democracy. Originally devised to extricate East European societies from excessive collectivism, the "open society" approach to postsocialist transformation considers liberal *societies* to be the prior condition for democratizing formerly authoritarian states.[29] In this view, civil society provides the moral and societal foundations for market and democratic institutions by aggregating societal interests, communicating values, ideas, and information, and providing crucial social services. Contrary to macroeconomic reform, civic democratic reform is conceived as a "bottom-up" grassroots effort. To hasten the revival of civil societies in Eastern and Central Europe, western assistance is funneled to local partner organizations outside the state, the leading parties, and the bureaucracy.

In the Czech Republic, the Soros Foundation and the emergence of more than 4,000 other nonprofit organizations have led this effort to democratize society "from below" ("Odpovědi Na Otázky . . ." 1997). Open Society Institutes, founded by Hungarian émigré financier and philanthropist George Soros, support the political and economic reeducation of citizens[30] as well as independent, social welfare initiatives.[31] Such initiatives seek to empower a "third sector," voluntary society to deliver public services, thus compensating for the limits of the marketplace while reducing the need for state social protection mechanisms. In sum, the political dimension of neoliberalism facilitates the absorption of postsocialist countries into a western market system, albeit with a little nudging from the visible hand of western-supported civil society (cf. Ignatieff 1995).

Contemporary Marxism

Karl Marx saw capitalism as the driving force of history. But he also warned of the divisions that capitalism's spread would bring and of how it could wreak havoc with the social order. Contemporary Marxists extend this analysis to explain the collapse of socialist regimes and the social and economic upheaval wrought by the expansion of market capitalism in Eastern and Central Europe.[32] In their judgment, postsocialist transitions have intensified the power of capital across the region and have left a situation of incomplete and ambiguous transformation. Socioeconomic "class" inequalities have been created at a pace unmatched in world history (UNDP 1999: 39). For instance, the Czech Republic once a fairly egalitarian society, saw income inequality increase exponentially in the transition from communism.[33] Growing unemployment and poverty resulting from market reforms have ensured that, surrounding the conspicuous winners, there are many silent losers in postsocialism.

I wish to highlight two forms of contemporary Marxism. The first, the world capitalist approach, offers primarily an economic explanation for communism's demise.[34] According to proponents of this perspective, socialist economies could not compete with or even play "catch up" with capitalist flexible specialization or with the global circulation of finance capital (Verdery 1996: 30–37). Moreover, those economies were dependent on western capital and trade to solve their internal structural problems. Thus, both local élites and western political and economic élites had shared interests in opening socialist states to the world economy. From the world capitalist perspective, these class forces have been driving the transitions since 1990.[35]

The second form of contemporary Marxism I wish to discuss is the neo-Gramscian approach, which draws on the political writings of Italian communist, Antonio Gramsci. This approach stresses the importance of culture and ideas in spreading capitalism around the world.[36] According to proponents of the neo-Gramscian view, capitalism expands where it has possibilities and untapped resources to do so. It takes advantage of the territorial fragmentation of the world economy, and of a whole range of existing social divisions and differences. These divisions and differences include gender, race, ethnicity, and so on, as well as class (Cox 1996: 23). Thus, neo-Gramscians analyze the consensual social interests as well as the coercive power behind capitalist hegemony within and across states and civil societies.[37] They focus on the state's moral leadership and the power of the ideas and identities that support capitalist social relations.[38]

Seen from a neo-Gramscian perspective, the Eastern and Central European revolutions against communism were prefigured by the dissemination, through clandestine transnational networks, of liberal ideologies and cultural norms.[39] These ideologies and norms have played a part in the transitions to capitalism as well. Their "common sense" appeal facilitates social consensus and masks the arbitrariness of the state's power, and the socioeconomic inequalities it is founded on (see Hanley 1999). For example, in the Czech transition, a combination of state strategies and private capitalist ideologies can be seen as contributing to the relatively broad consensus among different social groups for market reform between 1990 and 1994. They include the state's promotion of voucher privatization programs that appeared to give everyone an equal stake in capitalism (Appel 2000), the élite "civil society" ethic opposing state intervention, and the new globalized media's encouragement of consumerist lifestyles as symbolic of Czechs' membership in the European middle classes. However, in most postsocialist countries capitalism and democracy have been imported without the consent or participation of the majority. In those states, and in the Czech Republic after 1994, the emergent middle class did not have an adequate social basis for establishing hegemony (see Eyal et al. 1999). As a result, neo-Gramscians note that authoritarian politics have prevailed in Russia and other parts of the former Soviet Union, while political instability has been the norm in Central European countries such as the Czech Republic. Without sufficient domestic capital or social consensus, capitalist democracy has had to be forged from above, often with outside help and pressure.

Institutionalism

As a perspective, institutionalism is noted for its appreciation of the historical and social dimensions of systemic change. Less invested in grand theory than neoliberals or neo-Marxists, institutionalists offer contextually based explanations and draw upon a broad range of social science tools for understanding multilayered social, economic, cultural and political transformations.[40] For institutionalists, postsocialist societies are not a *tabula rasa*. Czechoslovakia's "embrace of defeat" after 1989, for example, was highly conditioned by its socialist past. The slow evolution of institutions, even in periods of radical change, renders them "path-dependent" on prior regulative, normative and cognitive institutions, for instance socialist production networks, the traditional family, and deeper set attitudes toward gender relations (Rona-Tas 1998; Bunce 1999).[41]

According to proponents of the institutionalist perspective, the new institutional frameworks in Eastern and Central Europe build on already existing socialist networks and practices.[42] Postsocialist states have responded to globalization in distinctive ways depending on their specific paths of institutional evolution, national and financial organization, industrial relations and so on.[43] However, reforms are filtered through these preexisting, embedded socialist institutions in ways that are not well understood and that often have unintended, negative outcomes. As a consequence, institutionalist scholars are critical not merely of the *direction* of systemic change, toward greater liberalization and social disembedding of the economy, but moreover, of the *pace* of change and its implications for the successful adjustment of different social groups.[44] For instance, in the Czech transition, radical reformers did not carefully consider the impact of market reforms on particular social groups and communities. It is now widely accepted that the rapid pace of privatization provided loopholes and opportunities for élite groups to feather their own nests by stripping the assets of former state-owned enterprises, at the expense of ordinary Czechs whose savings and future prospects were destroyed in the process (Mlčoch 1996; 1998).

As well as observing unintended consequences, institutionalists stress the importance of a society's accumulated social learning over time. According to sociological institutionalists, this learning is giving rise to new and hybrid institutional forms in Eastern and Central Europe, distinct from both western market and former socialist systems.[45] They maintain that global competition will produce further institutional and policy divergence rather than convergence among states. Future prosperity and social cohesion in postsocialist countries like the Czech Republic will therefore depend upon the local adaptation of state capacity, managerial networks, the social capital generated by the family, and other socialist survival mechanisms to a liberal global order (Poznanski 1999b; 2000).

The new institutionalism has emerged as an important corrective not only to the neoliberal orthodoxy but also to all who privilege global over local sources of continuity and change. After a decade of reforms, embracing global markets has not brought Czech women and men the fundamental democratic rights and freedoms promised by the language of capitalism and freedom. In the Czech Republic today, people no longer call for "capitalism without adjectives." Instead, giving credence to their socialist experience, Czechs now call for something closer to "capitalism with a human face."[46]

Institutionalist approaches represent an improvement upon neoliberalism and some variants of contemporary Marxism when it comes to guiding policy change. However, from the perspective of scholarship, institutionalist approaches merely underscore the dichotomy between the market and the state, the local and the global. Historically and socially embedded national state institutions are thought to *respond to* external market pressures and *resist* neoliberal — one size fits all — policies. But, viewed in this way, postsocialist states are seen as merely adapting to, rather than shaping or transforming, the globalization process itself. Local agency is given short shrift in this institutionalist telling of transition and its consequences.

Feminism

Seen from a feminist perspective, *gender* relations are as important as *class* and *ethnicity* for understanding postsocialist transformations. Gender, like ethnicity, became a fault-line of competition and means of distinguishing winners and losers in the restructuring of former socialist political economies, where class was initially less salient as a form of social differentiation (Watson 1993; 1997). As institutionalists might predict, the backlash against socialist states' official policy of women's emancipation after 1989 resulted in notions of men and women's equality being shunned in most Eastern and Central European states, and the differences between them being played up everywhere. However, feminist scholars attribute the significance of gender in postsocialist transitions to the introduction of capitalist social relations as well as to these institutional socialist legacies (see Gal and Kligman 2000).

The transitions from communism have been hailed in the region *as a return to what is natural*: to Europe, to private property, and to hierarchy between the sexes.[47] In this hospitable context, all the oppressive features of masculinist culture have been thrown into relief: unequal pay, employment discrimination, sexual harassment at work, sexist advertising, domestic violence, rape and sexual abuse, the feminization of poverty, lack of reproductive choice, lack of publicly-funded childcare and so on. Most of these forms of women's oppression existed during socialism, but were politically invisible; some of them have emerged only with the opening to the West and have been virtually unsanctioned.

Many feminist scholars have argued that women in Eastern and Central Europe have borne a disproportionate burden of the economic transition.[48] Women workers have been made redundant or become unemployed through privatization and restructuring at far greater rates than men in nearly all the countries in the region, including the Czech Republic. The socialist state's support of women as workers and mothers has been replaced by a new set of class identities based on an individualist male norm. Women have lost many of their previous social and economic rights as a result (Einhorn 1993: 67–68). According to feminist accounts, Central and Eastern European democracies are immersed in a "cult of domesticity," where women were encouraged to withdraw from the labor force after 1989, into the private world of the household and the family.[49] In addition, the backlash against socialism and the new capitalism have promoted the sexual objectification of women and given support to new dominant western — and *aspiring* western — masculinities in the marketplace.[50]

Western expatriate men in the region frequently talk about Eastern and Central European "emerging markets" as *sexy*; they are the adventure playgrounds for male managers, investors, and professional risk-takers.[51] (*Playboy* describes Prague, for example, as a "great multinational orgy of buying and selling") (Friedman 1993). The capitalist push eastward allows these men to claim "virgin territory," and to reassert their western hegemonic masculine identity vis-à-vis the "wild, wild East."[52] Meanwhile, Eastern and Central European men have sought to prove themselves (as "real men") to western élites by maintaining the image of committed reformers, reliable debtors, and potential members of Europe (Borocz 1999). After the "emasculating" experience of socialism, they have reasserted their masculinity through their power over women in newly defined, gender divisions of public and private. In the Czech case, the virtually all-male alliance between communist dissidents and neoliberal economists to restore capitalism was based in part on their common gender interest in extricating the economy from politics, and establishing an ethical, public sphere separate from the family and private life.

Czech (male) political élites have uncritically accepted western expertise and models. In contrast, feminists point out, Czech women's groups have resisted the wholesale adoption of western feminist ideas and struggles (see Šiklová 1997; Vodrážka 1994). This reticence reflects the determination among women leaders in Czech civil society to defend their unique subjectivities and moderate western influences in the process of globalization (see Šiklová 1998c). However, just as East-West business cooperation forges global integration and has been instrumental in ensuring the free entry and appropriate investment climate for transnational capital, East-West feminist co-operation has liberated public space for women in the region, offering an important inroad for global civil society in Eastern Europe (see Penn

1998). Paradoxically though, because these women's networks are often critical of the gendered power differentials (within postcommunist societies as well as between East and West), they are frequently received as a form of cultural imperialism *imported* from the West rather than a revival of indigenous Czech feminisms in the interwar First Republic or during the Prague Spring (Šiklová 1993). Yet, at the same time, western foreign investment, business practices, American constitutional expertise, and the onslaught of wealthy tourists from around the world are not seen as "cultural imperialism."

Neoliberal, neo-Marxist, and institutionalist approaches have typically overlooked the gender-differentiated experiences of postsocialist change. With the exception of institutionalism, these conventional scholarly approaches derive their analyses from investigations of formal political and economic institutions in the public sphere and in the realm of production identified with and dominated by men.[53] Neglecting the cultural reaction against socialist equality and "western feminism," and the gender dynamics in the family-household and consumer economies, which are part of the domain of political economy, among other things, they cannot fully comprehend the processes of structural change and the impact of globalization in postsocialist countries. As feminist scholars have shown, one of the main ways states have restructured is by cutting public expenditures and shifting the costs of social reproduction to families and households and, by implication, to women.[54] As in other countries, restructuring in the Czech Republic has involved "a struggle over the appropriate boundaries of the public and the private and the constitution of gendered subjects within these spheres" (Brodie 1994: 52).

Yet, feminists predict women's victimization by postsocialist states and global markets. They frequently view globalization only in terms of its regressive effects; as a dominating set of processes that will almost certainly reduce women's social and economic power relative to men and shrink the public space available for them to exercise their democratic rights. They have focused almost exclusively on women as the *losers* in postsocialist transitions and on the *negative* impact of these transitions. In so doing, feminist scholars have created the category of the victimized "Eastern European woman," not dissimilar to the "Third World woman" that Chandra Mohanty (1991) has located and criticized in western feminist scholarship (Jung 1994). They have overlooked women's agency and the aspect of local negotiation in globalization. Like some contemporary Marxists, feminists have overestimated the power of global structures — patriarchy and capitalism — at the expense of observing local actors and uncovering emancipatory potentials.

Engendering Post-Socialist Transformations

The argument thus far can be summarized as follows: each of the four perspectives I have discussed is inadequate for understanding the dynamic interplay between local practices and global forces in the postsocialist context. Both neoliberals and contemporary Marxists see global economic forces in the "drivers seat" of Eastern and Central European transitions, although they differ diametrically on the consequences of those forces. Both perspectives miss the local "responses," which create a much more dialectical process of transformation, one that can only be understood through looking at micro as well as macro processes of change and continuity. I argue that a focus on gender relations between men and women provides a vantage point from which to analyze these micro-macro linkages in political economy, culture, and civil society. A gendered perspective on the postsocialist transitions reveals new sites of power and sources of change at the interstices of local and global structures. In so doing, it overcomes some of the shortcomings of neoliberal, neo-Marxist, and institutionalist perspectives in theorizing the local processes inherent in global change.

In this study the particular is used to inform the general, and to illuminate the mutual relationship between postsocialist transformations and globalizing processes. Neo-Gramscian theory's focus on the bottom-up processes of change in civil society and their relationship to broader transformations provides an entry point for this study. Institutionalist approaches are also helpful insofar as they recognize that prior conditions do affect transition politics and the impact of globalization on societies. Thus, my analysis of the Czech transition combines aspects of neo-Gramscian, institutionalist and feminist theories. I use the concept of gender in three ways. 1) As a set of ideological representations and cultural practices that have become part of "common sense." 2) As an integral aspect of the social relations of inequality that condition material life. 3) As constitutive of political identity through the separation of the public and the private and the activities of production and reproduction.[55] Here, gender is conceived not merely as an ideological "superstructure," but as part of the material "base." Indeed, I view historically specific, *common sense* ideas about male and female human nature as being encoded in social practices. In turn, these encodings shape state and civil society, and the forces of production and reproduction in transitions to "capitalist democracy."

To examine the gendered processes of globalization in the Czech transition, this book looks closely at four sites of transformation. First, it explores the "crisis of social reproduction" and changing definition of the family as a result of reforms shaped by a global public policy agenda. Second, it analyzes how gender dynamics are shaping the emergence of a privatized labor market linked to a global division of labor. Third, it investigates changing gender identities in the expansion of a globalized consumer market. Fourth, it observes the stark gendering of formal and informal politics in the Czech Republic, noting in particular the dichotomy of men's dominance of formal democratic processes and women's empowerment in civil society, supported by transnational non-state actors. Integrated with these investigations, the book presents three puzzles with respect to the Czech Republic's transformations and shifting gender relations in the wake of state socialism and in the context of global integration.

The first puzzle relates to the construction of gender identities and differences during socialism and in the postsocialist aftermath. In socialist Czechoslovakia, although women's equality was official policy, gender was not a visible category of political identity or one to which men and women consciously subscribed (Scott 1974). The state's claim to have achieved the goal of equality and its repression of any political organizing not based on class closed off the possibilities for expressing gender identities and constructing common gender interests based on them. However, since the 1989 revolution, and the liberalization it set in motion, equality is no longer official policy in the Czech Republic. Ironically, in postsocialism, gender differences have become both more salient in the structures of political economy and more visible in everyday life.

The second puzzle of gender in transition has to do with the mixed impact of globalization on women in particular. For instance, in the aftermath of socialism, new norms of gender relations, ostensibly exports from the West, are *enabling* the extension of global markets and the commodification of human labor and human sexuality. Sexual objectification in multinational marketing, and the transnational sex market in women, are having exploitative effects in the Czech Republic. Yet, at the same time, the opening to western debates about gender relations and identities is having positive effects in the Czech context. New global norms, culture, and media are serving to *empower* women as individuals and citizens.

The third puzzle concerns men's presence in formal politics and women's participation in civil society. While many observers of the Czech transition have noted the drastic decline in women's political representation, and the consequent male dominance of politics, few have also noted the activities of women in civic organizations and other grassroots groups that have mushroomed in the period since 1989. Women may be absent to an extent from "politics" but they have certainly not been absent from the nascent Czech "civil society." Thus, while the Czech transformation can be seen to have closed off the few institutional channels for women's political representation that arguably existed under socialism, it has also opened new possibilities for women to participate in the emancipation of civil society within the Czech Republic and globally.

These puzzles suggest that women are both agents and victims in the Czech transformation from communism. But this book does not take the collective identity of "woman" for granted. Rather, it traces the paradoxical nature of female and male agency in the wake of the 1989 Velvet Revolution.[56] As we will see, processes of globalization and localization not only *affect* gender relations, they *construct* new gender identities and differences. The postsocialist transitions in the Czech Republic thus present rich opportunities for *engendering* our understanding of global and local change.

2   Gendering State Socialism

To closely explore how gender relations are both shaping, and in turn being shaped by, democratic and capitalist transformations in the postsocialist context we must have an understanding of the patterns of gender relations prior to 1989. A number of key questions need to be addressed: In what ways were gender identities, symbols, and divisions integral to the socialist state? How specifically did gender identities and differences structure the socialist political economy and ideological order? What has been the legacy of socialist "equality" and "emancipation"? How might we expect the preexisting socialist gender regime of Czechoslovakia to influence the regional and global integration of the Czech Republic?

By offering an overview of the specific Czechoslovak experience of state socialism, this chapter provides a benchmark for assessing how far and in what ways previous socialist gender relations and their attendant contradictions influenced the liberalization and democratization processes after 1989. Such a benchmark is critical if we are to fairly interpret contemporary developments, as I seek to do in subsequent chapters. Despite their repudiation of socialism, Czech actions and mentalities since 1989 have essentially continued aspects of the socialist period. The various experiences Czechs had during forty years of socialism have shaped both their expectations of capitalism and their engagement with the West.

The chapter contains two main parts. The first part examines the "gender regime" of existing socialism,[1] highlighting the inextricability of the organization of gender relations from the Czechoslovak planned economy (i.e.

the organization of production, consumption, and social reproduction). The second part of the chapter focuses in detail on the creeping democratization of Czechoslovakia in the late 1960s.

The attempt at reforming "socialism with a human face" during the 1968 Prague Spring was accompanied by the rise of a women's movement, which challenged the gap between the rhetoric and the reality of *emancipation* for women. However, these democratic developments were interrupted by the Soviet invasion and occupation of Czechoslovakia. In the latter part of the chapter I draw some contrasts between the Prague Spring and the Velvet Revolution in Czechoslovakia from the perspective of gender. For one, the political discourses in 1968 and 1989, while sharing dissatisfaction with their existing socialist regime(s), were radically different in other respects. Contrary to the ideas of "gender democracy" in 1966–68 that sought to make good on socialist ideals of women's equality and political participation, the transitions after 1989 popularized socially conservative ideas about appropriate gender roles among women and men, and sought to rescind many of the policies associated with women's equality.

In sum, I argue that real socialism shaped *gender* as well as *class* relations and that efforts to rethink and reform, and ultimately to overthrow, socialism both implicitly and explicitly took account of its gender dimensions. But while gender relations have changed alongside changes in the relations of production — with the mass integration of women into the labor force after 1948, and the transition to capitalism after 1989 — the foundation of a male-dominated hierarchy was preserved by the state, economic policy, and traditional practices in the family.

The Gender Regime of Czechoslovak Socialism

As in other East Bloc countries, socialism in Czechoslovakia was adapted from the Soviet, Marxist model. This model was founded on a "gender regime" that feminists argue serves to reproduce both the labor supply (i.e., concrete individuals) and the prevailing symbolic order, be it socialist or capitalist. Ilona Ostner and Jane Lewis (1995: 161) describe a gender regime as consisting of varying labor market structures, social policies, historical divisions of production and reproduction as well as differences in cultural norms and discursive practices concerning gender roles. This regime derives in part from the success with which various groups of men and women are able to articulate their interests and hegemonize their claims in any given state and society (Pringle and Watson 1992: 63). After 1948, Czechoslovakia's gender regime shaped and was shaped by both official communist ideology and policy, and by preexisting (pre-communist) gender divisions and cultural norms.

Official ideology held that the basic liberation of woman had been achieved by the victory of the socialist revolution. Legislative action guaranteed women equal rights in economic, political, and family spheres, and integrated them into the industrial labor force. But as the Czechoslovak sociologist Libuše Haková (1965: 76) noted in 1965, among government and party "eyes were closed to conflicting practice which offered a much less ideal picture." In reality, prior existing gender relations determined the distribution and division of production and consumption activities, as well as the responsibility for the social reproduction of labor. For instance, men and women's labor in the sphere of production was often allocated less with reference to levels of education, skill, or ability than according to traditional notions of gender difference. In the 1970s and 1980s a number of western scholars produced insightful studies that revealed this failure of state socialist governments to live up to their rhetoric of women's equality and emancipation.[2]

In what follows I argue that, contrary to the official ideology, Czechoslovakia's gender regime was not based on the equalization of men and women's roles. Rather, the gender regime that emerged under socialism was based on unofficial, embedded gender divisions that effectively homogenized women's lives and distinguished them from men's. To take just one indicator of this homogeneity among women, by the 1970s virtually all Czechoslovak women in their mid-twenties were married with a child and working full time (Havelková 1997; Fialová, Horská and Kučera 1995).

Labor and Production

State socialist regimes in postwar Eastern Europe claimed to have solved what Marx and Engels termed "the woman question." Engels' and Marx's, *Origins of the Family, Private Property and the State* (1884), attributed the cause of women's oppression to their confinement to a primitive mode of subsistence production within the bourgeois "private sphere." To allow women to realize their full human potential, Engels with Marx proposed

complete legal, economic, and political gender equality and the full incor-
poration of women within the advanced industrial mode of production. Following Engels, one of the first tasks of the new socialist regimes in postwar
Eastern Europe was to legislate principles of women's equal rights. As feminists have argued, socialism was always a *gendered* as well as a *class* project.

The legal changes prompted by state socialism prepared the ground for
assimilating all women into the laboring class (see Lampland 1990). In
Czechoslovakia women already constituted more than 30 percent of the
labor force in the 1930s, but the state socialist transformation integrated
them *en masse* into the labor force (Teichova 1988). In 1948 women made
up 36 percent of the total work force, by 1967 they were 46 percent — close
to half — of the workforce. Like men, women were required to be full-time
workers and guaranteed employment by the state. This opened the possibility
for all women to work and for many more women to complete higher education — something that women's movements throughout the western world
have struggled to achieve for more than a century. After 1948, as many
Czechoslovak women as men completed higher education. In the 1980s,
women in East Bloc countries were much more likely to be highly skilled
professional, specialist, and technical workers than women in western countries. In Czechoslovakia 25 percent of those in advanced technical education
were women whereas in the OECD countries on average only 12 percent
of advanced technical students were female (Heinen 1990: 44).

Between 1949 and 1953 the Czechoslovak communist government progressively changed the class and the industrial structure of the economy,
"giving marked priority to the expansion of capital-intensive sectors and
above all to coal-mining, metallurgy and engineering;" all consistently male-
dominated occupations (Heitlinger 1979: 137–38). Within *Comecon* (the
Council for Mutual Economic Assistance among the East bloc states) the
more highly developed Czechoslovak economy was to supply the newer
industrializing countries with capital goods and infrastructure. By 1968
only 15 percent of Czechoslovak capital stock dated from before 1948,
which gives an indication of the radical shift from light manufacturing to
heavy industrial production that occurred in the Stalinist years (Williams
1997: 21).

The socialist priority on heavy industrial production served to restructure
gender as well as class relations. Production for consumption and for human
needs, traditionally the province of women (e.g., convenience food, household appliances, clothing, housing construction, and the service sector) was

subordinated to commodity production for *Comecon* and industrial development.[3] Within the class of workers, the gender division of labor was startling. Women were generally located in the consumer-oriented, light industries, such as textiles, glass, and food processing, and in the health, education,
and social-service sectors, while men dominated the raw material industrial
sectors seen as most crucial to building socialism. Blue-collar men doing
manual work received superior wages to white-collar, better-educated women
doing work associated with care, social services, or administration.[4] But even
where unskilled women and men were working in the same firm they were
generally assigned different tasks in different areas, which thus became gender-
differentiated.

On the shop floor, the making and remaking of the socialist gender regime could also be seen. Because of scarce supply, goods and services for
production were procured through the hierarchies of the male-dominated
and led Communist Party. The organization of the workplace around supply
constraints and bargaining among party superiors and subordinates (e.g.
managers, bureaucrats, clerks, and customs officers) politicized the workplace, effectively creating two classes, "workers" and "party exploiters."[5]
These two groups were defined by *gender* as much as by *class*.

Women were typically excluded from the managerial and bureaucratic
networks of communist "party exploiters," which were equivalent to "old
boys clubs." Among the group of "exploited workers" they often found ways
to circumvent party plans and propaganda in their daily labor. Male and
female workers purposively ritualized practices of non-work and low productivity, adapting to the lack of incentives to be productive or efficient
under planning with the attitude summed up by the idiom (made famous
by Polish workers), "we pretend to work and you pretend to pay us." But
women workers made special efforts to socialize their workplaces, "making
them more like homes."[6] They sought to infuse the public, state-controlled
space with elements from the private, thus subverting the realm of production with the activities and symbols of social reproduction. For example,
during working hours women and some men could often be found queuing
for food, talking on the office telephone, visiting friends, and in some cases
"moonlighting" or organizing citizen initiatives with the use of state plant
and machinery.

The legacy of these socialist habits and dispositions can be seen in workplaces today; for example, in managers' offices where televisions and stereos
are frequently present and in government employees' practice of wearing

slippers at work. Institutionalists argue that these norms inherited from the socialist period shape the work ethic and thus economic productivity in Eastern European countries today as they make the transition to capitalism.

Consumption and Everyday Life

The state, through the planned economy, was also implicated in the perpetuation of gendered divisions and inequalities in the sphere of consumption. Successive governments in Czechoslovakia failed to incorporate many consumption-related economic activities into their five-year plans, or to prioritize reform of the consumer sphere. As Slavenka Drakulic (1993: 18) has written: "Every mother in Bulgaria can point to where communism failed; from the failures of the planned economy (and the consequent lack of food, milk) to the lack of apartments, child care facilities, clothes, disposable diapers or toilet paper. The banality of everyday life is where it really failed, rather than on the level of ideology."

The Czechoslovak regime took advantage of the gender-based division of labor in the family to provide key consumer goods and services and make up the gap in state production. But as one Czechoslovak woman author put it: "Shopping is women's domain, and as soon as something is laid down as women's domain, it is not advantageous" (Márová 1968: 4–5). The lack of a functioning socialist consumer economy had a particularly negative impact on women. Demand was limited in socialist states by the material allocation system: one could have money in the bank, but the bulk of goods, especially consumer goods, were effectively rationed (Nove 1991). Planners and party ideologists, moreover, viewed the "category of consumer demand" with suspicion because it was impossible to dictate and difficult to manipulate (Earle, et al. 1994: 4). Incomes thus tended to rise at a far greater speed than did supply under the system of planning (Nove 1991: 76–78; Kornai 1992). Between 1948 and 1971, for example, Czechoslovakia's Gross National Product (GNP) continued to gradually increase while the percentage share of personal consumption decreased markedly. Personal consumption registered a smaller proportion of GNP in 1971 than during the interwar period, 1919–39 (Mieczkowski 1975). However, while these statistics convey a relative decline in consumption, they hide the reality that women were supplementing family consumption through their unpaid work in the informal economy. Women were the ones who had to spend unpaid work time providing or procuring goods and services for their families to consume. As a consequence, they usually had less leisure time than men and were not rewarded for their management of consumption because it was not considered "productive" work or officially counted as part of GNP. When asked in a 1984 survey how employed women's situation could be improved, 88 percent of 2,200 respondents put a premium on "better distribution of consumer goods, a larger number of stores, shopping without waiting lines and greater availability of convenience foods" (Šolcová 1984).

During the 1970s and 1980s, crises in the Czechoslovak consumer market became increasingly evident in everyday life. The hard-line communist regime installed by the Soviet Union after the Warsaw Pact invasion in 1968 tried to placate citizens, especially women citizens, through *consumerism*. Because possibilities of exercising influence in an outward direction — in the public sphere — no longer existed, people diverted more of their energy in the direction of the least resistance, that is, into the private sphere. As Václav Havel wrote in a letter to Gustav Husák, First Secretary of the Communist Party in 1975:

> By nailing a whole man's attention to the floor of his mere consumer interest, it is hoped to render him incapable of appreciating the ever-increasing degree of his spiritual, political and moral degradation. Reducing him into a simple vessel for the ideals of primitive consumer society is intended to turn him into pliable material for complex manipulation. . . . People today are preoccupied far more with themselves, their families and their homes. It is there they find rest, there they can forget the world's folly and can freely exercise their creative talents. They fill their homes with all kinds of appliances and pretty things, they try to improve their accommodations, they try to make life pleasant for themselves, building cottages looking after their cars, taking more interest in food and clothing and domestic comfort. In short, they turn their main attention to the material aspects of their private lives." (Havel 1991: 58–59; see also Borocz 1999)

Indeed, the Czechoslovak government made available new consumer gadgets and household appliances while it promised vacations and the private ownership of a second home in the countryside to virtually all families. This "socialist consumerism" was often financed through western loans, increasing Czechoslovakia's technological, trade and financial dependency on the West as well as the Soviet Union. Despite these efforts to promote consumerism, the quantity and quality of goods produced in Czechoslovakia steadily declined relative to western European countries in the 1970s and 1980s (Havlík 1983). To deal with the shortage of consumer goods, in 1984 the Husák regime launched a plan entitled "one percent to the consumer market." It was designed "to compel large industrial enterprises to produce some shortage commodities in addition to their normal output." This policy however, failed. By 1986, "shortages became worse and consumer goods were being imported with increasing frequency from China, Yugoslavia, Egypt, and even South Korea" (Earle et al 1994: 9–11).

Contrary to the state socialist policy of emancipating women through collective labor, the existing socialist gender regime actually increased the prestige of private consumerism and the power of women within the family-household given its association with consumption and personal happiness. The embrace of western products after the Velvet Revolution in 1989 was therefore not new, nor just a product of global capitalism. Rather, this rampant consumerism was a continuation of the institutional legacies of Czechoslovak real socialism.

Social Reproduction

Following the socialist transformation, in 1950 the Czechoslovak law on the family legislated equality between men and women in all legal aspects of family relations. Similar laws were not instituted in western countries until the 1970s (and only recently in countries such as Brazil) (Wagnerová 1999). According to this law the authority over children was delegated from the state to parents, and men and women were given equal responsibility and authority within the family. However, with the gradual thawing of the Stalinist system in the early 1960s, the Czechoslovak communist regime's treatment of social reproduction came under scrutiny for the first time since 1948. Concerns about demographics, childcare, and family life were discussed as "woman questions." "Employed mothers," "incomplete families" (read: single parents), and "mother's holidays" (read: maternity leave) were singled out for Party political debate.[7]

In 1963 there was a public discussion of research by Czechoslovak psychologists and pediatricians, which provided evidence that infants in twenty-four hour state-run nurseries were not given sufficient attention and care to stimulate their normal development.[8] Later, between October 1966 and February 1967, a public debate about the effectiveness of women's employment was conducted on the pages of *Rudé Právo* (the major Party daily). In this debate, summarized by Heitlinger (1979), conflicting opinions were expressed about the "overemployment" of women, the feminization of whole sectors of the economy, the denigration of housework, and lack of quality childcare. Experts and readers placed the blame for the economic recession either on "the system" or on women.

The *Rudé Právo* debate was actually provoked by a letter from a woman living in a Bohemian village titled, "What have you got against us." She wrote:

> At the present time an employed woman is almost afraid to read the newspapers or listen to the radio or TV. It's not her life that's at stake but her peace of mind. . . . The employed woman is the cause of current economic difficulties, rising divorce rates etc., at work, she is insufficiently productive, and she does not show enough care or concern for her home and family. (Heitlinger 1979: 163)

Rudé Právo published dozens of reader's responses to this letter, some of which rejected existing policy by calling for a "family wage," and construing high female employment as the cause of economic problems, and others which strongly supported socialist equality, women's right to work and to economic independence. The debate was concluded by an editorial interview with the State Planning Commission, under the title "No new policy." *Rudé Právo* reiterated socialist ideology and policy by reinforcing state commitments to women's employment, promising increases in nurseries and kindergartens. They also countered economists' opinions about female "surplus labor" by pointing out that inefficiencies in state enterprises and planning involved all workers (Heitlinger 1979: 165). The state planners did not discuss any initiatives to socialize housework, or to improve the availability of consumer goods and services, nor did they dispute the idea that the work of social reproduction was an exclusively female function. However, planners did respond to concerns about population decline in the 1960s.

Czechoslovakia had achieved virtually full female employment by 1960. But this employment, combined with rising female educational attainment and continued shortages of consumer goods and housing, had the unintended consequence of decreasing fertility. After a decade of a declining birth rate there was widespread fear among Czechoslovak planners that the population would shrink, potentially jeopardizing future labor supply and socialist modernization. Responding to this fear, the state became actively involved in regulating and controlling women's reproductive capacity (Heitlinger (1979: 177–90). At the Twelfth and Thirteenth Party Congresses in 1962 and 1965 respectively, new pro-natalist policies were devised to encourage women to reproduce, while maintaining their "primary" contributions in the labor force.

Called "motherhood incentives," paid and unpaid maternity leaves were continually extended throughout the 1960s, as were generous family allowances and maternity allowances.[9] These incentives were also accompanied by disincentives, such as an increasingly restrictive and fee-paying service for abortions. Taken together, these government policies appeared to have their desired effect. Reaching an all-time low in 1968, the birth rate steadily rose after 1970.[10] One of the highest birth rates in Europe was recorded in Czechoslovakia in 1975 (on average 2.5 children per woman). Indeed, demographers estimate that the state incentives encouraged 200,000 more births during the 1970s (Možný and Rabušic 1999: 96).

But these socialist policies seriously undermined socialist commitments to equality. Employers responded to the motherhood incentives by effectively treating women's labor as less "efficient" than men's, and through the 1970s and 1980s this discrimination was reflected in the persistent gaps between men and women's remuneration and employment positions. Many women responded to government policy and employer perceptions by focusing more of their efforts on their family and household activities than on their state employment. The two income, two child family household became the norm in the 1970s (Fialová, Horská and Kučera 1995; Lhoska 1995). At that time, Czechoslovakia had the highest marriage rate in all of Europe, while the average age at which women married and had their first child was the youngest among European countries (20 to 22 years compared with approximately 26–27 years in West Germany and over 30 in Sweden for example) (Kuchařová 1996).

Herein lies a paradox central to understanding socialism as it actually existed in Czechoslovakia: the more the socialist state sought to address social reproduction by controlling population growth and ameliorating women's workload, the more it bolstered the family against the state and reinforced old, unequal, gender divisions of labor.[11] Czechoslovaks' withdrawal from public life once the oppressive climate of Soviet normalization had set in was "substantially buttressed [by] advantageous [state] material benefits and maternity leave" (Možný and Rabušic 1999: 96). Consumer and family roles often took precedence over production and paid laboring ones. Czechoslovak citizens resisted the intrusion of ideology and politics into their private lives at home. At work, they treated bosses and comrades as they would family members or friends, celebrating their birthdays as well as international worker's day together.[12] This valorization of "the private," raised the symbolic status of feminine domesticity, while the communist failure to adequately socialize reproduction, including childcare and house-work, concentrated more "executive" power within the family and in the hands of women. Pro-natalist state policies essentially guaranteed women's primary role in the private realm rather than in the socialist labor force, and reinforced traditional, bourgeois notions of gender difference within the fam-ily and in society at large (Wagnerová 1996: 106; Einhorn 1993). According to sociological surveys carried out just after the Velvet Revolution, "in the overwhelming majority of Czechoslovak households all usual chores were done by women, including caring for children" (Křížková 1999: 205).

Contrary to outward indicators of their strength, Ivo Možný (1991) argues that the family, trust among individuals and the work ethic were all begin-ning to break down in 1980s Czechoslovakia (cf. Tarkowski and Tarkowski 1991). The "family insurance" that generally worked during the 1970s, sub-stituting for the failing, paternalistic, state as a crucial source of economic redistribution and social reproduction, "was able to offer neither economic independence nor care in dignity near the end of one's life" (Možný 1994: 62). With the benefit of hindsight, Možný claims that tensions in the family "substantially contributed to the feeling that it was no longer possible to maintain the socialist social system" and added to "the economic and moral crises that led to the communist system's collapse" (1994: 62).

Summary

The political economy of state socialism was shaped by a gender regime, which often contradicted official communist ideology and centralized plan-ning. This regime emerged as an adaptation to government ideology and policy that did not take account of everyday social reproduction, and that placed priority on heavy industrial production over consumption and human needs. The Czechoslovak state did not acknowledge this actually existing gender regime, especially its economic reliance on women's double burden of labor. As a result, less visible but greater gender inequalities than in some capitalist countries developed under socialism (for instance, in work time and remuneration). Ironically, the policies of the socialist state reinforced the gendered distinction between public and private, and the liberal valorization of the individual family over the collective (Lampland 1995: 5), while officially denouncing them.

Experimentation with Democracy: The Prague Spring

In some socialist states, beginning in the 1960s, market forms of coordination were gradually introduced to address supply-side problems in the planned economy. Hungary, for instance, allowed a "second economy" governed by pseudo-market principles to emerge alongside and as a supplement to the state-run economy. But this creeping marketization in the Hungarian economy only reinforced its unequal gender regime (see Burawoy 1999; Goven 1993). Czechoslovakia, however, was unique among the Central Eastern European countries in introducing liberal reforms to encourage wider political participation.

As discussed in chapter 1, the "Prague Spring" period of unprecedented democratic reform of Czechoslovak socialism began in January with the election of Alexander Dubček to the post of First Secretary of the Communist Party. The new political system radically redefined the role of the Communist Party in state and society. Rather than dictating to society, the party would actively seek its consensus and participation in decisionmaking. To achieve that goal, power had to be redistributed and decentralized. As Kosík wrote in support of these reforms, "socialist democracy is either an all-inclusive democracy or it is not democracy at all." (Kosík 1995 [1968]; Oxley 1973). As part of the democratic reforms, new independent interest organizations were allowed to form to facilitate the expression of public opinion. These reforms gave rise to an autonomous women's movement. This new movement contested the existing socialist gender regime wherein women were exploited as double-shift workers and devalued *as women*.

The Flourishing of a Feminist Movement

It was during the Prague Spring and in its climate of democratic social and political change in 1967–1969 that an independent women's movement was first established in communist Czechoslovakia. This nascent movement developed a new de facto feminist discourse that challenged the gap between the theory and the practice of emancipation in state socialist policy. However, unlike western liberal feminism, especially the American type, the new women's movement viewed the state as a potential ally in women's advancement and did not identify individual men as a barrier to the goal of women's empowerment. In this respect, it drew on earlier legacies and feminist experiences with democracy in the interwar First Republic and in the Czechoslovak Communist Party prior to the state socialist transformation (Feinberg 1999; Garver 1985). Notably, the new women's movement did not see itself as a continuation of the short-lived women's section of the Communist Party active between 1948 and 1952.

State socialist ideology sought to promote gender equality in all aspects of collective life. Yet, the unfulfilled promises of this official ideology were particularly stark with respect to women's position and everyday lives relative to men's. Furthermore, women's political representation was a reality only in official numbers and not in actual political influence or decisionmaking. This was as true in Czechoslovakia as it was in other socialist bloc countries since independent associations and political organizations were for the most part disallowed. In 1965–1966, however, a group of women from the Central Committee of the Czechoslovak Communist Party and the trade unions put forward a proposal at the Thirteenth Party Congress for a new mass women's organization that would increase women's participation in socialist political, economic and cultural life (Scott 1974: 112–3: Heitlinger 1979: 68–69). The Congress agreed to the proposal and in July 1967, the Czechoslovak Union of Women (*Československý Socialistický Svaz Žen*, herein ČSSŽ) was founded.

The new women's organization, which was led by Helena Leflerová and a newly elected Central Committee, incorporated a vast countrywide network of local branches and town committees. Officially autonomous of the party structure (unlike the previous women's auxiliary), it became a member of the *National Front*, to which all non-party groups were affiliated. ČSSŽ was unique with respect to its legitimate role in publicly expressing opinions on social and political issues from the perspective of women's interests. But ČSSŽ could only influence policy through the existing bureaucratic state structure, responsive mainly to the Party from above, and it was not given any power of its own to implement policy.

Once the Prague Spring had begun in January 1968, frustrations mounted within the membership toward the leadership of the one-year-old women's organization. Drawn mostly from the upper ranks of the Communist Party, the Central Committee of the Czechoslovak Women's Union advocated Party policy rather than a women's agenda. At their April plenary session, the committee, which included the President, Helena Leflerová, was forced to resign.[13] A new committee and President, Miluše Fischerová, replaced them. Many of the new committee members had been involved in the interwar feminist movement and were intellectually active and practically engaged in building a new women's movement. After their election, the newly formed Central Committee of ČSSŽ spent the remainder of the plenary meeting deliberating over the future of the women's movement.

They laid out their new perspective in a letter to the government. The letter took issue with the democratization process for not addressing women's complex and difficult situation as a major society-wide problem to discuss and to act upon ("Nové perspectivy . . ."1968; Heitlinger 1979: 70). Having made a number of points about the failures of socialism in the context of women's rights as citizens, including the lack of quality consumer and childcare services for the many women workers and the relegation of women to subordinate roles in both the socialist workforce and the government, the Women's Union's letter sought a role for the women's movement as an equal partner in decisionmaking about the future of Czechoslovakia's democracy, through formal consultations with government. It served to usher in the women's movement as a force to be reckoned with, and not to be ignored by Communist leaders and society at large.

At the same plenary in April 1968, the new Central Committee of the women's movement prepared an *action program* explicitly articulating the ways in which the women's organization would go about defending and advocating women's demands and interests. In drafting this program the committee expressed a sense of urgency that in the interests of women the political opportunity opened by the democratic reforms must not be wasted. They alerted their members to a number of questions and problems relating to the difficulties of employed women and families, including childcare, the poor working conditions of rural women, the discrepancy between women's earnings and their qualifications, the conditions for and extensions of paid maternity leave, the time-consuming nature of public services in the consumer sphere, and the role of women in state institutions and social organizations. The *action program* set out to show that meaningful equality had not been achieved by the official state socialist transformation. While it is true, the committee argued, that "socialism in our country gave women the same citizen rights as men, by eliminating from our law regulations which discriminated against women and limited their opportunity for equal rights in the family, in employment, and in public life . . . the long journey from statements of principles to their practical realization is difficult, and sometimes not within sight" ("Nesmíme promarnit příležítost . . ." 1968). The program, however, did not criticize the socially-constructed gender relations between men and women that limited this practical realization of equal rights.

Adopted at the next plenary meeting in June, the final action program of the Czechoslovak Women's Union consisted of seven separate platforms, the most explicitly *feminist* being the last. This platform concerned itself with the development of a grassroots consciousness among its members and the strengthening of the role of the Women's Union in democratic politics and policymaking. Excerpts from the program were published in the official Communist Party women's magazine, *Vlasta*, and stated that:

> Through the medium of its organization women must have a direct influence on state policy, its formation and realization . . . [The ČSSŽ] puts forward proposals to parliament, government and other, accountable organs from the central to the local ones, and demands their realization. It participates in the formation of laws connected with the position and problems of women, families and children. And the condition for the Czechoslovak Union of Women to carry such weight in our political system is the fostering of voluntary membership and activities by the largest possible number of women of all ages, professions, positions and opinions. (Československý Svaz Žen má svuj . . ." 1968)

While the Central Committee of the Women's Union publicly expressed the need for one organization of sufficient power to be able to represent and defend the interests of women, its members were serious about making their new organization one in which as many women as possible could participate. In an open appeal, the leadership invited women of all political parties and those without party affiliation, of both Czech and Slovak nations and all creeds, to help fulfill the purpose of the new women's organization:

> We have decided to turn to you, all Czechoslovak women to discuss with us your situation in society. Give us your opinions, experiences

and capabilities to solve the difficulties which women face. . . . We welcome the democratization process, which our whole country is experiencing. It gives us the chance to objectively examine problems, which weigh heavy on us, and contribute to their resolution ("Otevřený list . . ." 1968).

Many women from around the country responded positively to this invitation from the new women's organization. "We need your organization," they wrote. "It is not sufficient to enact the equality of women, it is necessary to create the conditions in which it will be able to exist." "In today's times more than anything else, women need their own organization, but it must be on equal standing with other political organizations, one which women would not be able to lean against, but that would allow them to express their real demands, advancing them, until women in society have the same prospects as the rest of its members" ("Názory, Diskuse, Uvahy . . ." 1968). Once individual membership of ČSSŽ was allowed and Communist Party collective membership was abolished in June 1968, the membership of the organization grew rapidly. Six months later, at the beginning of 1969 approximately 300,000 women had become members.

Vlasta

By looking at what happened in the official Communist Party women's magazine, Vlasta, we can assess one aspect of women's democratic awakening during the Czechoslovak Prague Spring. At that time, Vlasta had the second largest circulation of any newspaper or journal in Czechoslovakia.[14] On the pages of Vlasta, beginning in January 1968 with the election of Dubček to the First Secretary post, we can clearly see the opening of a new discursive space for feminism. On these same pages, one can also see how this nascent feminist discussion was suddenly interrupted — by the Soviet invasion — and finally shut down, as state censorship was reimposed and the Communist Party restored to its leading role in the second half of 1969.

Other journals besides Vlasta played a part in the articulation of a critical female perspective on the state socialist regime. Literární Listy, for instance, which became one of the most controversial vehicles for political criticism and historical revisionism when it first appeared in February 1968, featured several articles written by women writers during 1968–1969 (e.g. Klauserová

1968; Klímová 1968).[15] They vigorously criticized the socialist policy of emancipation aimed primarily at women, in some cases because it was not truly egalitarian, in other cases for its asocial, homogenizing effects in daily life. For example, Eda Kriséová (1968) wrote on the pages of *Literární Listy*:

Women are torn in all directions by the demands on them at home, "relations in the family are so bad that [women] do not want to even be home, and so for them, work is the only social activity." Unfortunately "no institution exists which could represent the interests of women workers and solve their problems. Trade unions and the women's union are not fulfilling this function. Other social institutions are not concerned with social policy. Currently, therefore, much of our social inequality is greater and more flagrant than in contemporary capitalism."

In communist regimes even subtle changes in the media portrayal of public concerns and attitudes could affect major changes in official policy. In *Vlasta*, strong criticism of state socialist policies and their impact on women's lives was registered week after week in 1968 in discussions among women authors and readers. Consciousness-raising of the gap between the words and the actual deeds of the socialist regime was allowed to evolve even in the official communist women's magazine. This *de facto* feminism did not raise consciousness, as in the West, about a system of "sexual oppression" or "male domination," but rather explored the possibilities for democratizing socialism in a woman-friendly way. During the Prague Spring, women expressed great optimism in articles and letters to *Vlasta* that socialist democracy would improve their everyday lives by providing the space for them to advance their own interests and helping them to balance work and family responsibilities.

Both the form and the content of *Vlasta* changed in 1968, once the Spring awakening had begun. More and more frequent criticism of the socialist regime and its policies toward woman could be found amongst the conventional fashion and cookery columns. In February 1968, *Vlasta* doubled the number of its pages (to at least 32) and invited readers' critical comments and suggestions on how to fill them up ("Nad 32 Stránkami . . ." 1968). As a result of this feedback, its social and political content increased exponentially. *Vlasta's* editors spoke directly and earnestly to their readers, soliciting their views and life experiences, discussing political developments, coaching them in the art of democratic debate. Readers responded by writing to *Vlasta* with their complaints about the inequalities, injustices, and unfairness they encountered. On the pages of *Vlasta* an authentic voice emerged, one that was articulating women's diverse opinions and interests, and unmasking the actually existing social and political system. These can be grouped according to their content, in five different themes:

Theme 1: Representing Women   The first type of article was concerned with political action, specifically with advancing women's political interests within the new democratizing system. In March 1968, the issue devoted to celebrating International Women's Day proclaimed passionately that it was an "unforgettable month, full of excitement, expectation, hope and confidence in the creative and democratic power of our nation" ("Březen — Nezapomenutelný Mesíc . . ." 1968; "Komuniké Ze Zasedání . . ." 1968). Each week thereafter included articles, which scrutinized the reforms in the Communist Party, the forthcoming National Front elections, and the activities of the new women's organization. On the whole, these articles suggested that only when women — not men or the dictates of the Party — represented women, would solutions be found to the persistent inequalities and problems in their lives ("O Ženách . . ." 1968). Women, they proposed, were better representatives precisely because of their experience in positions of powerlessness, which more closely resembled the experience of most of the population. They encouraged women to get involved in politics and to elect women into positions of power, while acknowledging the discrimination that existed at all levels, making it difficult for women to even be placed on electoral ballots. *Vlasta* wrote that although women were not typically among "those candidates with the most time and space, to think and to voice" they are often the best candidates. A number of articles investigated the reasons for women's relatively low political participation. One based on a survey asked women factory workers in Eastern Bohemia what *they* thought were the barriers to women's inclusion in politics. The results of the survey suggested that "time was what handicapped women most in political life."[16] "Without changes in our lifestyle and in women's social conditions," the article stated, "our democracy will be incomplete" (Háková 1968).

Theme 2: Engendering Democracy   Another group of articles appearing in *Vlasta* stimulated both a philosophical and practical discussion of *democracy*, comparing democracy and socialism, and examining the role of women and men in a democracy (e.g. Petrová 1968). A map of the spread of women's suffrage around the world was featured in one issue (Zahlková 1968). Others provided discussions of democratic practice outside of politics, and guides to debating, deliberating, and criticizing effectively (Sedláková 1968). A series of articles over five consecutive weeks surveyed the opinions of five women from different walks of life (a writer, a teacher, a farmer, a chemist, and a scientist) on five different groups of questions; about professions, family, democratization, relations with their partners, and fashion respectively. The series aimed to draw readers into a discussion of women's everyday lives and put a "human face" on current social and political issues. The issue on democratization asked serious questions such as: "In the past, did the cult of personality deform your life in some ways? Did you see around you some flagrant examples of unfairness or injustice? Have you had the opportunity to correct these? What has changed in your life since the January plenary of the Communist Party's central committee? Do you believe democratization will be able to bring something good?" ("5x5x5: Demokratice" 1968).

Theme 3: Myths and Illusions about Women's Economic Equality   A third type of article in *Vlasta* engaged women experts and readers in a dialogue about the economic system and its reform. Critical debates about women in the economy were conducted over the course of several issues. These debates included a series entitled "How should it be and how is it in reality?" which pitted the theory of socialist equality against the reality of women's lives (e.g. "Jaké Chtejí Být . . ." 1968). Each article examined the problems and struggles of a different group of women, showing women's equality to be myth, a set of laws honored only in the breach. Another series of articles entitled "Controversies about women in our time," asked local and foreign experts (women researchers concerned with the gender regime) to contribute their answers to the same three questions: 1) Why are women employed, because they want to be or because they have to be for reasons of economic necessity? 2) Is it accurate in your opinion that men previously provided for the family whereas today they do not? 3) Is motherhood compatible with employment? The open discussion of these questions contested contemporary arguments that attributed crises in the economy to women's "overemployment" or their low skill-level, and those that considered social policies such as state-funded childcare and maternity leave to be a drain on the economy ("Spor O Ženu . . ." 1968).

Theme 4: Learning from International Feminisms   *Vlasta* also featured articles dealing specifically with cultural comparison and the international context of women's lives. Interviews were published with internationally known women, among them French feminist philosopher, Simone de Beauvoir and Eartha Kitt, the African-American performing artist and political radical. News was reported from international women's conferences, such as the World Congress of Women and the newly formed United Nations Commission on the Status of Women. Articles by Yugoslav and German women economists were commissioned on the economic situation of women in their countries. Other articles looked at the plight of women in far-flung countries, such as Iran, Vietnam, and America. One particular article dispelled a number of illusions about American women, including the prevailing view perpetuated by the communist regime that American women were all housewives. Most notable about this group of articles is the almost complete absence of any features on the Soviet Union. The Soviet model of the socialist woman was the daily bread of *Vlasta* during the 1950s; during the Prague Spring however, *Vlasta* looked elsewhere for inspiration.

Theme 5: Deconstructing State Socialist Discourse   The final group of articles appearing in *Vlasta* during 1968–1969 sought to deconstruct the existing state socialist discourse on women. Through the concrete analysis of women's experience, these articles simultaneously demystified the vocabulary and the daily reality of socialism in Czechoslovakia. For example, the editorial collective of *Vlasta* devoted a series of articles to inspire discussion, expression of opinions, and deeper reflections on the meaning of the word "emancipation." Readers were invited to respond to the opinion pieces and a lively conversation ensued over several months. One especially provocative author argued that women's difference from men was suppressed under socialism, while women's equality with men in the workforce was not supported by the socialist regime. In her words, "the emancipation of women in today's language really means the complete denigration of femininity, contrary to socialism's presumption that it would promote the full feminine development of women." The author went further in her criticism:

> Do you see women workers in foundries, in surface mines, as tractor drivers, this is so-called light work?! And what about those women in the frightful ČSD (transport service) working class rags? Are these women in keeping with femininity? And another thing, virtually all the permanent employees of the health service are women. . . . Is this your solution to the woman question? (Mikolášová 1968).

These articles sought to generate a new and more authentic perspective based on women's actual experiences in socialist society. The intellectual departure from "socialist realism" and its apparent resolution of "the woman question," required the creation of an entirely new language. Only by contesting linguistic truths could the exploitation of women under existing socialism be revealed. In this endeavor, old terms were discarded and new ones — such as "a-sociální — ismus" — were coined, that came closer to representing the reality of women's experience.

But all this discussion was ephemeral. The Soviets invaded Czechoslovakia in late August 1968 and this eventually changed everything. In the week after the Soviet invasion, *Vlasta* kept publishing, at first erratically, every few days and in varying lengths with almost all its pages taken over by news of the current political situation. The last issue of *Vlasta* before the invasion — a panel discussion of five women on fashion — now under Soviet occupation appeared utterly trivial, and in a special issue published in September the women panelists turned to discussing the realities of life since the invasion and their hopes for Czechoslovakia's future ("5x5x5: Moda" 1968). For a while it seemed that the conversations in *Vlasta* — which rendered the lacuna between the words and deeds of socialist policy toward women transparent — would actually empower women to take action and prod the socialist government to live up to its promises of gender equality. But in the post-invasion society, questions of gender relations and complaints about the existing gender regime seemed less pressing than before, less possible to resolve, and were haltingly put aside.

In the second half of 1969 *Vlasta* was still being published weekly but its main goal had become the reaffirmation rather than the critical scrutiny of the equality goals of socialism and of the government. Analyzing the content of *Vlasta* in the mid-1980s, Zdenek Salzmann (1990: 406) concluded pessimistically that, "while the magazine attempts to promote self-realization on the part of its readers and to assist women with practical advice in such areas as child care and household management, it does nothing to mobilize women" as a political constituency with political interests as it did in the late 1960s.

When Soviet tanks rolled into Prague on August 21, 1968, there was no mass or armed resistance to the invasion, although many were injured. Nonetheless, the Soviet-led intervention was not an immediate success. Dubček did not resign as First Secretary of the Communist Party until April 1969, nominating Gustav Husák in his place. In September 1969, the Soviet-installed Czechoslovak government began to reverse the reforms instituted during the Prague Spring. In that month also, the Central Committee of the Czechoslovak Union of Women was forced to resign and the autonomous, de facto feminist organization was brought back under the authoritarian command and control of the Communist Party. The flourishing of feminism was to be short-lived, due to the depoliticization initiated by the Soviet-supported regime.

From Women's Rights to Human Rights

As chapter 1 discussed, the founding of *Charta* 77 in January 1977 was the most significant political event in the period between the Prague Spring and the Velvet Revolution of 1989. With a repressive communist regime restored during the 1970s, most people escaped from public life, and the small number of dissidents who formed an alternative public sphere and parallel culture were united in their opposition to the state. They did not focus on their differences, but on their common enemy. As such, the solidarity between men and women in *Charta* 77 was much stronger than their gender conflict.

Family and kin relationships were conceived as a source of mutual resistance to power rather than a site of gender oppression.[17] Indeed, the dissident movement, as Mary Hrábik Šamalová has noted, politicized a substantial number of women.[18] Women were a significant presence among the original signatories of *Charta* 77, and they constituted close to one-third of the movement's spokespersons between 1977 and 1989 (without either formal or informal quotas).[19] Women risked police harassment, their careers and livelihoods and they also went to prison as often as men (Jancar 1985: 184). Havel, who is known to have dismissed feminism in the 1980s, commented in his *Letters to Olga* from prison that most of the dissidents were free from family commitments and thus they were able to participate more readily and take greater risks than parents with responsibility for children and their futures. But, this hardly seems the case in light of the many women involved in *Charta* 77, several of whom had sizeable families, and either they or their husbands spent considerable time in prison in the late 1970s and 1980s. Marie Haisová, for example, describes signing the *Charta* in 1979 just after her first son had been born. A second son was born and all the while for ten years she was typing out documents for the movement (Zelený Krůh 1996: 69).

Outside formal politics and electoral processes, women dissidents were able to adapt their own political resources — such as, networking at the grass-roots, organizing in homes, dealing with crisis situations at the same time as mundane everyday tasks — to the activities of dissent. Libuše Šilhánová, a Charta spokesperson at one time, believes that women were unrivalled as excellent organizers and interlocutors among the dissidents.[20] But they were also often able to elude the security police by acting dumb, claiming not to understand politics, and becoming pregnant. Eda Kriséová (1993: 133–4) observed that the security police "rarely locked up the mother of a small child," because they were constantly concerned with how things might look to the outside world. Women found a place within the Czechoslovak opposition to practice unconventional politics. Indeed, as politics got pushed into the private sphere under Husák, they came to control the very space for independent civic initiatives in Czechoslovakia. Because women were traditionally responsible for the private sphere they commanded both the representation of this sphere and the politics within it (see Bourdieu 1998: 11). As Mary Hrábik Šamlova (1996) explains:

> The dismissed intellectuals could no longer avail themselves of the *public space* such as universities, editorial offices, film studios, theatres, newsrooms or even meeting rooms. The locus of activities of the parallel culture and society [therefore] shifted to the only available *private space*, the home. Women, because they controlled the hearth, could veto all or any parallel culture and society activities.

And while *Charta 77* did not develop a specifically feminist platform, it did criticize women's dual burden of labor at home and in the workplace. One of the organization's original documents states: "the opposition of women is seen in the failure of the Czechoslovak government to provide adequate services and adequate pay to lighten women's burden and to promote greater equality for women in society."[21]

Twelve Women in Prague, a book published in *samizdat* in 1980 by Eva Kantůrková (1980, French trans. 1981), a *Charta 77* signatory (and earlier a leading writer and voice of the Prague Spring generation), reflects some of the broader questions about gender relations and political struggle in Czechoslovakia of the 1970s. Based on interviews of twelve other female dissidents, Kantůrková explained that her intention was not to advance a feminist cause, but rather to express a more authentic social reality through women's voices: "Women have so little sense of abstraction that ideas and reflection do not risk detaching them from the world as it really is," she noted. "In telling me their life stories, my friends have told me something basic about the world" (Fr. Trans. 1981: 227). This revelation appears to support the feminist notion that knowledge that emerges from women's experiences is superior to the theories produced by men. But because of the specific reality of the social and political world around her, in particular the Czechoslovak socialist state's hold over the language of oppression and emancipation, Kantůrková stopped short of advocating a universal feminist standpoint. Instead, she wrote:

> *Feminism* has been eradicated in our society by having been brutally transformed into a new form of women's slavery: obligatory work. Thus, if in Czechoslovakia there is one thing that a woman wishes to obtain for herself, it is to recover her undistorted *feminine essence* rather than to promote herself (Fr. Trans. 1981: 227).

A later book by Kantůrková (1984, English trans. 1987) published in 1984, *My Companions in the Bleak House*, gives an account of her time in a women's prison. It focused not on her story, but on those of the other inmates. Unlike her, these women were not dissidents, imprisoned for political "crimes," but ordinary criminals and prostitutes, members of the most marginalized class of Czechoslovak citizens. The book is testament to the fact that the women in the opposition movement did not want a *safe* space to express themselves politically *as women*, but rather a more *authentic* space to give voice to humanity. Thus, Kantůrková and her "fellow" female dissidents subsumed, or at least placed gender questions in the context of seemingly universal human concerns (Kirss 2000).

In post-invasion Czechoslovakia, democratizing communism was no longer possible, and nor was the establishment of an explicitly feminist perspective and autonomous movement. Men and women in the *Charta 77* movement joined in solidarity *against* communism rather than *for* its reform. Unlike the Prague Spring, women in the political opposition did not attempt to speak *as women* or to call for a feminist movement to promote women's interests. As Kantůrková's writings demonstrate, they vacillated between the struggle to recover an essential feminine identity in a homogenizing, authoritarian society, and to subordinate this identity to the quest for universal human rights. In this regard, Czechoslovakia's female dissidents simultaneously confronted a male-defined socialist equality that rendered their femininity invisible, and a state-defined equality that rendered both women and men *subjects* not *citizens* (see Šiklová 1993).

Postsocialist Transformation

Experimentation with democracy as in the Prague Spring and the civic movements between 1977–1989 was abandoned after 1989 when a radical experiment with market capitalism took precedent. The Velvet Revolution, which was in some respects a popular revolution — of civil society against the state — soon became a technical revolution led by experts, as chapter 6 further testifies. These western and local technocrats launched state-led transitions to integrate Czechoslovakia with the global capitalist economy. Ironically, it was these technocrats and not those associated with the civic movements who used *revolutionary* language; not, however, the language of class and Bolshevism, but of anticommunism, right-wing populism, neoclassical economics, and individualism.

While many contrasts can be drawn between the Czechoslovak Prague Spring and the Velvet Revolution, from a gender perspective, the political discourses of 1968 and 1989 appear especially at odds with each other. In 1968, a new de facto "feminist" discourse and movement emerged in the context of the broader democratic awakening. For a short time, they made visible the anomaly between the words and deeds of socialist policy toward women transparent, and prodded the socialist government to live up to its promises of equality. In 1989, however, these sentiments were nowhere to be found. Six months after the revolution, before the first democratic elections, liberal market reforms were instituted. This transition to capitalism was accompanied by socially conservative ideas about appropriate gender roles, rather than calls for greater gender equality by women themselves.

Socialism tended to *officially* deny the existence of gender differences, allowing class to be the only expression and principle of differentiation. As Slavenka Drakulic has explained, "just being a woman — not to mention a beauty — was a constant battle against the way the whole [communist] system work[ed]" (Drakulic 1993: 32). Communism was a very masculinized political model. After 1989, however, gender differences found renewed expression. In contrast to socialism's claim to emancipate women through labor, the choice *not* to labor but to express one's femininity became the idiom of emancipation. Playing up one's gender identity through consumption has been a popular marker of postcommunist freedom and individuality. Czech men and women have been extremely receptive to western consumer goods and capitalist market expansion. But it was the socialist regime that ignited these consumerist sentiments in the first place. Communist leaders sought to placate the politically repressed Czechoslovak population with promises of material comfort and a standard of living as good as the West's that they could not deliver on.

During the Czech transition, the media has consistently portrayed gender differences as unchanging "facts of nature" and typecast gender equality as either a foreign or former-communist artifice. Such a shift in discourse is starkly ironic, if not dialectical, when we remember the social transformations of the 1950s and 1960s, where "emancipation" rested on the "fact of gender mutability" and Communist Party newspapers routinely celebrated new socialist men and women. One of the legacies of this social transformation today is that there is no longer an immediately available or credible language in which ideas about gender equality and difference can be expressed given their association with the failed state socialist regime. In the postsocialist era, advocates of women's rights have had to seek out new, often unknown, spaces in which to articulate them, as chapters 5 and 6 show.

Conclusion

Czechoslovakia's "embrace of defeat" after 1989 was highly conditioned by its socialist past. Once again, Czechs were very optimistic that change would come to them all, this time through the omnipotence of capitalism and the benevolence of the West. As during the Prague Spring, they hoped that only the positive aspects of democracy and freedom would come to Czechoslovakia. Women especially had great hope about this, in part because of a lingering belief from the 1968 era that reforming the system would solve all other problems, including the relations between men and women. In 1968 the efforts to democratize socialism required addressing questions of gender and inequality. By 1989 this was no longer the case.

In 1989, as socialism was discarded for good, what little talk there was of the gender regime was couched in the rhetoric of markets and capitalism. The dominant ideology after the Velvet Revolution was *Friedmanite*; it essentially held that if the market rules were correctly put in place then all other rights and freedoms would follow. After a decade of reforms, however, women are now starting to realize that capitalism, like socialism, comes very gendered. Embracing unfettered markets has not brought women and many other citizens the fundamental rights and freedoms promised by the language of capitalism and democracy. In the Czech Republic today people increasingly call for "capitalism with a human face." In the following chapters, I argue that socialist legacies and democratic capitalist transformations have shaped Czech gender relations since 1989 in unequal, and often contradictory ways.

3 Refashioning the Family

In the socialist era, the Czechoslovak regime officially ignored the family and the intergenerational redistribution that compensated for the failures of the planned economy. By contrast, postsocialist governments have explicitly invoked family values as critical to the economic transition's success. The family has played a central role in the Czech postsocialist transition and process of restructuring. Indeed, the Czech constitution and all Czech political parties, with the exception of the Communist Party of Bohemia and Moravia, have hailed the family as the fundamental unit of the new market economy.

One of the most significant contributions of feminist political economy has been to show that the family-household, far from being a unified institution, is characterized by ongoing processes of bargaining, conflict and resource redistribution due to the inequality and hierarchy among its members. By disaggregating the family-household implicitly used as the unity of analysis in neoliberal and institutionalist frameworks, nonmarket activity that takes place in the family and women's well being, are revealed as integral to the process of economic development and change (see Sen 1996).

This chapter explores how successive Czech governments have used the family, and in particular women's labor in the family-household, to facilitate the shift from the state to the market system. The chapter contains three parts. The first part reviews the state of the Czech family before 1989 and the importance of family relations in the maintenance of the socialist system and in the revival of civil society in the 1970s and 1980s. The second part examines the changes to social policy after 1989, and the move away from a system of state support to a reliance on the family for the provision of social services. Here I argue that policies that seek to privatize social welfare not only undermine the socialist contract that supported women's participation in the labor force, but also assume a gender division of labor, in which men are the breadwinners and women are the unpaid care-providers. The upshot of these policies has *not* been to reestablish the traditional or nuclear patriarchal family in Czech society as intended. Rather, as I show in the third part of the chapter, the turn to the market has actually disrupted the place of the traditional family in Czech society, precipitating a dramatic decline in marriage and fertility and a diversification of family forms. If the socialist system was plagued by a crisis of production (and productivity), then the postsocialist market system faces a deepening crisis of social reproduction.

From Margin to Center: The Family Before and After 1989

During socialism Czechoslovakia had the highest marriage rate in Europe. At an average of 21 years, the age of the Czech bride was the youngest among European countries (Večerník and Matejů 1999: 98–9; Kuchařová 1996). Practically all Czech women had both a full time job and children, typically two children (Bransten 2001).[1] The interval between marriage and the birth of children was very close (Rychataříková 1995). Less than six percent of women remained childless in the 1970s and 1980s compared with approximately twenty percent in western countries (Večerník and Matejů 1999: 110).[2] Consequently, in 1991, 61 percent of all Czech households were dual earner families with children (Křižková 1999: 204).

The family in socialist Czechoslovakia relied on a system of intergenerational dependence, distinguishing it from the nuclear family in Western Europe (Večerník and Matejů 1999: 102). Extended families, social networks and households developed "manifold capacities, skills and strategies for survival," including informal trade, barter and economizing to make up for the shortcomings of the planned economy (Večerník 1995: 13). In the realm of social reproduction, women were able to retire as early as 53, which freed them to help with grandchildren while their sons and daughters worked (Možný 1994). It also allowed them to look after their own elderly parents, thus relieving the state of much of the responsibility for old age care.

In order to ensure the reproduction of the labor force, the socialist state depended on the reallocation of women's labor during their life course in addition to their double day of labor at work and at home.

However, difficulties and tensions could be observed in this informal, family system of care, which compensated for the failing social state. As divorce and mobility increased in the 1970s and 1980s, the younger generation began to react against prevailing norms (Možný 1991). Conflicts between men and women over the expectations of gender roles were no doubt also present. The socialist system was too reliant on strong ties, which were context bound, and becoming increasingly difficult to transfer from generation to generation. Indeed, the Czech sociologist Ivo Možný (1994: 62) has argued that the stress on the family system in the 1980s actually precipitated the Czechoslovak Velvet Revolution by contributing to the loss of faith in the socialist system. Other scholars argue that the family was at the heart of the reemergence of civil society in Central and Eastern Europe (Kurczewski 1996) and Czechoslovakia specifically (Šamlová 1996). Chapter 2 discussed how private family homes became sites for political organizing in the context of communist repression. Women were key players in dissident initiatives since they were also typically in charge of those private spaces *relatively* free from state control.

Dramatic changes have occurred in the Czech family since 1989; just at the time it has become the explicit focus on public policy. Family incomes have deteriorated, divorce rates have risen steadily, and fertility and marriage rates have plummeted. Although some of these changes can be seen as a part of a broader return to European norms, the speed at which they have taken place is striking. This pace of demographic change suggests that a deeper transformation in social relations has taken place in the Czech Republic than most scholars of postsocialist transitions have noted. At the same time, the strength and adaptation of the Czech family helps to explain the relative stability and maintenance of well-being during the postsocialist transition, especially the momentous upheaval of the period 1989–93.[3] Specifically, the Czech family has facilitated the economic transformation in two ways. First, it has served to cushion the transformation by redistributing resources and providing for needs in the presence of both government and market failure. Second, it has cushioned structural adjustment by reallocating labor (often women's labor) and/or deferring gratification, even biological reproduction, to increase economic productivity.

Privatizing Social Policy

Since 1989 changes in social policy in the Czech Republic have been uneven. Consistent with neoliberal principles, the Czech state has extricated itself from many of its public functions under communism, in particular the commitment to ensuring the full employment and the necessary social support for men and women workers. Between 1990 and 1992, the Civic Forum government preserved many aspects of the former socialist welfare system and reinvented other aspects. For instance, a subsistence minimum living standard above the poverty level was introduced in October 1991 to serve as a safety net during the transition. Czechs who fell below this standard could receive government assistance. Between 1992 and 1997, the ODS government led by Václav Klaus also consciously tried to maintain its electoral support through generous social compensation (Orenstein 2001). Social policy under Klaus was designed in compromising ways to mitigate the social and political effects of the macroeconomic adjustment. But it represented a marked change from the social democratic concept of social policy under the Civic Forum government, 1990–92.

Whereas the Civic Forum stressed universal benefits, earnings-related pensions, and generous social assistance, the ODS government sought to establish means-testing and to implement flat rate instead of earnings-related benefits, while advocating a neoliberal minimalist system where individuals would be held ultimately responsible for their own social and economic well being (Večerník 1995: 18).[4] The dominant forms of social regulation gradually changed from being pro-collective, protective, statutory regulations to pro-individualistic, market-oriented, fiscal regulations. Tax and social-benefit systems increasingly became mechanisms to control behavior through targeting and incentives structures (Standing 1998a). Many of these mechanisms privileged the nuclear family as the normative social form (Castle-Kanerová 1992).

Under Klaus, the entire social welfare system was to be overhauled by 1995. Following the policy advice of the World Bank, beginning in 1993 universal family benefits were replaced by targeted means-tested benefits, aimed at deserving, low-income families.[5] Enterprise-supported social benefits and state subsidies for childcare had already been eliminated in 1991, housing subsidies were reduced in 1993, the age of eligibility for pensions was changed in January 1996 (from 60 to 65 for men and from 53–55 to 60 for women to be phased in by 2006), and universal health insurance was introduced in 1995 (and private insurance funds appeared in 1996; see Večerník 1995). However, social benefits and education and health expenditures were not drastically cut as in other postsocialist countries such as Poland. Education and health spending actually increased slightly as a proportion of Gross Domestic Product (GDP) in the 1990s; (although GDP itself declined in that decade and did not reach its 1989 level until 1998).

The administration of public health and education was decentralized and transferred to local governments, but the comprehensive privatization of health, education, housing, and welfare sectors was strongly resisted by Czech citizens during the 1990s. As a result, some forms of government management, such as state sector rents and energy prices have never been fully deregulated. But those aspects of the state sector that supported women's employment in particular, received short shrift.

In a 1990 interview, a senior aide to the then Czech Finance Minister, Václav Klaus, criticizing the "overemployment" of women, noted that:

The Ministry of Labor and Social Affairs is preparing a program for young women so they can afford to stay home with small children, and we will aid them with social support. This policy in the end will save money because when women work they need state-supported care.[6]

Members of the Civic Forum's social policy group and officials in the Ministry of Labor and Social Affairs in 1990 and 1991 put forward proposals to increase maternity leave and other social welfare provisions in order to give women of child-rearing years incentives to return to the home and to their "natural roles as mothers."[7] The Civic Forum's initial manifesto on social policy read as follows: "A differentiation of incomes will gradually help to reduce the disproportionate economic activity of women, a rehabilitation of the family and the creation of better conditions for raising children" (cited in Castle 1990).[8]

In 1995, the ODS government changed the Czech Labor Code to extend legal *parental* leave to men as well as women, and increase unpaid *childcare* leave (the time during which leave may be taken from a job without terminating it) from three to four years. The combined parental and childcare leave in the Czech Republic is now the longest in the world (ILO 1997). However, few fathers have exercised this right. Men constituted only two to three percent of those who took parental leave in the 1990s.[9] Despite its apparent gender-neutrality, the new policy was designed and intended for women. Like the Civic Forum government between 1990 and 1992, the ODS government hoped to transfer much work of social reproduction — childcare especially — to the family, by encouraging women to stay out of the labor force. As the Civic Democratic Party platform, adopted by the 6th Congress of ODS in Hradec Králové, in 1995, stated:

> Only family is capable of providing a truly complete education to create mature members of society. The family is a place where moral and cultural values develop and are maintained, it is a place where people learn to respect and love each other, and experience feelings of authority and safety. The family is a significant factor of a fulfilling life. It is also the basis for appropriate functioning of municipalities and the state thanks to its mediating role. For all these reasons, we want to support an environment in which individual citizens wish to establish and maintain families.

Traditional notions about women and men's place underlie the Civic Democratic Party's stress on the family. As long as individual women are carrying caring values for society, both as individuals and in the family-household, society does not have to be collectively responsible for nurturing and for economically supporting care work.[10] The state can legitimately get out of the business of caring for citizens, leaving it to the family or in other instances, the market.

In addition to generous leave policies designed to encourage women to leave paid employment, the support services for women's employment were rescinded. Childcare and abortion facilities were privatized in 1991 and have operated on a largely user-pays basis since then In the case of childcare, the availability of places in nurseries for children under three years old declined rapidly from 78,555 places in 1989 to 17,210 places in 1991 (Český statistický úřad 1992). Between 1989 and 2000 the number of children between the ages of three and six years in nursery schools dropped by a third as well, as shown in figure 3–1.

In the case of abortion, the opening of borders after communism's collapse meant that the Czech Republic was susceptible to greater flows of people in and out of the country, and consequently to the effects of government policies to ban or tighten the availability of abortion procedures in the surrounding countries, including Poland, eastern Germany, and Hungary.

FIGURE 3.1   Children in Nursery School

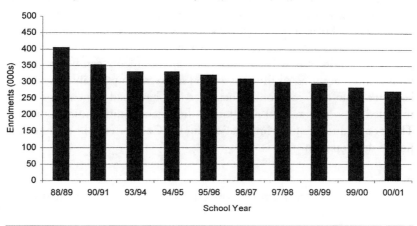

Figure created by author. Statistical source: Český statistický úřad 2001.

The Czech government sought to stem the inflow of women from Poland especially, by banning abortion to foreign nationals and privatizing abortion for citizens ("Facing a rush from Poland . . ." 1993; Cook 1993). A Czech woman who wants to terminate a pregnancy now is charged approximately one month's average pay. The intent of this policy was not explicitly to promote reproduction, but rather to cut state expenditures in light of global competitive pressures. But the two goals are nonetheless compatible and, in effect, the policy has served to limit the reproductive rights of Czech women. It has also reduced the number of abortions performed by two-thirds.[11]

Despite the high regard with which Czechs hold family life, attempts to reform the state social sector generated considerable public resistance in the 1990s.[12] Once the Civic Democratic government moved away from the so-cial liberal policies of 1990–1992 to neoliberal ones in 1993–97, its popu-larity quickly waned (Orenstein 1998). The financial austerity package in-troduced in April and May of 1997, following the collapse of the Czech currency, further increased the burden on women in the home, especially single parents, since it included a ten percent cut to education and health-care budgets (Čtk 1996). It raised the threshold for receiving family benefits, increased energy prices and rents and eliminated inflation-adjustments to social security benefits (Pehe 1997). In December 1997, the right-of-center

ODS government led by Václav Klaus fell from power and was replaced in June 1998 by a Social Democratic–Left coalition government, which ran on an electoral platform of preserving the social state.

Now no longer the showcase of neoliberalism, the Czechs may have proved the limits of how far neoliberal economic theory can be applied in postsocialist countries. As the next section shows, attempts to introduce market forces into the provision of social services have had some startling unintended consequences, in addition to their gender-differentiated impact. These consequences have implications for the Czech Republic's future economic development.

The Unintended *Family* Consequences of Market Reform

Housing Shortages

Housing policy shaped family formation and gender relations during socialism. At the end of the 1980s, there was a shortage of approximately 120,000 to 260,000 dwellings in the Czech Republic. Extended families, as many as three generations, frequently lived in one household. Nine percent of occupied apartments contained two or more households, while sixteen percent were shared with older relatives (Večerník and Matejů 1999: 107). Even after divorce, families were often forced to stay together because of housing shortages. The Czech writer Ivan Klíma's novel, A *Summer Affair* (1981), told the story of an ex-husband living in one room of an apartment, and the new lover in the other.

One of the only ways to secure a house or flat in the tightly controlled state housing system was to have a child: "Have family, will settle down, will get apartment" was the motto. Thus, young people faced incentives to get married as early as possible in order to gain independence from their parents and their parents' (or even grandparents') home. Forty-four percent of couples had flats when they married; forty-nine percent lived with parents in the first year after they were married. The socialist housing shortage thus functioned as a major constraint on diversification in the family and household formation of the young generation (Kuchařová 1996: 5).

Another way to secure housing was to build your own. Half of the housing stock constructed under socialism was built by individuals and not by the state. People "acquired their housing at artificially low prices for building

FIGURE 3.2   Housing Construction

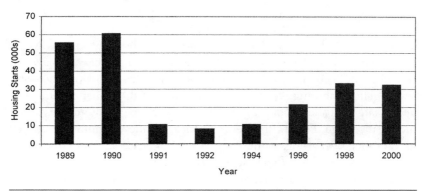

Figure created by author. Statistical source: Český statistický úřad 2001.

materials, public transport, cheap unofficial labor, and in many cases using stolen [state] construction and installation materials. All of these opportunities disappeared overnight in 1989" (Večerník and Mateju 1999: 106).

After the communist regime ended, a number of changes very quickly occurred. Immediately, the state housing policy which had privileged married couples and families over single persons in the allocation of new apartments was revoked. As a result, a key incentive to get married and have children as early as possible was removed. In the new *market* for housing, money counted more than family. Contrary to the post-1989 government rhetoric supporting the nuclear family, the creation of a housing market effectively discouraged the formation of new families. Housing construction also dropped off after 1990, as can be seen in figure 3–2. Approximately 61,000 new dwellings were started in 1990, whereas only 8,500 were begun in 1992.

According to the theory of neoliberal economics, one might think that freeing market forces would address the housing shortage. However, for most people the housing situation became worse after 1989, while the demand for living space increased. The State Institute for Territorial Planning estimated that in 1991 the housing need was 173,003 dwelling units, and 667,450 units by 2000. These estimates suggest a need for a housing construction program of 70,000 dwellings per year. The gap between the supply and the demand for new housing was far greater than during the 1980s for several reasons. First, under a new privatization program houses and other buildings confiscated by the communists in 1948 were restored to their former owners. By 1993, 10.5 percent of housing in the Czech Republic — 70 percent in central Prague — had been returned to private ownership (Sykorá 1996). This retarded the emergence of a functioning housing market in certain areas. Second, all state subsidies for housing construction were withdrawn. Third, housing mortgage schemes were in their infancy, and even by the late 1990s less than 10 percent of Czechs could afford to take out such a mortgage. Fourth, the new expatriate business community pushed up the price of housing, particularly in the major Czech cities, making it difficult for Czechs to afford new houses. As figure 3–2 shows, these factors as well as wage freeze regulations and rising construction costs resulted in an overall decline in apartment and home construction. While new home construction by 2000 was three times higher than in 1991 and 1992, it was still significantly less than in 1989 and 1990.

In the rental housing market, low rents remained an ideological objective of the ODS government to dampen wage demands and keep inflation down. Rent deregulation in the transition was thus gradual rather than "a big bang." In 1992 rent in the municipal (i.e. former state) sector was increased by 100 percent, and in 1994, by a further 70 percent. At that time, the government introduced new means-tested housing allowances that targeted low-income earners who needed assistance with basic expenditures (although these allowances covered just 20 to 25 percent of total housing expenditure). In the new private sector, however, rents could be fully deregulated after a change of tenancy, usually either by letting housing to foreigners or by selling property to commercial developers. In prime areas, landlords displaced poorer local residents to peripheral areas in order to charge inflated rents. Nationally, "the rich," often foreigners, gain 20,000 apartments every year because of such conversion.[13]

Market deregulation has not alleviated the housing situation for most Czechs. Rather, in Czech cities, the lure of tourists and the liberalization of the labor market have privileged expatriate professionals and a small "nouveau riche" class over the needs of the local population (Cooper and Morpeth 1998). The transformation from plan to market has reversed the socialist incentive to "settle down" by establishing a family. The nascent market instead encourages young people, young women especially, to stay single and remain in the labor market. Here we see how the inextricability of postsocialist housing, labor, and family markets is reshaping gender rela-

FIGURE 3.3   Decline in Marriages

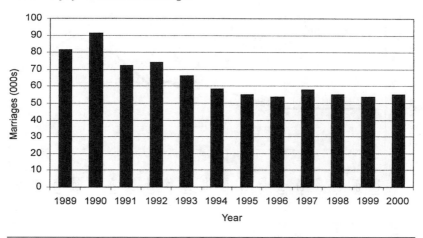

Figure created by author. Statistical source: UNICEF-ICDC Florence database.

tions as well. Although successive Czech governments have hailed the family as the fundamental unit in society, market forces have undermined much of the economic basis for family-formation. Beyond unpaid childcare leave provisions, governments have done little to align their policy settings with their rhetorical support of family. Ordinary Czechs have taken note, and adjusted their behavior accordingly.

Marriage in Decline

After 1990, the numbers of new families being formed greatly declined and the breakup of existing families seemed to accelerate overnight. During the six years between 1990 and 1996, Czech marriages fell by 41 percent. As figure 3–3 reveals, in 1990, there were 90,953 marriages recorded, a figure slightly higher than the year before. By 1996 this level had fallen to 53,896, where it would remain relatively stable for the rest of the 1990s. In addition, the average age of marriage rose nearly three years between 1990 and 1994 to 26.1 and 23.9 for men and women respectively, in the direction of that in western countries (Kuchařová 1996).

As marriages were decreasing, divorces were rising steadily. Figure 3–4

FIGURE 3.4 Divorce Rate

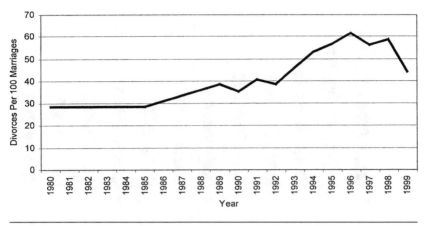

Figure created by author. Statistical source: UNICEF-ICDC Florence database.

shows that the divorce rate was rising in the 1980s to 38.6 per 100 marriages in 1989. But by 1996 this rate had practically doubled to 61.4 divorces per 100 marriages. Such a gradual increase peaking in the late 1990s suggests that the heterosexual, nuclear family has been as much a casualty of, as a cushion for, the postsocialist transformation. The stress and uncertainty generated by wide-ranging social and economic changes clearly have had a toll on the social institution of the family.

Fertility Strike!

Since 1991 Czech society has experienced a dramatic and unprecedented decline in fertility, which implies a spontaneous collective strike on the home front by young women. Whereas the socialist state used to provide incentives for women and men to form families while they were young and in the labor force, the introduction of the market economy has had the opposite effect (see Erlanger 2000; Fiálová, Horská and Kučerá 1995). Registered births dropped by almost a third in the first six years of transition, as seen in figure 3–5. Births registered in 1990 were 130,564, but six years later in 1996, the number was just 90,446 (Český statistický úřad 1997).

Jitka Rychařiková, the head of the Czech Academy of Science's Demo-

FIGURE 3.5   Live Births 1989–2000

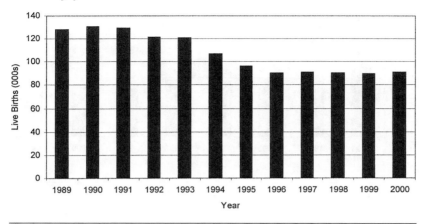

Figure created by author. Statistical source: Český statistický úřad 2001.

graphic Society, does not believe the low fertility rate will reverse any time soon:

> We speak about delaying, but we've been talking about delaying chil-
> dren until a woman is older for a very long time. This discussion has
> been ongoing for ten years. But we know that it is a fact that when
> childbirth is put off, fewer children will end up being born. I think
> fewer children will be born here, because it a combination of this
> desire to delay and the economic situation (Bransten 2000).

In the context of a long economic recession accompanied by market reforms that have removed the support for families with children (socialized childcare and other public services), young women have not merely deferred motherhood After more than a decade, some have clearly foregone it altogether. Contrary to government and societal expectations, young Czech women have chosen to keep their jobs and pursue new career opportunities in the market system rather than fulfill traditional mothering roles and "reproduce the nation" (Erlanger 2000). This behavior is the opposite of what the Czech government tried to encourage in 1990–91, when they provided incentives, such as family benefits and extended leave provisions, for women to exit the workforce and "return home."[14]

FIGURE 3.6   Women on Maternity Leave

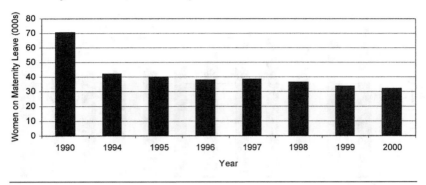

Figure created by author. Statistical source: Český statistický uřad 2001.

FIGURE 3.7   Women on Childcare Leave

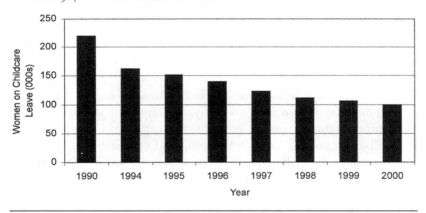

Figure created by author. Statistical source: Český statistický uřad 2001.

Even when young women now choose to have children they do not stay out of the labor force for long. Although the combined maternity and childcare leave was extended to four years in the early 1990s, most women take twelve months leave and the average leave is less than twenty-four months (Research Institute for Labour and Social Affairs 1998). Mirroring the declining fertility rate, there has been a steady decline in the number of women taking either maternity or childcare leave during the transition, as figures 3–6 and 3–7 show.

FIGURE 3.8   Natural Population Change

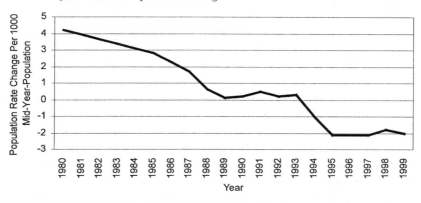

Trend Figure created by author. Statistical source: UNICEF-ICDC Florence database.

Women's choices are stark in the new market society: On the one hand, combining family and employment increasingly involves discrimination, career interruption, and the physical exhaustion of a "double day," since men rarely contribute to household work (see Křižková 1999). On the other hand, being a full-time mother usually involves economic dependence on a male breadwinner or a targeted state benefit that is barely enough to live on. The "fertility strike" by young women has externalized the burden of this tradeoff in the form of a steadily declining, negative population growth rate, shown in figure 3–8.

Markets are embedded in social institutions and attempts to create "unfettered" markets often have unintended consequences. In the Czech case, radical reform has indirectly put a brake on the birth rate and formation of new families. As the below-replacement level population rate since 1994 illustrates, society's ability to reproduce itself both biologically and socially has been called into question by the shift from the state to the market. Although neoliberals might interpret the decline in fertility as a response to structural change, designed to preserve resources for existing people in families, as much as a weakening of the family itself.

The economist Robert Chase (1997a) argues that the sudden contraction in fertility in the Czech Republic cannot be explained by conventional factors like alignment with western reproductive behavior, increases in women's labor force participation, or changes in family support policies. In his view, a phenomenon such as a rapid decline in fertility can be explained only by changes in economic conditions and expectations such as anticipated un-employment, declining wages, and high inflation, which increase the costs of marriage and child-rearing and counteract pronatalist state policy (Hei-tlinger 1993). This situation represents a serious policy problem for the Czech Republic: women who are barely past fifty were pushed out of the workforce on small pensions after 1989, while younger women are discrim-inated against if they interrupt their work to start families (Paukert 1995b: 7).

Without a doubt, the economic transition has had an impact on social reproduction, but changes in family forms as a result of economic uncer-tainty and public policies have also affected the economic transition (Chase 1997a). The rapid demographic change, for instance, will likely have serious economic consequences for the Czech Republic, among them a shortage of skilled workers and a potential collapse in the state-funded pension plan, already $500 million in debt (Bransten 2000). The Czech Republic is the only postcommunist country where the mortality rate has begun to decline significantly, particularly in older age categories (Legge 1998b). Taken to-gether, the declining birth rate and the improved mortality rate mean that in the future the Czech Republic will have proportionately far fewer eco-nomically active adults paying taxes and proportionately more old people receiving state pensions.

At present 2.33 Czech workers support one retiree, that ratio of economic dependence is expected to drop to 1.66 workers per retiree by 2030. Such a ratio forewarns a fiscal crisis even though the pension age has already been raised by several years. Czech neoliberals suggest that the state pension sys-tem should be privatized. The Social Democratic government has re-sponded by suggesting the introduction of child-friendly subsidies as incen-tives to parents to have more children (Bransten 2000). But this policy proposal does nothing to level the playing field between men and women on the labor market, and is not enough to reduce the disparities in living conditions between families with children and those without children.

In sum, although market-based reforms in the former state sector might appear to be gender-neutral, they have actually had an important impact on Czech gender relations. The full extension of the market mechanism, for instance, encourages young women — like young men — to participate fully in the paid labor-force, and leaves them little time and few social resources to assist with family life. This has resulted not only in what Pope John Paul has called "the demographic winter" in Central and Eastern Europe but in a "crisis of social reproduction" which is reflected in the declining marriage and birth rates and the general well-being of the population (cf. Pearson 1997, 1998). Just as some women and men have "opted out" of the nuclear family, state actors have resorted to conservative and discriminatory policies to reestablish the traditional gender regime in the family and in civil society. However, as the evidence presented here shows, these efforts have had serious unanticipated effects.

A Crisis of Masculinity?

If Czech women respond to the tumultuous economic transition by avoiding the "double burden" of work in the labor force and at home that their predecessors endured under socialism, how have Czech men responded? Peggy Watson (1995) argues that, "there is a male identity crisis" in the former East bloc. This crisis is a product of widespread masculine anomie, reflected in the rising male suicide and mortality rates, alcohol abuse, and unemployment and crime rates across the region. One of the reasons why Russian men have been more vulnerable to death, suicide, and illness in the transition, Guy Standing (1998b: 33) suggests, is that "women were made more resilient by their need to adjust to difficulties in the Soviet era, [whereas] men were accustomed to a rather passive role in that period."

Men's job security and status as head of household were basically ensured under communism. In Hungary, the sociologist Julia Szalai (1997) contends that men have experienced greater stress and difficulty in adjusting to the new economic system than women. Unlike in Russia, however, the Czech male mortality rate has not drastically increased, nor as in Hungary has their rate of unemployment been more than 10 percent or greater than women's. In fact, the life expectancy of Czech men has climbed more quickly in the 1990s than that of other Central European men (Legge 1998b). Yet, many Czech observers of the transition have expressed similar concerns about Czech men. Psychologist and former *Charta 77* dissident, Helena Klímová compares men's anxiety in the current postsocialist transition to the rapid social change Czechoslovak women experienced during the Stalinist drive to integrate them into the labor force:

What happened in the 1950s and 1960s was a massive change in the lives of women but compared with this, the changes in the 1990s are mainly influencing men. I would say the communists did some of the dirty work and as a result, women became very independent. In the 1980s, we did not feel any oppression by men, as *women*. We were oppressed by the regime, not especially as women, but together with men. When we entered the 1990s new values spread, I mean the values of the free market economy, of career and money. All this has had a much greater influence on men. This phenomenon, I think, is somehow connected with the fate of women in the 1950s and 1960s. It seems that we underwent something that men are only now undergoing. When I work with patients and clients, I see that indeed it is men who are subject to greater change; they are living through these social changes more intensely than women I would say.[15]

Men, of course, were exploited as laborers during communism but unlike women, the experience of working a double shift in a full-time job and in the family-household, of being demoted or laid off is relatively new to them. During socialism, women's identities rested less on laboring than did men's, and as much on their private family and domestic roles in spite of the official rhetoric of equality. In the harsh days of normalization, these traditional family roles gained importance and power, as havens from the repressive state. Ironically, as Klímová suggests, they may have helped some Czech women to adapt psychologically and practically to today's rapid postsocialist change.

Conclusion

Institutionalists observe that capitalist social relations typically rely on noneconomic institutional arrangements. Feminists pay attention to the culturally specific patterns of gender relations that enable both production and the work of social reproduction. Consistent with both perspectives, the shift toward market principles in Czech public policy has at the same time displayed an explicit normative preference for the traditional family. To make up for the shrinking state sector and the market's inadequacies, Czech reformers have drawn on conservative ideology and the socialist pronatalist legacy in order to strengthen the family.

In the Central and East Eurobarometer polling, Czech citizens consistently approve both of market principles and a strong state. Without a doubt, opening markets has offered them some new opportunities. However, it has not dealt with such basic human needs as employment and housing, and has, at the same time, allowed human vice to flourish as chapter 4 shows. In addition, one of the consequences of market reform has been severe economic and psychological insecurity that not even the bedrock of the family has been able to alleviate. Market democracy, as it has been introduced in the Czech Republic, has begun to erode its social basis in the family system of reciprocity and redistribution. Although the dramatic decrease in new births and marriages and the growing divorce rate may not signal the breakdown of the Czech family *per se*, they do not bode well for the survival of the traditional family system that compensates for government or market failures. In the next chapter we will see that , women value paid employment highly in state and market sectors. Indeed, women's participation in the new labor market is as strong as it was in the state socialist workforce.

4 Establishing Labor Markets

This chapter shows how gender is shaping the processes of establishing new, niche labor markets in the Czech Republic. In turn, it also reveals how the nascent capitalist labor market is serving to restructure gender relationships by reconfiguring public/private and national/international boundaries. Transforming the socialist economic system not only involves integration with global markets; more fundamentally it involves the alteration of human relationships.

In order to effectively embed capitalist institutions and practices in formerly state-run economies, social space and social relations must be changed. For Czech policymakers, getting the market rules right was seen as the fount from which all social and economic transformations would occur (Potůček 1993). Postsocialist market reforms aimed to permanently change old social relations. Yet institutionalist scholars observe that socialist *nomenklatura* networks and practices of stealing from the state, among other norms, have proved remarkably durable in postsocialist countries despite the introduction of the global homogenized market. Neo-Marxists point out that market reforms have yet to create a sufficiently large middle class to support capitalist relations. Feminists, for their part, argue that breaking up socialist networks and bringing a middle class into existence depends on removing inherited gender divisions of labor and power. However, gender divisions have become fault lines of competition in the Czech transition to capitalism. Rather than being deemphasized, gender relationships have become salient distinctions used to sort out new labor and property relations in the Czech lands since 1989 (cf. Watson 2000).

The chapter contains three parts. In the first part I review the critical feminist debate about the plight of women in transition countries that took place in the first half of the 1990s. In the second part, which presents the major evidence for my argument, I assess some of the initial feminist predictions about women in postsocialist labor markets in light of the Czech experience of more than a decade of reform. I show how changes and continuities in gender divisions have been an integral part of the establishment of a three-tier labor market in the Czech Republic. Taken together, the legacy of socialist occupational gender segregation and the rapid integration with the global market created a voracious, hyper-masculine, Czech brand of capitalism in the 1990s. As I show, both women and men have been among the losers of this new capitalism, although I argue that women have been more negatively affected by the formation of the labor market than most men. Finally, in the third part of the chapter I consider how market forces have advanced eastward through commodification processes that operate with an explicit gender bias. Opening borders to foreign investment and rapidly privatizing the formerly nationalized Czech economy has not only brought disproportionate female unemployment, it has also intensified employment discrimination against women and sexual harassment at work. These gendered processes take place in the top two tiers of the labor market and have contributed to the emergence of a thriving sex market, including many well-documented instances of the forced trafficking of women and girls for prostitution. This sex work and illegal prostitution constitute an officially invisible, third-tier of the Czech labor market.

Gender in Transition

Postsocialist transformations are complex, socially mediated processes. As in previous extensions of the global market, the transitions in Central and Eastern Europe are bringing both new forms of exploitation and opportunity to women and men. In the early 1990s, however, feminist scholars tended to emphasize women's victimization rather than their opportunities for empowerment in transitions from communism. These scholars saw women in postsocialist countries bearing a disproportionate burden of the social and economic transition (Rueschemeyer ed. 1994; Mies and Shiva 1993). Nanette Funk (1993) stated in her introduction to the first volume on gender issues in post-communism that, "women's interests are being sacrificed to the transformation" (Funk and Mueller, eds. 1993: 2). In her book, *Cinder-*

ella Goes to Market, Barbara Einhorn (1993: 67–68) stressed women's loss of significant rights to work, childcare, and welfare as neoliberal austerity caused the state in Central and Eastern Europe to rescind from its previous commitments to social equality. In addition to these trends, Peggy Watson (1993) argued that the new market democracies were immersed in a "cult of domesticity." Chris Corrin (1992) also analyzed women in the region's "double-day" burnout and their retreat to the home. Elzbieta Matynia wrote that, "in Czechoslovakia one of the most puzzling trends . . . post 1989, has been the expressed desire of women to withdraw from the world of work into the world of the household, domesticity, and the family" (1995: 386, 390).

On the basis of some early cross-national research, Valentine Moghadam argued that the privatization and restructuring of state industries was marginalizing women in postsocialist labor markets. Her data showed that women workers were being made redundant or becoming unemployed at greater rates than men in nearly all the countries in the region. Moghadam attributed this new reality in part to the perception of employers that women workers were more expensive and unreliable than men since they can become pregnant and/or take parental leave. Consequently, she suggested that female labor would play an essentially more important role in the continued restructuring of postsocialist labor markets. In her words, "the global integration of Central and Eastern Europe will in effect reduce female employment just as the peripheral integration of third world economies has increased the employment of women workers on the global assembly line" (Moghadam 1992: 62–63; also Einhorn 1995: 221). In contrast, Susan Gal (1997: 39) argued that women's double work day, which was a constant burden under socialism, could become a model of flexibility in postsocialism. In her view the postsocialist female subject is ideally suited to the new flexible specialization of the globalized labor market (see McDowell 1991).

There is some truth in all of these observations about the postcommunist region, but when scrutinized in the Czech context, they reveal only part of the picture of the transformation, and lack much country-specific detail of the processes of gendered restructuring. Feminists, like neoliberal and neo-Marxist scholars, have approached the study of postsocialism from a teleological rather than a gendered perspective. They have by and large focused exclusively on Central and Eastern European women as the *losers* of the transitions. Moreover, much of the early feminist research on transitions did not adequately analyze gender *relations*. By concentrating almost solely on the situation of women, feminist scholars did not attend to the relational aspects of gender, that is, to the change and continuity in men and masculinities as well as women and femininities. For example, women are not the only ones to be adversely affected by the establishment of labor markets in Central and Eastern Europe. Some men have also experienced labor market insecurities and a loss in personal status (as the main household earner for instance).

In postsocialist transitions, gender is being restructured in a combined and uneven process of social change that includes the endurance of socialist practices, the local effects of political and economic liberalization, and the influence of global, supranational forces. Thus, many Czech women resent the western feminist assumption that they are, or will be, the new victims of global capitalism. Many women are well educated and the influx of foreign capital and spread of markets since 1989 has opened up new employment opportunities for them, and as chapter 2 showed, nationalization of private property and integration of women into the wage labor force under state socialism did not eliminate material gender inequalities. Most women did not consider themselves to be liberated but *overworked* by state socialism.

Cushioning the Transition — Women Go Home!

So how have gender relations shaped the formation of the postsocialist Czech labor market, and to what extent have they been changed in turn? A common assumption of neoliberal as well as feminist accounts is that there was a massive withdrawal of women from the Czech labor force after 1989 (Murray 1995; Matynia 1995). Mitchell Orenstein (1996: 210) claims that 10 percent of working-age women dropped out of the Czechoslovak labor force between 1989 and 1992. Indeed, the *Economist* argues that this phenomenon explains the Czech success in keeping unemployment down between 1990 and 1997 (The Czech Republic, the New Bohemians." 1994). But these assertions are largely unqualified. Rather, they are based on government discussions in 1990 about how to reduce the size of the labor force and prevent anticipated unemployment.

Despite their many disagreements, former dissidents and technocrats in the Civic Forum government agreed that high unemployment resulting from macroeconomic stabilization and liberalization policies could be avoided by encouraging women to exit the labor force. As the last chapter noted, the Czech government sought to use the traditional family to rewrite the collectivist social contract in 1990–1991. Former dissident, Jiřina Šiklová commented in 1990 that most of the Civic Forum leaders, all but one of whom were male, basically agreed on the benefit of women returning to the home. "They see it not only as a wise way of dealing with the potential high unemployment but also as the natural order of things" (cited in Rosen 1990: 12).[1] Finance Minister Václav Klaus's (1991) idea, reminiscent of the nineteenth-century notion of the night-watchman state, was in a nutshell that the development of Czech capitalism could be facilitated by a gender division of labor with men in the entrepreneurial driver's seat and women in supporting roles in the family.

Czech policymakers apparently believed that policies to get women to leave the work force would receive public support and support from women themselves. Indeed, public opinion polls in 1991 suggested there was a wide-spread belief in Czechoslovakia that women's employment was too high (Wolchik 1994). Yet despite all their intentions to induce women of child-bearing age to exit the labor force, the proportion of working women has remained virtually unchanged since 1989. In 1988 women constituted 46 percent of the total labor force; in 2000 44.8 percent (Český statistický uřad 1989, 2001; also Chase 1997b). Although the total Czech labor force was reduced by an estimated 10 percent in 1989–1991, as both women and men took early retirement (Paukert 1995a; Čermáková 1996; OECD 1995).[2]

An ILO study conducted in 1994 concludes that during the early phase of transition *age* rather than *gender* was the crucial factor in labor force reduction, although the study noted some gender differences (Paukert 1995b: 4). The Czech case stands in contrast to Hungary where there was a 10 percent or more drop in the labor force participation of women between 15 and 40 years (ILO-CEET 2000). But there was a noticeable decrease in the participation of Czech women compared with Czech men of retirement age. The withdrawal of women between the ages of 53 and 57 was relatively large, constituting the majority of the reduction in women's economic activity as a result of opportunities for early retirement immediately following the Velvet Revolution (Paukert 1995a: 18). Moreover, as shown in Table 4–1, every year since 1989, substantially more Czech women than Czech men have registered as unemployed, indicating their desire to find a job rather than to withdraw from paid work altogether. Women are currently more than 55 percent of unemployed persons, registered and nonregistered, in the Czech Republic.

The perception that after communism women withdrew into the private

TABLE 4.1 Registered Unemployed (Annual average, thousands)

Year	Men	Women
1990	19.2	20.2
1991	94.6	127.2
1992	57.1	77.7
1993	81.6	103.6
1994	69.8	96.6
1995	64.9	88.1
1996	81.2	105.1
1997	105.1	151.8
1998	181.5	205.4
1999	239.5	248.1

Source: UNICEF-ICDC Florence database

sphere of family and domesticity appears to be based in large part on rhetoric rather than reality. Among working-age women, the striking development since 1989 has not been their retreat from the labor force but the continuity with women's near full employment for at least two if not three generations during socialism. Some Czech men express the opinion that life in the transition is difficult and a family can only survive if the husband devotes himself to pursuing business projects while his wife plays a supportive role, not only doing the housework but also the typing and officework. However, although women's level of participation in the work force has not been greatly altered by the transition, the forms of their participation have.

A Three-Tiered Labor Market

Robert Cox suggests a framework for analyzing the differential impact of globalization on various groups of workers. According to Cox (1995; 1999), workers around the world can be categorized as "integrated," "precarious," and "excluded." These three categories only partially capture the many ways of being a worker, particularly *an excluded* worker, in the global economy. Yet, they provide an important heuristic for analyzing emerging hierarchies in the Czech labor market.[3] Indeed, the Czech Republic is a site in which all the three categories of workers are readily observable.

Since 1989 the Czechs have seen the most rapid rise in wage inequality in the region (Kapoor 1996/7). A three-tiered labor market has emerged. The Czech labor market consists of a first tier akin to a *labor aristocracy* of integrated, skilled, and professional workers who command high-salaried, secure jobs with fringe benefits and the possibility of promotion. The second tier consists of those precarious workers, low-paid and unskilled, whose employment is insecure, while the third tier comprises unofficial workers, often Romany Gypsy or those operating underground and transnationally in illegal economic activities. While women are increasingly among those employees in the first tier, they are the majority of those precarious workers or unemployed in the second tier and as sex workers and trafficked persons, they are an integral part of the unofficial, third-tier of the labor market.

The top two tiers of the labor market increasingly resemble the growing distinction between those employed in the former socialist *public* sector and those employed in the nascent *private* sector. In addition to this public-private differentiation, the Czech transition has seen the emergence of a division between *domestic* firms producing mostly for the national market and *foreign* firms producing mostly for export markets (in 2002 an estimated producing 70 percent of Czech exports).[4] Foreign firms generally offer the most lucrative salaries and employment benefits. In 1999, *Business Central Europe*, the regional journal of the London-based *Economist*, argued that the Czech and Hungarian economies were "split down the middle"; with foreign-owned companies making high-value-added products for export and attracting the most productive labor, and locally owned companies starved of investment and equipment, and competing solely on the basis of low wages (Nicholls 1999; Komínek 1998). In what follows, I analyze the public-private sector division, the domestic-foreign division, and the sex industry, noting how they have structured the labor market in gendered ways.

Female Public Sector, Male Private Sector?

In 1990, the Czech private sector began to expand rapidly, and it was overwhelming dominated by men. They made up 84 percent of private sector employees in 1990, 64 percent in 1992, 62 percent in 1994 and 61 percent in 1998. In addition, men were three quarters of all self-employed entrepreneurs and employers in the late 1990s (Český statistický uřad 1999: 301).

During the restructuring and privatization of state firms between 1990 and 1994, Czech managers, more often than managers in Poland, Hungary, and Slovakia, admitted that they used gender as a high criterion (second only to low productivity) for making employees redundant (Paukert 1995a; 1995b).[5] Unions too, accepted redundancies in "feminized" sectors that were female labor intensive as a legacy of gender-segregation in the socialist economy. According to Peter Rutland (1993: 125), when approving female redundancies Czech union officials volunteered comments such as: "a lot of these girls were not really productive workers anyway." However, male-dominant industries were largely protected and losses/debt written off by the government in the initial macroeconomic, "shock therapy" phase of the transition.[6] For example, the engineering industry was considered by top union officials to be "the mother of Czech industry" that must not be lost.[7] Industrial production output fell by 30 percent between 1990 and 1994 while employment fell only 20 percent. By contrast, employment in the female-dominated textile industry was reduced by half, from 155,000 workers in 1990 to 86,000 in 1995 (Cohen 1997).[8] Organized labor's adaptation to transition restructuring occurred along gender lines as women's jobs were sacrificed to save men's jobs in state-owned and privatized industry. Table 4–1 supports this finding, showing higher numbers of women were registered unemployed, especially in the first transition years.

As Czech men moved into the new private sector beginning in 1990, the public or *civil* sector became even more feminized than during the socialist regime. Women were 46 percent of state employees in 1985, remained at that level in 1990, and by 1998 they were approximately 60 percent of all public sector employees, and more than 75 percent of the employees in the education and health sectors (Český statistický uřad 1999: 278). ILO analyst Liba Paukert (1995a) argues that this outcome is due to the combined effects of the socialist occupational structure of female employment, private firms' gender bias in recruitment, women's greater sense of security in public sector employment, and their lack of time for retraining due to family responsibilities.

Postsocialist transitions have amplified and accelerated the structural changes occurring in the global political economy; for instance, they hastened the rise in the service sector and the concomitant demise of the manufacturing sector, especially of heavy industry. Such transformations have the potential *in theory* to improve women's structural position in the labor market and counter any effects of gender discrimination (Fodor 1997, Fodor and Van der Lippe 1999). An institutionalist perspective might hold that the knowledge capital women acquired under socialism, for example, their higher education, foreign-language competency and experience in service-related areas such as banking and finance, is an advantage under capitalism. The demand for labor in the service sector especially in finance, tourism, information, and administrative services has grown steadily over the last decade, and women were expected to benefit from this trend since they long dominated socialist employment in service occupations (Fong and Paull 1993).

The Czech Republic has fostered a strong service sector more quickly than other countries in the region as a result of booming tourism, small privatization (22,000 shops and other state-owned services were sold to private owners between 1991–1993), the rise in financial sector employment (from 5,000 to 55,000 persons) and the close proximity of the Czech lands to Austrian and German markets (Kapoor 1996/7). The Czech service sector remains female dominated, containing 62 percent of all women workers (which includes public sector education and health). However, women's comparative advantage in this sector has diminished since 1989 and, contrary to institutionalist predictions, no transitional advantage has accrued to women from their socialist experience on the postsocialist labor market.

In private banking and financial services, which have grown exponentially in the transition because they are so fundamental to the operation of capitalism, the greater demand for male labor has resulted in a greater increase in men's share of employment in services (Shen 1994: 8A1). In 1988 more than 80 percent of those employed in financial and banking services were women, in 2000 this proportion had been reduced to 65 percent, as figure 4–1 reveals. Average wages and salaries in the financial sector in 1998 were seven times greater than in 1990 (Český statistický úřad 1989: 198; 1999: 278).

Men have also been attracted to the lucrative job opportunities in the tourism industry where profits can be readily made. Consequently, as shown in figure 4–1, the proportion of female employees in tourism-related services has been reduced from approximately 71 percent in 1990 to 55 percent in 2000. Further, according to the ILO, newly privatized trading and retail businesses are registered mainly in the names of men and have resulted in

FIGURE 4.1   Gender Wage Gap by Occupation

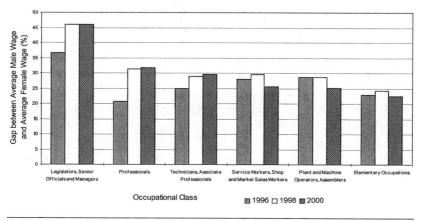

Figure created by author. Statistical source: Český statistický úřad 2001.

unemployment for women who formerly worked in the state retail sector (Paukert 1995b: 11–12).

A 1995 ILO study notes that, "the pattern of employment shifts from the public to the private sector has been detrimental to women in all countries of the Central European region, in an alarmingly similar way" (Paukert 1995b: 15). As the majority of public sector workers, women experience the negative outcomes of rapid privatization. Wages are on average higher in the private sector than in the public sector.[9] Gender segregation in public sectors (e.g. education, health, and social welfare) versus private sectors (financial services, business entrepreneurship) could be seen as a form of "disguised discrimination" considering that there are over three times more women employed in the former areas, where working conditions are substandard and wages are consistently below the average (Kollonay 2000).

Despite the strong association between labor and the core male-dominated industries, it is non-core (women) workers in highly feminized sectors such as education and health that have engaged in most of the labor militancy and strike action in the Czech Republic. This is not surprising given the declining, below-average wages in those sectors and the under-funded, impoverished state of hospitals and schools — both legacies of communist priorities that privileged industrial production.[10] By negotiating a low-wage, low-unemployment compact with the male-dominated unions and business sector in the early 1990s, the Czech government maintained the preexisting socialist occupational wage structure that placed education and health workers among the lowest paid state employees.

Labor costs in the Czech Republic are among the lowest in the Central European region.[11] Tellingly, gender is the single most important variable in determining wage differentiation in the transition (Večerník, Hraba and McCutcheon 1997). In 1989 wages in the feminized health and education sectors were approximately 90 percent of the average wage, in 1997 wages in the health sector were still 90 percent of the average wage, while wages in the education sector had dropped to 88 percent of the average wage. Compare this constancy with the massive increase in relative wages in the more masculinized banking and insurance sector. In 1989 wages in this sector were 98 percent of the average wage whereas in 1997 they were 175 percent of the average wage (Večerník and Matejů 1999: 120).

Manual, low-skilled, occupational categories, whether in the public or private sector, are now at the bottom of the income scale. A process of "equalizing down" has taken place; as men's wages in less skilled occupations and lower wage sectors have been reduced during the transition they have achieved near parity with women's wages in the same sectors (see table 4–2; figure 4–2). Traditional labor, as represented by mainly male core workers in strategic industries, has lost the privileged place it obtained under state socialism.

Foreign Enclaves?

Not only does gender structure the division of public and private sector employment, it also structures the division of the private sector of the Czech economy into foreign and domestic-owned firms. Between 1990 and 2001 more than $23 billion was invested in the Czech Republic. After incentives for foreign investors were introduced in 1998, $6.5 billion flowed into the Czech Republic the next year (OECD 1999a: 110–113).[12] The Czech Republic has received the most foreign direct investment per capita among those former Soviet Bloc countries since 1994. By the end of the 1990s, a large proportion of the world's best-known multinationals had all set up operations in the Czech Republic, including ABB, AssiDoman, Bell-Atlantic, Coca-Cola, Daewoo, Ford, Motorola, Nestle, Procter & Gamble, Renault, Siemens, Toray, and Volkswagen. In total, there were more than

56,000 foreign-owned companies registered in the Czech Republic at the end of 1998. Currently, they employ about 10 percent of the Czech workforce.

Foreign direct investment has so far concentrated in capital-intensive areas such as automobiles, rubber and plastics, machinery, electronics, printing and publishing, chemicals, telecommunications and less so in female labor-intensive industries (light industries such as foodstuffs, glass and ceramics, textiles and garment manufacturing) (OECD 1999b: 48–49). In the former industries, the vast majority of employees are men (Bednáček and Zemplínerová 1997). The only export-processing zone established in the postsocialist Czech Republic is the textile manufacturing industry on the Western Bohemian border with Germany, where unsurprisingly most of the workers are Czech or immigrant women. Foreign multinationals in the Czech Republic employ nearly 20 percent of the industrial sector work force, and on average pay 25 percent above the average wage in domestic-owned private firms (OECD 1999b: 22).

The average wages in these foreign companies are 50 percent greater than the average wage in the female-dominated public sector. They exceed public sector wages by an average of 50 percent, and this gap is increasing. Higher wages are paid despite the punitive government tax, designed to keep wages down, incurred by companies that pay wages above the state-mandated ceiling. In 1997 the Czech Ministry of Industry and Trade reported that the average wage in the public sector was 9, 913 Czech crowns (ČZK), in the private sector 10,962 ČZK and in foreign firms 14,704 ČZK. Foreign firms also reported the greatest increase in wages. The lowest average wages, 7,484 (ČZK), were reported in the private (*Czech-owned*) female labor-intensive garment manufacturing industry. The highest average wages, 33,386 (ČZK); were reported in the *foreign-owned* financial sector (Český statistický úřad 1999: 281–84).

The wage differential between managers and workers, the lowest and highest paid is also far bigger in foreign firms, disproportionately affecting women who are generally at the low end of these corporate hierarchies. Coopers & Lybrand's half-year study of employee wages in foreign companies in the Czech Republic showed that a joint venture director earned ČZK 171,000 approximately $5,000 per month in 1998 while the most highly qualified worker at the same firm earned ČZK 13,214. According to the Czech research company Trexima, in 1997 the average salary of a male general director or CEO was 61,000 crowns a month. Women who were general directors received 38,500 crowns a month, that is, 66 percent less than a man in the same position (McClune 1998).[13]

Gender wage gaps present in Central and Eastern Europe countries are explained by discrimination in the remuneration received by men and women who share similar characteristics and jobs, in contrast to western countries where the gap is largely explained by differences in men and women's education level, skill, experience, and occupational sector (ILO-CEET 2000). As table 4–2 indicates, the gender gap in remuneration in the Czech Republic is still large, between 17 and 40 percent. The gap is sizeable in those nascent private sector industries, such as finance and insurance services, restaurants and accommodation, which have seen the most growth and profit since 1989.

Although the aggregate Czech gender wage gap has grown smaller since the 1980s, it has actually been widening in the upper income, managerial and professional job categories ("Ženy v České Republice . . ." 1998; Chase 1998). Figure 4–2 reveals that the greatest gender wage gap is between men and women legislators, senior officials, and managers. Moreover, it is likely that we would see further variation if this data could be disaggregated

TABLE 4.2 Average Female Salary Share of Average Male Salary
In Some Professions in 1998 (In %)

Profession	Female Share of Average Male Salary
Agriculture and Hunting, Forestry	78.1
Construction Industry	81.3
Trade, Repair Services	60.5
Restaurants and Accommodation	70.6
Transportation, Storage, Postal and Telecommunication Services	83.2
Finance, Insurance Services	65.6
Health Care, Veterinary and Social Activities	76.6
Education	68.5

Source: Ministry of Labor and Social Affairs

FIGURE 4.2 Change and Continuity in the Gender Structure of Economic Sectors

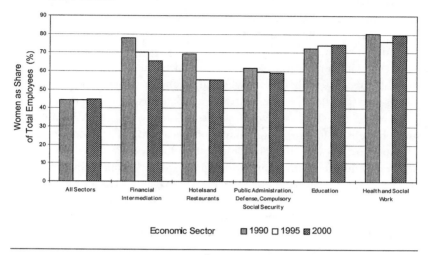

Figure created by author. Statistical source: Český statistický úřad 2001.

by sector: state, domestic private, or foreign private. For instance, Věra Kuchařová's (1999: 188–189) analysis of the Czech 1996 Microcensus survey reveals that women in state-run companies receive more than 80 percent of the income of men, while women in foreign companies earn less than 60 percent.

Foreign capitalism is premised on a masculine gender bias. Human resources firms admit that foreign firms using their services prefer to employ male managers and staff. They view women employees as less productive and more expensive because they may take between two and four years of maternity leave.[14] Whereas the socialist organization of labor worked in favor of women's dual roles as workers and as household managers, allowing them to take the time to stand in queues for groceries and to take their children to the doctor for instance, in the market system, these dual roles are the basis for discrimination against women workers. As such, gender-neutral English and German job descriptions are converted into Czech gender-specific forms. Advertising preferences for male or female employees are usually also within a certain age range (Jedličková 1996a: 30).[15] Local Czech and foreign executive search and personnel services reproduce this discriminatory environment on behalf of their clients. When asked if foreign firms discriminate against Czech employees, Petra Vanková of the Commercial Union responded that most people prefer men of a certain age group as executives or managers ("Jsou čest zaměstnánci . . ." 1998). Jana Novotná, managing director of "Manpower" a human resources firm in the Czech Republic has also publicly acknowledged that her firm often has to deal with clients who specifically request a male candidate for a management position: "Of course," she says "we always ask the client why he prefers a man. Normally he tells us that men don't have complications with children etcetera. The standard answers" ("Jak trnitá je cesta žen . . ." 1998).

Young educated women with foreign language competency are an exception. Western companies needing local managers and expertise often find them appealing because they can be rapidly socialized into western corporate culture; they are even more appealing as trophy secretaries (Dvořák and Solčová 1998). Petr Zahradník comments that Czech women who are secretaries or assistants to foreign managers are expected to work overtime and respond to their requests beyond the workday. Unlike during socialism, little consideration is apparently given to the fact that these women employees may have small children and family responsibilities ("Jsou čest zaměstnánci . . ." 1998).

Personnel firms openly acknowledge the corporate preference for young male managers. For their part, young men are attracted by the masculine, slick image of western corporations, regardless of whether this involves marketing Coca-Cola or feminine sanitary products (Ascoly 1994; Wheatly 1992; Brdečková 1994).[16] Curiously, expatriate women working in the Czech Republic have remarked that they have achieved greater experience, more prestigious positions, and are treated with more respect as managers and executives than would be the case in North America or Western Europe.[17] They are taken seriously because they are *foreigners* with so-called "expertise." Czech women managers, by contrast, are often not taken seriously precisely because of their gender (Orol 1998). They are seen to have none of the expertise or cachet of foreign women, and all of the baggage of the socialist era.

Stereotypical perceptions and prejudices against women in foreign and multinational sectors have strategic implications for the gendered restructuring of the entire labor market in the Czech Republic. Economists generally hold foreign firms to be key actors in the diffusion of innovative knowledge, management, and technology to domestic public and private industries in transition countries. Their "best practices" in the region are strategically thought to raise the standards of local firms through competition and demonstration effects (e.g. resulting in institutional isomorphism with the West) (Eichengreen and Kohl 1998; Nielsen 1995).[18] However, if foreign firms in the Czech Republic are routinely practicing gender discrimination in their recruitment and employment policies, consciously preferring men over women and thus restructuring the labor market in explicitly gendered ways, what may be diffused to domestic firms in this case are not "best practices" but discriminatory practices that are often illegal in the home countries of these multinationals.

Gender and age discrimination has gone unsanctioned due to vague laws, poor enforcement of labor codes since 1989, and a society that has unconsciously has turned a blind eye to such practices even during communism (Kobešová and Dvořáková 1998; Zachvalová 1999). However, the requirement that applicant countries to the European Union (EU) harmonize their legislation with European law, including the body of European equal opportunities legislation and policy, before joining the EU makes this lack of action in the Czech Republic viable only in the short-term (see Fuchs 1998; Paraschiv 2002).

Sex and Power in the Labor Market

Sexual Harassment at Work

In addition to the increasing gender-based discrimination against women in the nascent Czech labor market, recent public investigations have exposed sexual harassment as a major problem. Academic feminists such as law professor Catherine MacKinnon first developed sexual harassment as a concept in the 1970s in Canada and the United States. MacKinnon extended the Marxist analogy of capitalists exploiting their workers to sexual harassment, which she saw as a metaphor for capitalism's exploitation of women by men (MacKinnon 1989).[19] In this view, "men . . . in corporate America, use their favored position in the capitalist system to dominate and control women" (Paul 1999: 94–95). Along with other feminists, MacKinnon saw sexual harassment as the vehicle for prostituting women in the workplace. When a woman is fired for refusing the sexual advances of a male supervisor, it is because she is a *woman* and not because of the personal sexual idiosyncrasies of her boss. Since the late 1970s then, employers have been held responsible for the infractions of their supervisory employees, as agents of the firm. More recently, employers have been made liable for any actions by co-workers that contribute to a "hostile working environment," when the employer knew or should have known of the harassment and failed to take remedial action.

In the postsocialist Czech Republic sexual harassment is widespread by all indications. A 1999 study commissioned by the Czech daily *Lidové Noviny* found that nearly half of all working women have been subjected to sexual harassment at work. To the shock of many Czechs, the study found that 45 percent of Czech women had been sexually harassed, many of them repeatedly. More strikingly, one-third of those women quit their jobs as a result of unwanted and unpleasant sexual advances by a male superior in their workplace, and only 2 percent informed the police (Sofres Factum 1999).[20] An institutionalist perspective explains sexual harassment as a legacy of the way in which communist paternalism infiltrated the workplace and overly personalized work relationships. But the communist experience alone is not responsible for this male treatment of women workers. Following MacKinnon's feminist perspective, it is also possible that, in the highly-charged atmosphere of the transition, Czech men are sexually harassing Czech women to ensure their power in the new capitalist system.

Under communism, the personalized workplace — where personal relationships take priority over party ones — emerged as an adaptation to the state's attempt to collectivize everything. Ironically, it was this antipolitical resistance to communist authority rather than the communist system itself that rendered public and private spheres transparent. Obscene jokes, suggestive remarks, unwelcome advances, gentle slaps were apparently all part of "the culture" of communist workplaces. Despite the avowed gender egalitarianism of the socialist state, most working women did not complain for fear of state retribution. This fear has apparently endured in the transition to the market economy.[21] In today's capitalist labor market, the political function of harassment is the same; to subdue, intimidate, and stigmatize women workers. However, in addition, sexual harassment drives its victims out of the competition for the new benefits the capitalist workplace has to offer, leaving only a select group of core, privileged workers.

The experience of communism may have normalized sexual harassment at work, but the phenomenon cannot be attributed to the communist system by itself; indeed capitalist systems have also provided a home for it to flourish.

Even foreign multinational companies, who are required by law in their home country to have policies against sexual harassment, rarely publicize these policies in their local headquarters or translate them into local languages so that they reach actual workplaces. Moreover, the priority placed on economic reform over institutional legal reform (with the exception of property law) under neoliberal governments in the Czech Republic has engendered a situation where there are no local mechanisms to prevent the incidence of sexual harassment and few legal remedies for its victims. This postsocialist environment has encouraged the institutionalization of sexist attitudes in the new labor market, even though for employers operating in a competitive marketplace, one would think men's harassment of women at work would be a hindrance to the efficiency and productivity of their employees. The lack of concern for sexual harassment in the Czech context suggests that the Czech version of capitalism has been closely fused with old socialist workplace norms and patronage networks.

With the opening of a democratic discussion since 1989, awareness among women about the problem of sexual harassment has grown. Women's rights advocates in Central and Eastern Europe have persisted in raising this issue of men's maltreatment of women at work. However, discussion of the topic has been taboo among postsocialist citizens in a context where freedom from communism has often been expressed through sex and sexuality. Sexual harassment itself is a western term that was imported to the Czech Republic after 1989. Early on in the transition, it was widely seen as a form of American radical feminism that threatened to spoil the "natural" relations between men and women. Indeed, sexual harassment was first translated into the Czech language as "sexuální harašení" by the Czech-Canadian émigré writer Josef Škvorecký, which roughly means "sexual buzz or rumble" something akin to flirting rather than a flagrant abrogation of a woman's rights (Škvorecký 1992a).[22] He attributed sexual harassment laws in America to the frustrations of frigid feminists and decried the scourge of political correctness that these laws had engendered. The sensational media dialogue between Škvorecký exiled in Canada and a Canadian feminist living in Prague had the effect of squashing any serious discussion of the problem of sexual harassment in Czech workplaces in the first half of the 1990s (Busheikin et al. 1992).[23]

Surveys of women's opinions in the early 1990s found sexual harassment was a particular problem for only five percent of Czech women. Women's rights advocates suggested a new Czech translation, "sexuální obtežování," that came closer to the intended meaning of the English term (Jedličková 1996b). Sexuální obtežování is defined as "that behavior of men which either directly (e.g. offers of employment on the condition of spending the night, the opportunity to become physically or emotionally familiar) or frequently indirectly (e.g. offers to spend the weekend together) demands or at least suggests intimate physical contact" (Sofres Factum 1999: 4). However, in the late 1990s sexuální harašení was still being used alongside the new, more correct term, sexuální obtežování. Not until 1996 was an actual sexual harassment case successfully prosecuted in the Czech courts as a violation of the labor code, which provides a vaguely defined right to a harmless work environment (McClune and Stojaspol 1996; Perlez 1996). In this high-profile case, a manager at the major state bank Komerční Banka was dismissed after a secretary filed a sexual harassment complaint against him. In a previous case involving the same man filed the year before in 1995, the bank had refused to act.

The second woman to win a sexual harassment suit was a student at Olomouc's Palacký University, Dagmar Frýsaková in 1999 (Plotová 1999). A few weeks before getting married, a teaching assistant in the university library approached Ms. Frýsaková. When she refused his advances, the man forced her hand to his genitals and ejaculated on her skirt. The parallel with the story of Monica Lewinsky's dress did not go unnoticed. The stained skirt allowed Ms. Frýsaková to win the lawsuit, although the man only received an eight-month suspension from Palacký University ("Sexuální harašení před . . ." 1999; Bauerová 2000). At the same time, following the Clinton-Lewinsky debacle in the United States, several articles were published in the main dailies under the headlines, "sexual harassment is not a Czech problem," "sexual harassment is not present in the Czech lands" and so on ("Sexuální obtežování . . ."1998; "Sexuální harašení . . ." 1998). However, when *Lidové Noviny* asked five well-known Czech women, three of them politicians, whether they thought sexual harassment existed in the Czech Republic, four replied that they thought it did ("Co říkájí významní . . ."1998).

The initial court cases of sexual harassment have underscored the weakness of the Czech legal framework for dealing with gender injustices in employment. One would assume that sexual harassment actually existed before 1989, but could not be broached in a system which did not allow for freedom of expression, had few mechanisms if any for the protection of human rights, and in which there was no conceptual language to articulate the power relations between men and women. What has changed since 1989 therefore, is the introduction of a new conceptual language and set of legal principles adapted from western countries that together have made visible different forms of discrimination and harm. This diffusion of western concepts has sparked a public discussion, taboo under communism because of its ideological blindness to conflicts not based on class (see Vizdal 1998). Moreover, the EU accession process has given incentives to EU applicant countries such as the Czech Republic to provide adequate legal protection and institutional mechanisms for ensuring there are equal employment opportunities (European Parliament 1998; Paraschiv 2002).

In order to fulfill the requirements for EU admission and remove any barriers to market making, the Czech parliament discussed a draft law on sexual harassment designed to harmonize Czech law with EU law in December 1999. This law was passed in 2000. However, male experts, psychologists, and politicians publicly expressed their skepticism toward the law. The Minister of Labor and Social Affairs is on record as stating that the draft amendment to the Work Act, which will define the term sexual harassment, is not a Czech initiative but rather appeases EU demands. These critics of the new law argue that it is impractical in the Czech context where "a different view of morality exists than in America (from whence they see the law deriving), and where the integrity of the law will be undermined by everyday practice. Although they do not deny that sexual harassment is present in Czech workplaces, like Škvorecký earlier, they claim that passing a law against it "will elevate human foolishness to a new height" (Kučera 1999a). These arguments only go to show that legal protection of equality is a necessary but not sufficient mechanism for changing deeply embedded attitudes toward women among Czech male élites in particular. The Czech sexual harassment law is gender neutral and also protects men who have experienced harassment at work, although it is designed with the expectation that the majority of cases will involve women plaintiffs. Yet, such a law conflicts with Czech neoliberals' skepticism toward legislating morality and violates the boundary around private life, which many Czechs, including those former-communist dissidents and civil society advocates, wish to defend (Neunerová 1999).

Sex Work — a New Type of Labor or a Market in Women?

Just as sex at work is being outlawed, the sex industry is becoming a thriving business in the Czech lands, part and parcel of rejoining the European fraternity. Sex work, and other informal, often underground, economic activities constitute a third, less visible, tier of the new Czech labor market. This third-tier sex market shapes the overall labor market environment for Czech women and the perception of women workers in the more visible first and second tiers of the labor market. However, equal opportunities law covers only those who experience sexual harassment in legal workplaces; in no country does it address the gender and socioeconomic class differences that cause women to become sex-workers. The burgeoning global sex market has profited handsomely from the liberalization of Central and Eastern Europe. As poverty grows, unemployment rises, and the economic situation gets worse in the Czech Republic and other former East bloc countries, prostitution is one of the few jobs left that pays a living wage. Women's bodies are commodities in the newly privatized Czech marketplace and tourism industry. Prostitution existed under communism, albeit illegally. But in the wake of socialism's fall, prostitution was less stigmatized since it was no longer a crime against the regime and the market for it expanded greatly with the opening of Czech borders to the West.

Prostitution is just one aspect of a much larger, globalized sex industry that spread quickly across Eastern Europe after 1989. Other products and services include the trade in pornographic books and films, strip/sex clubs and sex tours. The opening of borders within the EU and between Eastern and Western Europe along with wider print media and Internet access to proliferating erotic images is facilitating not only economic integration, but also a Europeanization of sexual desires and practices (Borneman and Fowler 1997). The European integration process has created geographic locations where sexual practices that are illegal in most states are not only legal but the basis for an entire growth industry. John Borneman and Nigel Fowler (1997) call these places "Eurogenous zones." The zones are all well-known sex tourist sites, with both customers and "suppliers" often coming from elsewhere to be someone else; one of these zones is the Czech-German border; another is Central Prague.

In the northern Bohemian towns of Dubi, Chomutov, and Teplice close to where the E-55 highway (which runs from Prague to Dresden and then to Berlin and is called "the longest beat in Europe") crosses the German border at Zinnwalk-Gerogenweld-Cinovec, the sex trade is prospering. Under communism, E-55 was already notorious for offering a variety of sexual services to truckers making the long haul from Scandinavia to the Balkans (as described in Iva Perkařková's 1993 novel, *Truck Stop Rainbows*, where the main character is a young woman environmentalist who makes her living this way). When the borders opened in 1989, E-55 became a magnet for international criminals practicing more sophisticated activities, including pedophilia, drug trafficking, forced transportation of women and girls for prostitution, and smuggling immigrants to the West. The police chief in Teplice, Petr Zelasko explains: "There is a great demand by foreigners in this area for all sorts of perverse sexual activities. It's cheap, very accessible and totally anonymous" (Mortkowitz and Stojaspol 1996). In addition to the border region, Prague 1, the historic core of the capital city of the Czech Republic, is acquiring the reputation of "Central Europe's Bangkok," in the words of the head of the Prague police vice squad chief, Petr Vosolsobe. He estimates that Prague alone has 300 brothels holding some 15,000 women. Moreover, Czech police estimate that about 70 percent of all missing Czech women between the ages of 10 and 40 have been abducted and sold into sex slavery (Mortkowitz and Stojaspol 1996).

Soliciting prostitution is illegal in the Czech Republic, not as a criminal act as under communism's social parasitism clause, but through other violations of the law. After little public discussion of the sex industry during the first six years of transition, in 1996 the Czech government sought to legalize and closely regulate the industry by registering and taxing sex-workers (Sarah 1996). A bill proposed in the Czech parliament that year, estimated that $10 billion in taxes had been lost each year through untaxed prostitution (Donovan 2000; Štástná 1999; Kabat 1998). The author of the bill, Jitka Gjuricová from the Ministry of Interior, said there are some 25,000 Czech women making their living from prostitution, excluding sex-workers from other countries resident in the Czech Republic. But community leaders and women's rights advocates generally agree that while the legalization of prostitution may help to contain the industry in appropriate spaces, prostitution is primarily a social problem that has its root in poverty and unemployment. As the Prague police chief saw the problem in 1996: "If the exchange rate between the German mark and the Czech crown were reversed all our problems would simply slip across the border" (Mortkowitz and Stojaspol 1996).[24]

In the Czech Republic, as in other Central and Eastern European countries, prostitution is inextricably intertwined with trafficking of women to Western Europe, but also to Israel and Asia (Heinrich Boll Foundation 1996; Specter 1998). Since 1989, there has been a huge recruitment of women from Eastern Europe, especially Russia, Poland, the Czech Republic, and

Bulgaria, to service West Europe's heterosexual male desires. The Czech Republic is in the unique position, poised as it is on the Eastern border of the EU, of being both a sending and a receiving country for trafficked women. Conservative estimates put the number of women smuggled each year into the EU through the Czech Republic at 300,000. The United Nations estimates that worldwide, approximately 1.2 million women and girls are trafficked for prostitution annually (UNDP 2000: 4). The International Organization for Migration put the annual figure for Central Europe at more than 500,000, while the Ukraine government estimates that many of the 400,000 women who have left the country since 1992 have been drawn into the sex trade and industry. The sex business in Europe is thought to be worth some $9 billion a year ("Trafficking in women . . ." 2000; Cohen 2000). Due to the illegality of the trade though and the obvious difficulties in accurately observing it, estimates vary widely (Kempadoo & Doezema 1998).

Mafia-type traffickers take advantage of women from Central and Eastern European countries who are looking to the West for opportunities. Lack of opportunity at home "compels East European women to take risks their peers in Western Europe would never contemplate." ("Trafficking in women . . ." 2000:38). Advertisements lure them. "Single, tall and pretty? Want to work abroad? Often seemingly honest women standing in for male traffickers, promise the girls legitimate jobs once they are over the border ("Plenty of muck . . ." 1999). Since the Czech Republic is a point of origin, sale *and* transit of women, there are 600 brothels or so across the countries with an estimated 20,000 trafficked women. Large criminal rackets are centered in the Czech Republic because of its proximity to the West. As many as 40 percent of female sex trade workers in the Czech Republic are estimated to be foreigners, of whom 25 to 30 percent are said to be Ukrainian. (Other common countries of origin are Bulgaria, Romania, and Slovakia).

Of those Czech women who have been trafficked since 1989, some have returned to tell their horror stories. For instance, in 1992 the Yugoslav mafia smuggled three Czechoslovak women to an Amsterdam hotel. They took their passports and locked them up. The girls finally ran away to Germany and went to the Czech embassy there. They were the lucky ones, however (Waxman 1993; Brussa ed. 1999). A recent unpublicized United States CIA report indicated that the Czech Republic is one of the countries from which more than 50,000 women are trafficked to the United States each year and forced into prostitution.[25] Indeed, in 1996 a transnational women-trafficking team was broken up in New York City and a Czech employee at the American embassy in Prague was found to have issued false tourist visas and to be working in cohort with the male traffickers (Bauerová 1998). The trade in women is a very profitable business in postsocialist countries such as the Czech Republic because of the relatively easy corruption of the police and other local bureaucratic authorities as well as the poor economic situation of many young women.

In 1994, *Profem*, a Czech women's advocacy organization held Europe's first East-West conference on trafficking in women. The conference brought together former and current working prostitutes from around Europe to discuss the issue. As one street worker from Liberec, Czech Republic noted,

[t]rafficking in women and possible abductions, are among the most secret things. Nothing is said about them. . . . The truth is you cannot help but notice the frequent changes of girls standing on the streets, their sporadic disappearance, redeployment and returns. . . . At the beginning the girls told us they were ill, that they went home or something like that. In recent times some of them seem, at least to us, to show signs of anxiety about their friends who are gone and from whom there is no word. We know that the pimps sell these girls among themselves. The women are sold abroad and also to other places in the Czech Republic or directly to Germany. (Heinrich Boll Foundation 1996: 31)

Sex trafficking is a criminal activity, which because it is by nature underground, has hardly been acknowledged let alone adequately addressed by the Czech police or government as a grave gender injustice and a serious abrogation of international human rights law. In their press release after the first conference on sex trafficking in Prague, women's rights advocates protested:

The absolute lack of any policies protecting the rights of women working in prostitution places women completely at the mercy of pimps. . . . Marginalization and stigmatization further strengthen the grip of criminal networks on these women and make them subordinate to various forms of exploitation, as well as violations of their human rights (Heinrich Boll Foundation 1996: 1–2).

Yet, at the same time as large numbers of young women have been sexually abused and left with few rights in foreign countries, a group in the Czech Ministry of Interior and Parliament has been working to have prostitution recognized as a trade in the Czech Republic so that the allegedly fantastic sums prostitutes earn would, in their opinion, come into the state treasury in a proper way (Heinrich Boll Foundation 1996: 28; Šťastná 1999). There are some in the Czech government who would like to see Czech foreign exchange reserves boosted through the remittances of young women working as prostitutes abroad, roughly following Thailand's rise to economic prosperity through the marketing of sex tourism or the Philippines' remittances from foreign female domestic workers (see Chin 1998). While pursuing this economic interest, it is also possible that the state, by recognizing the legality of sex work, may be able to extend some protection to sex workers. Recently, the European Parliament passed a report on the Czech Republic's progress toward EU membership. It called on Prague to pay "urgent attention to the problem of sex tourism, child prostitution, and trafficking in women in the border area between Germany and the Czech Republic" (Radio Free Europe 2000f). Thus, if the Czech Republic is to court EU membership whether or not it succeeds in economically benefiting from the sex trade, it will have to use some of its resources to prevent the export of young women.[26]

Return to European Norms?

In 1998 the screening process for the Czech Republic's entry into the EU began in earnest. This process precipitated the establishment of a department for the equal status of women and men inside the Czech Ministry of Labor and Social Affairs[27] and an interministerial working group (including representatives from civil society "social partners" in EU parlance) on discrimination against women in employment.[28] On December 22, 1999, after two successive negative report cards from the European Commission, the Czech government approved an amendment to the Labor Code bringing it in line with European legislation (Radio Free Europe 1999). This amendment includes among other things, provisions for equal employment opportunities for men and women designed to prevent gender-based employment discrimination (Karat Coalition 1999). The first report by the Czech Ministry of Labor and Social Affairs to the European Commission noted that legal and illegal discrimination based on gender is a common occurrence in the Czech Republic. It concluded that there should be further discussion of the potential institutional mechanisms that could monitor equal opportunities in the Czech Republic, drawing on the external models of the United Kingdom where there is an autonomous agency for equal opportunities or Germany, where a governmental ministry with many regional branches is devoted to this task (see Castle-Kanerová 1996).

The diffusion of EU gender politics and equal opportunity policies has stimulated public discussion about gender issues in the Czech Republic ("Ženy patři k plotne . . ."1998; Čapová 1998; Karat Coalition 1998). Seminars and newspaper coverage of discrimination against women in employment proliferated once the negotiations with the EU began in 1998 and 1999.[29] But while this process has forced the Czech Republic and other countries seeking admission to the EU to emulate its legislation, it has also provided an incentive for Czechs to disguise their difficulties in implementing laws, such as the equal opportunity law and policy.

The Czechs can easily pass an equal opportunity law; they passed many such equality laws under communism. But what concerns the Delegation of the European Commission in Prague is the government's failure to properly implement these laws and the informal culture that effectively undermines their integrity.[30] Reacting against the communist legacy, and yet reproducing it at the same time, Ministry of Labor and Social Affairs officials are reluctant to implement legal or institutional remedies for discrimination against women in the labor market.[31] They interpret equal opportunities as the absence of discrimination rather than a positive endorsement of the equal treatment of women and men workers (Castle-Kanerová 1999: 237). What is more, women themselves are not willing to take cases of discrimination to court for fear of being branded feminists in an anticommunist culture, according to Czech sociologist Maria Čermáková (Zachvalová 2000).

At a three-day seminar in the Czech Republic on the position of women in European legislation, many of the sixty or so women participants shed doubt upon the credibility and purpose of EU equal opportunities policy (Český Svaz Žen 1998).[32] Some women drew parallels between the imposition of Soviet norms from above and the current requirement for the Czech Republic to comply with EU law. More than just a reaction against communism, the seminar discussion exposed some of the key weaknesses of EU gender policy, its lack of enforcement mechanisms, the expense of litigation, the law's failure to acknowledge women's roles as mothers and caregivers, and any legitimate distinctions between men and women. Although there are many similarities in the material forms that gender inequality takes in

EU states and in postsocialist states, there are important normative differences between women in these states, especially in their attitudes toward equality and gender identity.

In the race to join the EU, Czech government officials have focused narrowly on the legal aspects of equal opportunities seeking to prove that the Czech national law and traditions accord with EU law and policy, rather than initiating proactive measures to monitor equal opportunities and equal treatment. According to Mita Castle-Kanerová (1999), the EU integration departments in Czech ministries were instructed to speed up the process of harmonization. The European Commission let the Czechs know that "the time of actual implementation when real sanctions might apply was still far off" (Castle-Kanerová 1999: 238). Certainly, there is no indication that the Czech Premier, Miloš Zeman, has changed his sexist attitudes in light of the Czech Republic's bid for EU membership. In 2000, he stated that holding a referendum on EU entry before knowing the conditions of the union would be tantamount to "facing the decision whether or not to marry a woman whose age, size of breasts or waist, or dowry are unknown."[33] So the Czech government has used a considerable amount of EU financial assistance to translate documents and make amendments to national legislation, none of which has resulted in any change in the sexist culture Czech politics let alone in Czech workplaces.

Conclusion

Policymakers advocated radical economic reforms in the Czech Republic. After 1989 they argued that the falling rate of productivity, high inflationary pressures, and poor quality of goods and services inherited from the system of economic planning gave them no alternative but to rapidly adopt structural adjustment policies, including liberalization, privatization, and reductions in state expenditures. However, as institutionalist, neo-Marxist, and feminist scholars have all argued, because they are based on theoretical models deduced from North American and European experiences, these neoliberal prescriptions neglected the social and political context in which market reforms were instituted in Central and Eastern European states. Certainly they failed to anticipate the gender-differentiated impact of these reforms.

The evidence presented in this chapter has revealed some of the gender-differentiated consequences of the Czech capitalist transition in the nascent labor market. As in other parts of the world, women have generally been more disadvantaged than men by more than a decade of labor restructuring in the Czech Republic. In addition to altering class relations, commodifying labor in an emerging market has promoted a three-tiered labor force and given rise both to employment discrimination against women and their egregious sexual exploitation. In so doing, it has engendered a new "common sense" about masculinity and femininity.

The standards for judging what are appropriate workplace relations and who is an appropriate employee in any given economic sector or job have been conditioned by stereotypical assumptions about gender. Although pre-1989 socialist gender relations have clearly shaped the divisions in the new labor market, market forces have reshaped socialist gender relations. For instance, by reconfiguring the boundaries of public and private, state and society, national and international market forces have heightened the feminization of the public/state sector and produced a highly masculine private sector, in both its domestic and foreign-owned forms. At the same time, state downsizing and replacement by an almost religious faith in market mechanisms have reinforced rather than eradicated previous, deep gender inequalities in remuneration and occupational status.

Moreover, the absence of gender awareness on the part of Czech reformers and lawmakers has effectively allowed for unfettered discrimination against women in the labor market. Political discourses of anticommunism and the market moreover provide no avenue for addressing rampant sexual harassment and predatory cronyism in Czech workplaces. These very practices may well be continuous with communist shop floor routines, yet they effectively undermine both the freedom and efficiency, which are apparently the hallmarks of a contract-based labor market. Just as the myths of socialism told us that exploitation and oppression had been eradicated, the myths of capitalism are that freedom and efficiency will weed out all injustice and discrimination (see Friedman 1962). Sexist practices at work have been contested and debated in the Czech public realm, suggesting some hope for future remedies supported by the EU. Yet, the sex industry and illegal market in trafficked women and girls remains officially invisible and if not taboo, then rarely on the public agenda for discussion let alone government action. The Czech government has so far failed to develop institutional mechanisms or shown the political will to rectify pervasive gender biases in the labor market, and even less so the exploitation associated with the thriving sex trade located within and across the Czech Republic's borders. However, given the penetration of western investment capital and imports in Central and Eastern Europe, the saturation of marketing media and new forms of consumption may be as important as labor market dynamics in interpreting and explaining the gendered outcomes of postsocialist transformations.

5   Expanding Consumer Markets

This chapter argues that capitalist expansion in Eastern Europe has been promoted by the marketing of gender identities in global culture industries and consumer advertising.[1] This marketing has created new class and gender distinctions. Multinational firms that capitalize on emerging market opportunities in Central and Eastern Europe — the likes of Coca Cola and Citibank — do not merely trade goods and services; they also profoundly alter existing social relations.

Reinscribing gender identities and desires is a sound multinational corporate strategy for maximizing profits and increasing consumption in this region. But the interplay between the local and the global is not straightforward. The case studies of Czech-*Harlequin* and *Cosmopolitan* Magazine presented in this chapter show how this global marketing is contested in the postsocialist context. In the aftermath of communism, new norms of gender relations, ostensibly exports from the West, enable the extension of markets and consumerism, while also empowering women as individuals and consumers.

Recently, institutionalist scholars have studied the economic growth as well as the new inequalities that have resulted from extending trade and financial markets to more and more parts of the world. In so doing, they have developed a deeper understanding of the nature and limits of globalization.[2] But institutionalists have rarely analyzed the gender dimensions of economic growth and inequality arising from globalization. Some international relations studies have revealed the salience of norms and cultural identities in the post–cold-war period, as political and economic structures undergo change.[3] However, while these approaches have been useful in explaining the collapse of communism,[4] they have yet to be systematically applied to the subsequent transitions from communism in East-Central Europe. Several feminist political economists have documented how changes in gender relations are tied to the globalization of market forces.[5] But even feminist political economy has tended to overlook the cultural dimensions of structural change and their implications for changing gender identities.[6] This chapter investigates the dual processes of expanding markets and marketing gender distinctions in the Czech Republic.

Transitions in modes of consumption offer important lessons for the study of international political economy, revealing just how pervasive gender symbols and identities are to the representations and rituals of the capitalist mode of production. In Eastern Europe, the saturation of advertising media and consumer marketing suggests that representations of difference conveyed through gender identity are a "strategic nexus" of globalization (cf. Sassen 1998: 85). The association between the growth of an acquisitive consumer society and the creation of new gender roles has been noted before in both the West and the East.[7] Craig Murphy and Cristina de Ferro (1995) argue that these practices of representation are integral aspect of the globalization of political economies. In their view, "the power of representation in IPE [international political economy] lies in the universalization of the categories of capitalism and of the application of laissez-faire principles to all aspects of history regardless of cultural, racial or gender differences" (1995: 66). These practices of representation produce new identity politics but not any unity of identity although they seek to draw all human beings into the fold of global capitalism.

The cultural dynamics in postsocialist transformations and the global integration process revolve around gender. Debates about globalization generally refer to *economic* globalization, that is, to global flows of trade and financial capital, and the spatial dispersion of innovation and production. However, this transaction-based conception of globalization fails to analyze the intangible but powerful cultural representations, products, and dispositions that are *practices* of globalization. More so than economic and political spheres, the realm of cultural production has been de-linked from any national or stable locations and thus cannot be adequately captured by the notion of "flows" (cf. Appadurai 1996). "Transnational, for-profit, 'culture industries' (loosely defined as sectors that use symbols, stories, images, and information to generate profits) are now the world's most powerful cultural institutions" (Budde 1998: 77). Contemporary capitalism's reliance on ephemeral images and brands "have made the cultural realm the most globalized arena," as more and more of our meaning producing activities take place in that realm (Palumbo-Liu and Gumbrecht 1997: 15; Klein 1999).

Culture industries, especially American popular culture, play a more important role than ever before in global capitalism. It is worth noting that *culture*, such as Hollywood films and television programs, now constitutes the largest single export industry in the United States. According to the United Nations Development Program (1999: 33), Hollywood films grossed more than $30 billion worldwide in 1997. With the globalization and acceleration of production, consumption in general must be continually increased if firms are to grow and survive in a competitive environment. David Harvey (1996: 246) argues that capital penetration of the realm of cultural production is especially lucrative "because the lifetime of consumption of images, as opposed to more tangible [industrial] objects like autos and refrigerators, is almost instantaneous." Moreover, most groups in society, young and old, the "haves" and the "have-nots," men and women, can afford some object of cultural distinction, however small, a chocolate bar or a lipstick, a movie ticket or a flashy magazine. Thus, the market for cultural production is readily made in boom-times as well as in "transitional recessions."

Cultural capital, particularly American cultural capital, may be one of the most potent forces for global transformation, and I suggest, for the transformation of postsocialist Europe. Neoliberal "shock therapy" did not have its desired effects in realm of production, given the slow and stagnating growth rates in the Czech Republic during the 1990s. However indirectly, in the realm of consumption, market reforms were widely popular, as new merchandise filled stores and new shopping centers appeared after 1989. Integrating Eastern Europe entails more than a transition to a new global order and a market-based way of satisfying material needs. It also means assimilating to a new ideological and symbolic system suffused by new gender and class distinctions (Bourdieu 1984).

The closeness of Western European lifestyles, consumer goods, travel, and media during communism fed a desire for all things western among many Central and Eastern Europeans and thus prepared the ground for the tumultuous changes of 1989–90. When the Czech Republic was frequently lauded as one of the most successful cases of transition from socialism to capitalism following a neoliberal reform program, one aspect of that case was that personal consumption sharply increased, exceeding increases in wages and production output.[8] Real wages had barely returned to their 1989 levels ten years later and yet consumption continued to rise. I argue that global marketing and advertising has driven this unprecedented trend by linking the ownership and consumption of goods and services to new class, gender and generational identities.

The objectification of gender is facilitating the extension of markets and capitalist market culture in the Czech Republic. Products that exploit gender differences and firms that target gender-specific consumer markets appear to have a strategic advantage in generating profits and greater market-share as I show below. One of the reasons for this development since 1989, I suggest, is the ubiquitous identification by Czechs and other post-communist citizens with the West, specifically with western masculinity and femininity. Indeed, in the Czech Republic, the diffusion of western culture and the saturation by western commodities have in many ways preceded the actual restructuring of the socialist political and economic system. In contrast to this discussion of how gender enables the eastward expansion of markets, in the second part of this chapter I explore how this market process empowers women as much as it subjects them to new forms of discipline. Here, I introduce the cases of two multinational enterprises, *Harlequin* Enterprises and *Cosmopolitan* Magazine, that are having a significant impact on Czech gender relations. These cases illustrate how gender identities are both pervasively marketed by multinational companies and contested in the local postsocialist context. *Harlequin* and *Cosmopolitan* reveal moreover, that social and cultural transformations result from even the seemingly most trivial penetration of western imports and advertising media.

Socialism officially denied gender differences. In contrast to socialism's claim to emancipate women through labor, capitalism offers the choice *not* to labor but to *consume*. Consumer choice expresses one's identity, and difference from others; thus expressing one's masculinity or femininity can be seen as a new form of emancipation. In contrast to socialist images of working women, postsocialist images depict beautiful women as aids to consumer transactions and virile men as the new face of Czech banking rather than Czech industry. At the same time, however, new feminist discourses are burgeoning and some individual women and men's life chances have expanded. I turn now to explore how this postsocialist remaking of gender identity and difference is facilitating the extension of markets and consumerism in the Czech Republic.

Expanding Markets: Conspicuous Consumption and Gender

In established capitalist societies images of naked women selling cars and niche marketing for men and women appear commonplace. In the Czech Republic the creation of a capitalist economy has reinscribed gender distinctions to extend markets into the most intimate areas of everyday life. Myths of the market and consumerist forms of desire have proliferated since 1989 because of the way communist regimes impeded the spread of the global market, and harbored massive shortages, thus controlling citizens' consumption (cf. Humphrey 1995). Slavenka Drakulic (1993) described the material deprivation and yearning for western commodities aptly in her book, *How We Survived Communism and Even Laughed*. Western consumer products are powerful crusaders for capitalism in Eastern Europe (Belk 1997; "Poland's market," 1999: 52). In the Czech Republic, the new *Škoda* model (now owned by German *Volkswagen*) *Octavia*, is heralded as ushering the Czech lands into the European "middle-class" (and the middle of Europe) once again. Likewise, *Marks and Spencer* claim that now they have set up shop in Wenceslas Square, Prague is a truly western city.

A conspicuous paradox of the Czech transition has been the increase in private consumption of positional and luxury goods in spite of the otherwise unprecedented fall in national income and output (Cook et al. 1997).[9] This new consumption has been funded through the depletion of preexisting savings and new wealth generated in the nascent private sector and the unofficial, shadow economy (World Bank 1996: 71). Initially in 1991 and 1992, domestic demand, which includes household consumption and fixed investment, fell dramatically in Czechoslovakia, by as much as one third. This was due to price liberalization and the resulting considerable increase in consumer and manufacturer's prices. However, after the first two years of transformation, domestic demand recovered. Since then, the increase in consumer demand has been so great that imports have been necessary to complement domestic production of goods (Earle, et al. 1994). Between 1990 and 2000, imports went from 43 percent of Gross Domestic Product to 75 percent (World Bank 2000a).[10] In 1995 alone, half of the increase in Gross Domestic Product was attributable to increases in household consumption, and imports of goods and services grew 20 percent (Český statistický úřad 1998). Indeed, there have been large increases in the consumption of durable goods (as shown in Table 5–1) such as televisions and cars. These increases have occurred at the same time as overall production and

TABLE 5.1 Changing Patterns of Consumption
in Czechoslovakia/Czech Republic

Year	Televisions per 1,000 People	Cars per 1,000 People
1989	122	173
1994	388	287
1997	447	344

Sources: World Bank Atlas 1990; *Financial Times*, April 17, 1990; *World Development Indicators* 1998.

TABLE 5.2 Increase in Consumer Durables per 100 Czech households

Consumer Durable	1995	1999
Refrigerator	134.3	149.4
Automatic Washing Machine	93.7	100.0
Color TV Set	95.8	112.3
Video Recorder	28.5	43.6
Microwave Oven	13.3	38.2
Dishwasher	0.5	4.2
Phone Fixed	37.8	70.3
Phone Mobile	7.1 (1998)	14.2
Passenger Car	64.6	69.3

Source: Český statistický úřad 2001.

real income have declined, resuming their 1989 levels only very recently ("Eastern Europe Recasts Itself 1997; Wieniecki 1996; World Bank 1996).

In Prague, retail sales grew by more than 20 percent in 1995 and 25 percent in 1996, *The Financial Times* reported in their December 1996 survey of the Czech Republic. "Some retailers say what attracts them to the Czech Republic is relatively high levels of disposable income . . . . There is growing evidence that consumers are increasingly prepared to spend money rather than save it" (Survey of the Czech Republic 1996). Given that the average retail sales per head in the United Kingdom is $3,750 and only $1,560 in the Czech Republic, foreign retailers expected to capitalize on the gap in consumption ("Retailing Revolution" 1996: 2).

Not surprisingly, western imports make up the bulk of postcommunist "conspicuous" consumption. Introducing western goods into East European markets has greatly increased the number of consumers of a whole range of products from subsistence categories such as food and shelter to clothing and textiles, footwear, furniture, electrical and household goods, and other durables, pharmacy and personal care and so on. As something of a counterweight to the massive decline in output in 1990–93, *BMW's* and *Armani* suits, *Elle* and *Playboy*, *his* and *hers* Marlboro cigarettes, mobile phones, and garden gnomes have all done extremely well in Eastern European markets. In 2001 imports in the Czech Republic amounted to approximately $36 billion compared with around $5 billion in 1988. According to a market study by International Business and Research Services in Prague, Czechs generally prefer foreign-made goods: *Sony* and *Panasonic* to the Czech electronic brand, *Tesla*; goods made in Switzerland, the United Kingdom, USA, and Germany over those made in the Czech Republic. Young people, in particular, prefer American brands that are heavily advertised, such as *Levi* jeans and *Coca-Cola*, according to a 1997 survey by ANER Nielsen Research (Bauerová 1998a; "Czech Youth" 1999; Giordano 1998). Different generations of women and men in the Czech Republic respond differently to the impact of marketization depending on whether they reached adulthood before the Prague Spring, during the normalization era, or around the 1989 Velvet Revolution (See Heitlinger and Trnka 1998; Nagle 1994). For the younger generation the demand for western goods and services is more likely to be a quest for social distinction as in the West, but for older generations it often represents a rejection of communist identities and symbols (Verdery 1996; Holý 1996). Embracing western influences — in entertainment, sexuality, and *life-style* — allows the revolution against the old regime to continue.

During the revolutions of 1989 men and women all over Eastern Europe expressed their new won freedom by wearing short skirts, and high heels or mauve Armani business suits, and by flaunting their new foreign cars and sexy mobile phones. Such performative displays of masculinity and femininity overturned the old symbolic order and took back the public space (cf.

Butler 1990). Accentuating one's sexual self was a political act, subversive of the socialist regime's monopoly on legitimate expressions of (collective) identity (Hobsbawm 1982). After communism, the freedom to express gender difference was one form of Havel's "the power of the powerless," reclaiming personal identity and the right to publicity. As Dagmar Degrínová, (Managing Director of *Harlequin* Enterprises in the Czech Republic), put it "since 1989 there has been a revolution in culture. The market reacted positively to ideas and products that were forbidden under communism."[11] She credits this revolution to the psychological censorship of male and female desire under communism, akin to the actual shortage economy. It is not surprising in her view that products and images stressing sexuality, gender identity and difference have been very popular in the postsocialist Czech Republic. On this account, the highly masculinized character of the Czech transition discussed in the previous chapters, is a natural response to the liberation from socialism as well.

The growth of consumption in the Czech Republic is partly explained by the low consumption levels for many consumer products relative to per capita income during socialism. But there is a definite class dimension to the rise of the new consumerism. As in all capitalist societies, liberalization has extended the scope of inequality. For some the consumption of luxury goods is now a way of life (A millionaires club was set up in Prague shortly after the revolution in 1991 by a former dissident). The dual labor market discussed in chapter 4, where employees are paid vastly different wages, has expedited the emergence of a consumer culture (Kohák 1997; Wheatly 1992). For much of the population, though, conspicious consumption is still an unreachable dream. According to a 1995 survey, 22 percent of Czech households did not even have enough income to maintain food consumption at 1990 levels (Millic-Czerniak ed. 1998).

There is a common perception that the liberalization of the market and the spread of consumerism have improved women's lives, and their status in Czech society. As was discussed in chapter 2, consumer goods, convenience foods, household appliances were limited in supply in the socialist economy, and these shortages particularly disadvantaged women who spent hours queuing to procure goods for their families' basic needs (Yeznikian 1981). Now, we are told goods-filled supermarkets, Sunday openings, cheaper and more widely available mixers, microwaves, washing machines, and dishwashers save time and make shopping and housework less arduous. As one author declares, "the convenience of Western consumerism is revolutionizing women's lives in Central and Eastern Europe more than Western feminism has ever done." Consumerism has presumably been "brought about by those who actually make the purchasing decisions: women" (Stroehlein 1999). But this view is more wishful thinking than verifiable truth, and the resentment of western feminists in the Czech lands is irrelevant here, albeit a significant issue treated in its own right in the next chapter. If anything, Czech women have born much of the brunt of economic reform in their traditional domestic roles in the family. By redistributing resources in a self-sacrificing way and doing more, not less, work in the home, women have often cushioned the transition for members of their families and communities. To be sure there are emancipatory potentials arising from the growth of the consumer market. But there is also evidence of the increased exploitation of women's labor and women's bodies in the postsocialist transition.

Mapping Profits, Mapping Eastern Europe

Most multinational companies and foreign investors seeking to enter new markets are motivated by the desire to expand their market share, increase revenue, and ultimately to reap the greatest profit. They develop strategies to achieve these goals, and this includes mapping specifically where profits lie. It is no different in Eastern Europe. The main motivations for multinational firms and investors entering Eastern European markets include liberalized trade and investment policies, expanding (global) market share, acquisition of assets for sale (particularly former state monopolies) and cheaper labor costs (Estrin, Hughes and Todd 1997). Profit concentrates in certain sectors, geographic regions, customer segments, distribution channels, and product types; and firms strategize to maximize their profits by mapping all of these coordinates. Foreign direct investment has been motivated in particular by the high profit margins available in protected markets characterized by pent-up demand and weak domestic competitors, especially in the consumer sector of postsocialist economies. Capitalizing on new consumer markets and potential market share however, provides a greater impetus for firms to establish themselves in Central and Eastern Europe than apparent lower labor costs (Estrin, Hughes and Todd 1997). As Hugo Radice (1999) has pointed out, the costs involved in reorganizing production and management, and coping with infrastructures and cultures designed for a command economy often outweigh the gains made by cheaper labor.

Marketing and advertising is particularly important to profit-growth in

Eastern Europe, where the scope to raise prices is limited (given the local incomes) and cost cutting has already been exploited. In former socialist societies, marketing and advertising are also doubly important in cultivating tastes and seducing consumers because the market mentality has been largely absent. (Under socialism, costs such as advertising and marketing were considered nonproductive). I have argued that, because they are globally recognized, the market pull of western brands that were virtually nonexistent in Eastern Europe before 1989 has been especially powerful there. Similarly, because gender differences were officially downplayed by state socialist regimes, their popular reemergence under the guise of the free market has been striking. Thus, it would seem that where market expansion has been successful in the East, it has benefited from an understanding of the former socialist system and from strategies that have deliberately played on the deficiencies and predispositions that have carried over from this system.

Transitions to the market system have facilitated the entry of transnational companies that consciously employ sexist advertising and marketing, usually heavily sanctioned in their home countries. "Eastern Europe is the last remaining frontier in terms of what companies can get away with," says Mark Wright, Client Services Director at the global advertising firm, *Ark J. Walter Thompson* in Prague. "There are no women's groups claiming offence and consumers respond quite well" (Burgess and Tůma 1997). Marketing strategies that would be considered reprehensible and are often illegal in western countries are standard operating procedures in Central and Eastern Europe. Firms take advantage of the minimal legal requirements and lack of state regulation and censorship in the East, especially with respect to gender discrimination and sexually explicit material (as compared with established western markets). Of the top twenty advertising companies in the Czech Republic, only five have their headquarters there, three-quarters are multinationals; of the top ten only two are local companies. Annual growth of advertising firms in 1995–1996 averaged around 30 percent. The combined capitalized billing of these advertising and market research companies in 1996 was approximately $200 million (Prague Post 1998). The lion's share of this capital belongs to multinational firms. It is multinational and not local firms that are making new markets through research designed to ascertain demand tendencies, identify niche markets, and saturate them with advertising. An average large multinational in the Czech Republic for example, will spend approximately $100,000 in a given year on market research, whereas a Czech firm might spend none (Bauerová 1998a).

In particular, global advertising and marketing industries exploit gender identities and differences to generate new needs and market niches. Multinational firms have developed distinctly East-Central European gender-specific marketing strategies. *Marlboro*, for example, has developed a new line of *his* and *hers* cigarettes, especially for this regional market in order to gain a competitive edge over more popular local brands (Perlez 1997).[12] Likewise, *Eurotel* uses daring images (of naked men) in their mobile phone advertising that are intended to appeal to masculine fantasies of control or feelings of penis envy. In the Czech Republic risqué advertising that crosses the boundary of what is publicly appropriate in most western countries is unremarkable. Female nudity is ubiquitous in selling everything from sportswear to bathroom tiles. Sexually explicit poses and slogans (such as *Raveli* boot's "fuck the world" and *IP Reklama's* billboard of a crucified woman reading "Everything needs advertising") are also not unusual on the streets of Prague. Similar trends in the practices of multinational advertising companies have been noticed in other emerging capitalist markets such as South Africa ("Free at Last" 1998).

In her study of billboard advertisements in Prague, Libora Indruchová (1995) observed that in all cases these "signs" were directed toward two gender-specific groups — either to men or to women, rather than to such disaggregated groups as those with different income levels. While some of the goods and services advertised luxury commodities, appealing to upper-income groups, the playing up of gender differences in these billboards addresses — and persuades in the pleasures of consumerism — a society whose class structure is unstable and in which inequality is growing. Gender differences evoke desires that are apparently successful in selling a whole range of new commodities on the nascent Czech market.

In all of the billboards visible, Indruchová noted that women performed traditional role activities with "agency as actively aspiring sexual objects," while men were depicted as the receivers of their services and of new consumption pleasures. Indruchová stresses that none of the billboards in 1994–1995 represented a man, either as a father or a sexual object, seeking to satisfy a woman. Marci Shore (1995) analyzed a Czech billboard in 1995, and noted its use of a double-entendre aimed at specifically male consumers. In her article for *The Prague Post*, "Listen or Obey — Either Way, Women Should Not Take this Lying-Down," she deconstructed this billboard slogan designed to sell *Sony* stereos. In translation it read: "Men like women who listen." But since the Czech verb for *listen* and *obey* is ambiguously the same, Shore made the point to English-speakers that the slogan could be read quite differently by a native audience and, she added, quite offensively by a western female audience (Madden 1996: 9b). Yet, regardless of which sex is placed in the dominant role, the emerging capitalist social structure is symbolically defined by the power relations of gender, as Indruchová argues. As audiences become increasingly desensitized, advertising becomes both more powerful and increasingly subtle in its ability to reinscribe a gendered social structure.

Mobile Fantasies and Penile Phones

In a departure from billboards depicting women as passive objects, the late 1990s saw a splurge of advertising depicting sexually attractive male bodies seemingly fulfilling female desires. Male as well as female bodies were being inscribed with consumer messages. *Eurotel* GSM Global in the Czech Republic sold its services with a naked man and a mobile phone strategically placed over his genitals, with the slogan — "Small phone; Big coverage." (This billboard was later turned into a promotional Valentine Day's card reading "Small phone; Big love," see illustration 5–1).[13] Likewise, *Velké Popovice* brewery designed a billboard in 1994 that resulted in unprecedented sales of the particular brew advertised (Burgess and Tůma 1997). It showed a woman atop a sexy, naked man with the double entendre "Enjoy your goat" — Kožel, the beer brand name, means "goat," which can also mean a sexually virile man.[14]

Several interpretations of these billboards seem plausible. The objectification of the male body here signifies the way in which East European men are placed in subject positions relative to western men in global capitalism. Men are constructed as secondary, incomplete subjects, not yet rational or masculine enough to "return to Europe." On billboards, they can therefore be depicted as bodies that are lacking, in need of "mobile phones." This view confounds universal notions of gender as the domination of masculinity over femininity. It suggests rather, that constructions of gender are plural depending on racial, sexual, and national hierarchies and must be located within a global social field of dominant and subordinate, western and *aspiring* western masculinities and femininities (see Williams 1996).

These images are not inconsequential in the postsocialist context. In the transition, men and women are paying attention to all possible direction and assistance they can garner to help them make choices. Advertising and mar-

FIGURE 5.1 A Mobile Phone Advertisement

Eurotel GSM Global Mobile Phone, 1997.

Courtesy of Eurotel Praha.

keting in addition to promoting particular products and brands provide an education in market culture. In Central and Eastern Europe, Ina Merkel (1994: 63) writes, "advertising acquires an entirely new function. It teaches the population quickly and easily how western society and culture function; it offers advice on managing within this new *life-style*."[15] Under socialism, people self-actualized through high-culture and the clandestine cultural sphere of the musical underground, dissident theatre and *samizdat* publishing. But since the fall of communism, the market has very nearly dropped out of this realm, as people have turned to consuming and defining themselves through identification with new "things." For instance, reading western pulp fiction in translation, "how-to" self-help books and so on has replaced the reading of Czech and other serious literature in the transition (Anyz and Vrba 1998). The spread of market civilization has lowered the cultural and intellectual tastes of the Czech public, and in so doing created new class distinctions in society, rather than merely responding to an already constituted market and set of desires.

Direct sales are effectively a form of consumer socialization in Eastern Europe. Although door to door sales have met with resistance in the region because there is little familiarity with often confrontational techniques of selling (Perlez 1998), there is evidence that *woman to woman* sales are doing very well. Multinational cosmetic companies such as *Estée Lauder, Mary Kay* and *Margaret Astor* have been remarkably successful in the Czech Republic using their direct method of selling beauty products to groups of women in their homes and via promotional mailing ("Ženská Otázka" 1998: 11–13). In April 1998, Marcela Speert, Director of Czech *Mary Kay*, reported that the Czech Republic is the fastest growing branch worldwide. According to her, in just one year of Czech operations, Mary Kay's growth outpaced that of *Coca Cola*.[16] That just goes to show that capitalism is great for women, remarked Peter Magurean III, an American businessman in Prague.[17] Woman to woman selling is particularly popular in transition countries like the Czech Republic, Ms. Speert explained, because women need to be shown by other women how to use beauty products (of which they had few before 1989). Akin to missionaries, Ms. Speert and her consultants described their role in the Czech lands as schooling women in the art of femininity (see also Newman 1995).[18]

Advertising and marketing, of course, have the same function in the West as in the East. However, if we locate the Czech examples of advertising and marketing mentioned, not only within the symbolic system of capitalism, but also in terms of the socialist order, they take on different meanings. These sexually explicit images and marketing of gender stereotypes can be viewed in more than one way. They simultaneously negate the former socialist order, where identity and community was tied to labor, and affirm a new order of individualism, sexual identity, and gender difference. The two social orders are superimposed one over the other: "Hastily erected billboards [stand] where before there were slogans" (Hell 1997: 942). Both socialist and capitalist discourses are lived contemporaneously in postsocialist transitions. Their coexistence means that images and dispositions that may offend in the West are often greeted in the East as denoting new-won freedoms. A Czech survey of the public perception of advertising containing sexual connotations for instance, found that most people either like the use of the naked female body in advertisements or are not bothered by it (Vajnerová 1998). This is not to dispute that the intent of these representations is to facilitate the consent of postsocialist citizens to a new consumer economy. Such a consumer economy may well create precarious inequalities and insecurities, as much as it provides new freedoms and opportunities.

Marketing Gender: Global Culture Enterprises and De-Facto Feminism

A universal meaning cannot be assigned to the representation of gender in postsocialist marketing nor can the eastward expansion of multinational cultural enterprises be seen as a one-way process. Local receptiveness to global cultural production is often complex and contradictory. *Harlequin* Enterprises, publishers of romance novels, and *Cosmopolitan* Magazine, show how gender identities enable the extension of market capitalism in Eastern Europe, while also providing new spaces of empowerment for women. Alongside their profit-making mission and promotion of consumerism, these multinationals are having a profound, and often positive, impact on gender relations. They not only persuade women to consume but also encourage their role as citizens by responding to non-consumer needs such as physical safety and sexual abuse, employment discrimination, and political education. *Harlequin* and *Cosmopolitan* demonstrate that multinational companies do not have a global blueprint and are open to alteration by the local social context. Like *Vlasta* during the Prague Spring period of socialist democratization, Czech-*Harlequin* and *Cosmopolitan* are providing a public forum where women can air the problems of daily life and their dissatisfaction with the gender regime of state socialism and postsocialist democracy. In the following discussion I explore how they are helping to facilitate women's public participation, and in various ways, to challenge prevailing gender stereotypes and inequalities in the Czech Republic.

Harlequin

In 1997 *Harlequin Inc.* made $81.3 million in profits, with sales of 165 million books in twenty-three languages in more than 100 countries. *Har-*

lequin is the global leader in serial romance publishing. One of the most significant opportunities for future growth, states the 1997 annual report, lies in geographic expansion by means of controlled entry into new markets. In 1994 *Harlequin* entered Russia; in 1995 it launched its series in China in association with two local publishers; and in 1996 *Harlequin* began selling Spanish-language editions in Mexico, Central, and South America. In spite of difficult economic conditions for consumers in these particular regions, especially women consumers, Torstar Corporation, the owner of *Harlequin*, reports very encouraging initial results, with increased profits in all markets. *Harlequin* has developed a global brand, which uses a similar marketing strategy worldwide. For instance, one poster, featuring a woman reading a *Harlequin* book in a bathtub with the slogan "A *Harlequin* book makes any time special," has appeared in Russian subways as well as in British bus shelters (Torstar Corporation 1997: 10–12).

A global strategy is not the only approach *Harlequin* takes to selling books, however. Since 1992 *Harlequin*–Czech Republic has sold romance novels to an estimated one in four Czech women; that is, 256 titles per year in Czech translation from English and 35 million books for a population of approximately 10 million.[19] This is the result of a highly strategic, *local* marketing plan. As part of its quest to expand markets, *Harlequin* has introduced both Valentine's and Mother's Day celebrations to the Czech calendar (Fronk 1998). International Women's Day on March 8 used to be the day for celebrating women during the communist era. After the fall of the regime, people stopped celebrating the old communist holiday and happily replaced it with Valentine's Day.[20] Since 1994, *Harlequin* has promoted this day as a celebration of romance, love, and women, sponsoring television specials, media events, and most recently a Valentine's night at the Prague town hall.

Czech-*Harlequin* also has a social conscience. The Director of *Harlequin*, Dagmar Degrínová, with a doctorate in psychology, acknowledges the poverty and difficult living conditions of her readers (78 percent of *Harlequin* readers borrow their books for instance).[21] She is quite aware that *Harlequin* provides only a fictional escape for these readers and yet wants to do more. So in 1995 she initiated a social program to support battered and abused women, funded by one percent of net profits, and provided a radio program and drop-in center at Prague headquarters for women seeking counseling and advice. All of these activities are unique to Czech-*Harlequin* and are not shared by Torstar Corporation's more than 100 other *Harlequin* country operations worldwide.

Czech-*Harlequin* produces more than pulp fiction. Each month *Harlequin* novels come with an interactive newsletter magazine that includes news about *Harlequin*'s social activities, advice columns, features about readers, discount coupons, and letters from both the editor and readers. At the end of each novel there is also an interactive section, "Keyhole," that provides a forum for discussion and advice. The release of each *Harlequin* book/series is deliberately scheduled in a 28 day-cycle like a menstrual calendar.[22] In the Czech context, *Harlequin* has become as much a social forum for women as a book club. *Harlequin* novels are actually considered "magazines," not books. By being registered as magazines that include some regular content, such as the newsletter and *keyhole* section in addition to the romance story, the novels can be sold *en masse* in Czech towns and cities by local street vendors.

Harlequin has a positive image in Czech society, in contrast to western countries. "*Harlequin* is not something to be embarrassed about," Degrínová says; "women do not hide their books." In fact while 10 percent of women have stopped reading and buying books since the 1989 revolution, and the number of book titles has decreased, *Harlequin* readers have continued to grow (Strauník 1997: 11), even though *Harlequin* novels are hardly bargain-books by Czech standards. Their price is roughly the same as in North America, which with purchasing power adjustment makes them two to three times more expensive. However, like other products marketed by using gender-specific advertising, *Harlequin* offers a new identity for women, and a chance to escape from their old lives. Banned after the 1968 Soviet occupation, in 1989, western romance novels were a symbol of liberation for many Eastern European women; an escape from the past exhaustion of communist emancipation — the double day of paid labor and unpaid household work. Pleasurably indulged, they offered the fantasy and hope of a new and better life.

Degrínová believes that *Harlequin* books have helped promote a revolution in values, "a return to what is natural: personal lives, strong families and human relationships over socialism and ideology." In her view, the former regime sacrificed "women's position in society and their rights as mothers, while femininity was given up for careers." Whether or not we agree with Dagmar Degrínová, it is hard to deny that *Harlequin* has tapped an enormous longing on the part of many women. Innovative in its profit making, it has also opened up a new space for women to express themselves in the nascent Czech democracy.[23]

From a western feminist point of view, *Harlequin* fiction exudes patriarchal imperialism. In the typical narrative an initially resistant woman is won over by a virile man or Prince Charming.[24] Yet, in an unintentional way, *Harlequin* romances have actually popularized questions of gender relations in the public domain for two reasons (Hauserová 1997).[25] First, the actual narratives of *Harlequin* novels in the 1990s have undergone considerable change. Indeed, the characters and plots in these romances reflect significant social transformations in western countries with respect to gender roles and women's sexuality in particular. Gone is the damsel in distress, or pathetic female victim who is saved by a manly man. Today's *Harlequin* protagonists are feisty, career women, young and middle-aged balancing multiple roles as decisionmakers, workers, lovers, and parents. Men figure in these narratives not only as "manly men," but also as vulnerable, often caring beings who are incomplete without a woman. Tension is evident between the male and female characters who both have strong egos, but it is resolved in a way that is mutually beneficial; the female does not give up her career or ambitions, nor does the male. Certainly the novels are heterosexist in their assumptions about proper sexualities and family forms, but they are not in fact as conventionally sexist as one might think.

There is another reason for disputing the impression that *Harlequin* is merely a tool of patriarchy. The novels in Czech translation not only diffuse the changes in sexual and gender roles which feminism has evoked in North America and the West generally over the past two or three decades, they consciously refashion the characters so that Czech readers can identify with the heroines (Vešínová 1996). Two Czech-*Harlequin* translators, one male and one female, discussed with me how the actual process of translation allowed them certain liberties with the narrative. The male translator said he would frequently change the endings of the English language romances, reverse the roles and introduce new characters. He also found ways within the translation to make the novel more racy and the heroines more complex and thus more appealing to more sophisticated young Czech readers who prefer an absurdist twist to the formulaic "happy ending."[26] The Czech-*Harlequin* Director, Degrínová, keeps her letters from Czech women readers, using them to help her make decisions on what stories and translations to publish in the future.

FIGURE 5.2   A Czech-*Harlequin* Cover

"Czech Harlequin Desire," 1998.

According to Czech-*Harlequin*'s own survey of readers the most popular *Harlequin* happy endings involve: an independent, successful career woman who falls in love with an American Indian, a cowboy or equally a favorite, a single Mum who traps a single Dad and combines families with him (e.g. Hudsonova 1997; Cresswellova 1998; Cruiseova 1998). Eva Hauserová describes a typical *Harlequin* romance where feminist assumptions are embedded in the core of the story. In *Dívčí kopána* ("Soccer Girl" by Heather Allisonová) the main protagonist is a young girl (with whom the reader is expected to identify) training as a soccer player, who dreams about playing with the same aggression and feeling of competition and "sportsmanship" as young men soccer players." Hauserová (1995: 42–43) notes that this female character "runs contrary to the usual imaginary, where a girl practices ballet or plays the piano, flirts with boys in a group of girlfriends as did women of a previous generation."

As a result of innovations in both translation and marketing, *Harlequin* has been extremely successful in Eastern Europe. (It is the second largest foreign publisher in Poland, and has operations in Hungary, Bulgaria, Russia, and other former East bloc countries). *Harlequin*'s popularity in the Czech Republic demonstrates how discourses associated with former communist times and those associated with western consumerism deflect one another in complex ways, provoking new potentials for social and democratic change. It also demonstrates how in the process of postsocialist transformation global cultural influences are interwoven with local social relations, in particular historically specific gender identities.

Former Czech-*Harlequin* translator, Eva Hauserová, has gone on to write the first popular books that describe a variety of western-style feminist ideas for the benefit of Czech society (Hauserova 1995; 1998). She has no qualms about calling *Harlequin* feminist. A question lingers though: if there were indeed a democratic revolution in gender relations in the Czech Republic (and women were not overworked but satisfied in their everyday lives), would there still be such a large female market (1 in 4 women) for romance *Harlequin*-style?[27]

Cosmopolitan

Cosmopolitan magazine, published by Hearst Corporation, is a U.S.-based global enterprise catering to an increasingly empowered female market. It is the world's best-selling women's magazine and also the world's largest magazine franchise. It has a circulation of 2.75 million in the U.S. and 4 million readers abroad, who buy one of forty-one foreign editions from India to the Czech Republic in twenty-five languages. The *Cosmopolitan* woman exudes independence, sexual freedom, and glamour. For conservatives, *Cosmopolitan* is seen as radical. In a *Wall Street Journal* op-ed piece, journalist Evan Gahr (1997) argued that women's magazines like *Cosmopolitan* go beyond helping you to stay slim and hold onto your man. They're also tub-thumpers for liberal causes from government health-care to gun control. "When the subject is politics," wrote Gahr (1997: A14), "a *womyn* lurks behind every story written by a *Cosmo* girl."[28]

If anything suggests a global wave of American feminism, *Cosmopolitan* does. Launched in Russia in May 1994 *Cosmopolitan* now sells 480,000 copies there each month, more than in any other country outside the United States. Its popularity is such that *Cosmopolitan*-Russia has released its own website in association with a model agency. The catch is *Cosmopolitan* costs about four dollars in Russia, as much as its cover price in the U.S., except that an average women in Moscow earns about one-tenth of her U.S. counterpart. In April 1998, *Cosmopolitan* arrived in China, in a joint venture with a local women's magazine approved by the Chinese government ("Cosmo gains toehold" 1998). "It's a general rule of thumb that women's magazines lead the march [of the media industry] overseas" says Chuck McCullagh, international marketing director of the media/investment banking firm *De Silva and Phillips* (Greenberg 1998). In emerging markets, *Cosmopolitan* provides an outlet for an advertising onslaught, and is thus a trailblazer for fashion, beauty, and other gender-specific consumer industries.[29] Although *Cosmopolitan* is at the forefront of global market expansion with its emphasis on female freedom and beautification, it has a distinctly indigenous face in most of its markets. The female face of *Cosmopolitan's* foreign editions is often more explicitly feminist than the current American version, as is the case in the Czech Republic.[30]

The first issue of Czech *Cosmopolitan* appeared in April 1997. Over the past few years, Czechs have talked enthusiastically about the new *Cosmopolitan*.[31] The Czech writer, Eva Hauserová (1997) has no qualms about calling it feminist. Why? Because Czech *Cosmopolitan* regularly features articles about sexual harassment, trafficking of women, discrimination in the labor market, women and politics, interviews with prominent women activists, and suggested strategies for political lobbying in the Czech Republic and the European Union.[32] For example, after *Cosmopolitan* ran an article on all the ways in which women could lobby their politicians, the Czech Parliament was inundated with telephone calls from women.[33] Another article gauged the potential support for a Czech woman prime minister (Imrých 1998: 30).

Cosmopolitan has run several articles on what the European Union can do for you, as a woman and as a Czech citizen.[34] Editorials columns in Czech *Cosmopolitan* moreover, frequently remind readers that gender equality is a condition of the Czech Republic's entry into Europe, and therefore, that the government must pay attention to discrimination and violence against women (and norms in European countries for instance).

Editor Anaztázie Kudrnová writes columns that discuss issues such as homosexual partnerships and the lack of government action on domestic violence, and that are generally critical of the state of gender relations in the Czech Republic. A column ironically entitled "Brothel Instruction" addresses gender discrimination in employment. Another editorial entitled "Only for Women" makes a case for celebrating International Women's Day. The editorials "Oblivious World" and "the Case of Killing" condemn the scourge of domestic violence in the Czech Republic and pressure the government to draft special legislation. Domestic violence is no longer a "family secret" thanks to *Cosmopolitan*. Its prevalence and the lack of remedy for battered women have been consistent topics for discussion in *Cosmo*. In the April 1998 issue, Kudrnová suggested a special police force division trained to deal only with domestic violence cases.

In her January 1998 editorial entitled "Breasts Between Tractors" (a pun on socialist metaphors), Kudrnová comments on the use of female bodies to sell all kinds of commodities in the new Czech marketplace. She writes:

On our post-socialist market it's possible for models similarly making their living with their bodies to sell tiles, central heating, tractors and steel piping. The resulting advertising photos perhaps fulfill whatever kinds of secret desires of influential proprietors, but about their effectiveness one could further polemicize.

Further, she related the objectification of women's bodies to the gender discrimination faced by women in the nascent labor market in this editorial:

It is like when one peruses the pages of the newspaper with the help-wanted ads. Try to find a firm looking for a female director, executive or manager. And some companies, in the interest of being perfectly clear, write explicitly that they are only interested in men.

Following this latter editorial Kudrnová encouraged readers to write to *Cosmopolitan* with their experiences of discrimination and harassment at work. A subsequent issue thus featured a lengthy article about some truly outrageous reader's experiences (Kucerová-Turková and Jungrová 1998: 72–73). The title of the subsequent article with reader's responses featured an accompanying photo of a young woman in a leopard print mini skirt with the slogan "do you need to look this to get a job?" If this is not feminist consciousness-raising then what is? *Cosmopolitan* has been an agenda-setter in Czech media and civil society, first raising and documenting the rampant sexual harassment in Czech workplaces two years before the major liberal daily, *Lidové Noviny*, commissioned its focus group survey on the issue (for a discussion, see chapter 4).

Kudrnová and her staff appear to be pushing the limits of *Cosmopolitan* in the interests of empowering women and bringing a critical perspective to bear on the transformation of Czech society. They seem intent on shaping a new feminist awareness in the postsocialist Czech Republic, where the local media have been largely hostile to discussions of feminism. Further, they are doing this in a foreign-owned publication that is part of a multi-national business enterprise, not in one of the many local women's magazines that purport to be for — or so their subtitles read — "the intelligent, modern woman."[35] *Cosmopolitan* for the most part stands alone among Czech women's magazines, the majority of which — in spite of these subtitles reminiscent of the socialist era and its manifest contradictions from the perspective of gender relations — shy away from serious issues and questioning traditional gender roles (Szymanowski 1997).

But *Cosmopolitan* is also Janus-faced, and only ambivalently Czech. Approximately half of its contents are local; the other half is translated from English without regard to the specific needs and issues Czech women face.[36] The same American cover appears on all Czech editions of *Cosmopolitan*. But this universal cover masks the two faces of the magazine as found in the Czech Republic. One face looks approvingly upon women as a group who deserves and is desirous of social change in their public and private lives.

FIGURE 5.3 "The Cosmo Girl."

Czech Cosmopolitan cover 9/1997.

Courtesy of Hearst International and Cosmopolitan, Czech Republic.

The other face teases them, enticing them to join the new class of consumers and promised fulfillment through makeup, diets, and the possession of luxury commodities. Two faced, in this perspective, the magazine presents feature articles that question the objectification of women cheek-by-jowl with advertisements vigorously cultivating a new market of women consumers.

Cosmopolitan editors in New York frankly admit that their goal is to shape women's identities and interests. *Cosmopolitan's* maiden editor (and author of *Sex and the Single Girl*, 1961) Helen Gurley-Brown who now heads up the international edition believes moreover, that "women are basically the same the world over — we all have a vagina, heart, and brain" (1998). Yet, this identity of woman as body and as consumer is contested within Czech *Cosmo* (cf. Slobin 1997). Women are enticed not only to *forget* their real world troubles by the global infomercials and focus on sexual fantasy, but also to *remember* them by the Czech content, which focuses on women's experience of overwork, discrimination, and sexual exploitation.

Although bearing the same global brand, local editions of global magazines are usually given enough freedom to be able to produce and market their product locally. But they are also expected to conform to a similar set of standards and values in order to uphold the global reputation of the brand. Should a local Central or Eastern European edition of a global magazine step outside of what is deemed appropriate practice for upholding the brand, then we can expect to see the tanks come rolling in. A recent example from Romania serves to underscore this point. The Romanian edition of *Playboy* magazine — not known for its feminism — published a satirical article entitled "*How to beat your Wife . . . Without Leaving Marks on her Body*" with by a step by step procedure for spousal battery accompanied by a series of photographs of a woman being beaten by a man. Although this article, which is clearly beyond the pale of appropriate practice in the West, made it to publication, *Playboy's* New York headquarters and American President moved quickly to rein in and sanction the Romanian local publisher. "We know the physical abuse of women is a problem in Eastern Europe and the editor is being reprimanded as we speak."[37] The imperial relationship between the multinational headquarters and the Romanian edition had to be firmly asserted in this instance.

While American control and values had to be reasserted in Romanian *Playboy* Czech *Cosmopolitan* shows that this local/global power relationship can work in an oblique fashion with potentially positive effects. The Czech *Cosmo* editors are free to promote more progressive, pro-feminist, social values than the American version. Feminism is marginal in Czech culture, but it is acceptable in Czech *Cosmopolitan*. The *Cosmopolitan* brand, founded on a tradition of female sexual and economic independence, has given local Czech journalists and editors the freedom to experiment with feminist ideas, which are relatively new to the region, as long as they continue to sell magazines. At Hearst International, the editors of the 41 franchised magazines meet each year to discuss the Hearst philosophy, things that have worked, things that have not, and things that are appropriate. In this way, best practices, including the regional appeal of feminist ideas in Eastern Europe, can be diffused across the various country editions. Ironically, Czech *Cosmo* is far more effective in getting across the message of feminism to young women than the western academic literature or "fly-by" feminists evoking the liberation struggles of 1970s women's movements.

New Publics for Women?

Nancy Fraser (1992) has suggested that there are more dimensions to the public sphere than the realm of formal politics from which women have historically been mostly excluded. Rather, there are many publics, which include the so-called private or marginalized or alternative arenas and activities initiated by women. It seems to me that Czech-*Harlequin* and *Cosmopolitan* are nascent examples of such *counter publics*, constituted mainly of women who have few avenues for voice in their transitional society dominated by male élites.

Postsocialist representation often takes the form of an explicit gender hierarchy, contributing to women's subject status and relative absence from public space and political power in Central and Eastern Europe. *Harlequin* and *Cosmopolitan* however, suggest the possibility for gender equality and women's transformation of public space. Their dual focus on consumption as well as on women's particular problems is important given that postsocialist women are generally better educated than western women and have had a history of emancipation and inclusion in the labor force for at least three generations. As Czech journalist Barbara Osvaldová (1998: 15) points out, western women's magazines have a limited notion of women's emancipation: stressing sexual freedom, de facto marriage, and managerial careers while promoting cosmetics, advertising propaganda, entertaining movies, and mediocre fiction. These lifestyles are *not* for the most part shared by Czech women, although they are certainly appealing to them at the level of fantasy as evidenced by the huge numbers of women reading *Harlequin*.

What the cases of *Harlequin* and *Cosmopolitan* have in common is that they both have had to adapt the form, and to some extent, the content of their global or "American" product in order to be successful in a postsocialist society. It is their very *localization* that has liberated spaces for women's expression in the Czech Republic.[38] That is, Czechs have a degree of agency in their reception to and adaptation of global culture. Any intelligent reader looking at the U.S. *Cosmopolitan* magazine will see immediately that it is schlock, selling products primarily through sex, and by conditioning women to view themselves through the approving and disapproving male gaze. In stark contrast, in the Czech Republic, the editors have deliberately used *Cosmo* as a site for popularizing feminist thinking — and made it a commercial success. It is an irony that contemporary global market forces, and not the official socialist gender equality policy, have given rise to what I call "de facto" feminism in the Czech Republic. But is what this chapter has documented in the Czech Republic only a transitory phenomenon? Will these women's magazines ultimately become more like their frivolous western sister versions? Or, is there something new that is being produced in the Czech context? *Harlequin* and *Cosmopolitan* Czech style are more than temporary phenomena; they reflect dynamic processes of globalization.

Globalization cannot be comprehended simply as a process of westernization or homogenization that renders cultural norms and daily life the same everywhere. The *Harlequin* and *Cosmopolitan* cases counter the assumption that there is a simple one-way relationship between global markets and gender identities. In contrast to neo-Marxist scholars who argue that the forces of globalization are increasingly constraining and overpowering nation-states and democratic governments, and feminist scholars who predict women's victimization by global markets, the gendered perspective presented here suggests that we need to view global processes *dialectically*. One way to do this might be to distinguish between the *form* and the *content* of globalization. Seeing the globalization process dialectically raises the possibility of recognizing that local groups can exhibit considerable, often ingenious, even refreshing agency in transforming the content of patriarchal cultural exports or neoliberal economic models.

Conclusion

Multinational enterprises view Central and Eastern Europe as the newest and perhaps last frontier for accumulation. The emergence of a market-oriented, consumer economy is manufacturing new gender-specific needs and desires and engendering new identities. Marketing stresses masculinity and femininity to sell goods and services in this region. However, in the aftermath of communism, these new identities are as much a source of liberation as domination. For the first half of the 1990s, the majority of Czech citizens favored a government purporting to bring about a "free" market economy.[39] They associated that liberalized market economy with the freedom to express previously repressed, identities and differences.

Harlequin Enterprises and *Cosmopolitan* Magazine highlight the double-edged role of multinational enterprises in the Czech Republic that not only enable the extension of markets but also empower women as individuals and consumers. One way to look at these case studies is to see them as yet another instance of Coca-Cola capitalism or American cultural imperialism. The wall comes down and all the cultural detritus of America comes oozing in. But a more subtle reading is to notice the differences in how local cultures receive and redefine global or American influences and the potentially positive aspects of this.

Harlequin and *Cosmopolitan* dispel the conventional wisdom that gender identities are merely exports from the West (to the East), even in the realm of popular culture (Elshtain 1995; Šiklová 1993). They reveal in microcosm how the postsocialist subjects are ideologically constructed in dynamic relation to both local traditions and western cultural forms. Expanding markets and marketing gender distinctions in the Czech Republic do not represent an inevitable marriage between patriarchy and capitalism on the road to postsocialist freedom. Instead, they show how seemingly conventional approaches to gender can be deconstructed to rearticulate power relationships, thus facilitating postsocialist transitions.

6 Importing Civil Society

Gender is shaping and being shaped by postsocialist transformations in the state and civil society. Change and continuity in gender
relations have both been critical features of the transitions in Central and
Eastern Europe. The restructuring of the local labor market and the cultural
processes of global integration illustrate how gender relations have under-
pinned and facilitated postsocialist transitions, as well as how the identities
and interests of "women" and "men" have been reconstructed by systemic
reforms. Czech postsocialist civil society can also be read in the context of
an emerging global civil society and in a gendered arena.

Civil society is the space lying between the public realm of the state
and the private realm of the family. Following Antonio Gramsci (1971)
and Robert Cox (1999), I define civil society as a source of both domination
and empowerment. In Gramsci's terms, civil society has two distinctive
meanings. It is the space, which "sustains the dominance of the bourgeoisie
in capitalist states" as well as the space in which "an emancipatory counter-
hegemony can be constructed" (Cox 1999: 3; Chin and Mittleman 1997:
27).[1]

Since 1989 male élites in the Czech Republic have masculinized the
public realm.[2] In response, many women have turned away from the world
of formal politics and sought to build democracy from below. Thus, as it has
emerged in postsocialism, civil society has been founded on a new division
of public and private that, while structurally marginalizing women as political and economic subjects, has opened up new possibilities for their empowerment (cf. Sen 1996: 822).[3]

Contrary to most of the world, where women's access to political power is the newest fad, Czech women have been made to feel out of place in the new formal political structures of their democracy.[4] They have become increasingly engaged in the informal realm of civil society and have reached out beyond the borders of traditional national politics. In so doing, they have joined an emerging global civil society that is constituted by transnational networks of nongovernmental organizations (NGOs) and discourses of democracy and human rights, which have been more open to women's concerns.[5] International organizations see grassroots civic organizations in post-socialist countries as crucial sites for democratization, and many women in these states, including the Czech Republic, have taken this opportunity to develop and extend their transnational linkages.

In their efforts to build a Czech civil society from below, some women's groups have drawn on western assistance, but on their own terms. In contrast, in the realm of formal politics, western institutional forms have been imported, lock, stock, and barrel, even as male politicians have rhetorically shunned western interference. Ironically, while the realm of state-centered Czech politics stagnated in the late 1990s, with the steady decline of voter participation after the first democratic elections, Czech civil society flourished.[6] While designed to empower women in civil society, transnational projects have sometimes tended to privilege western agendas and interests more than local development. Differences between American and European approaches to civic development have played themselves out both through contests within the western camp as well as between eastern and western conceptions of civil society and appropriate gender norms. Political scientists who focus solely on formal political institutions and power structures in Central and Eastern Europe miss a big part of the story of democratic transition. Without the independent activities and organizations in civil society currently led by women, democracy is not likely to be consolidated in this region.

The Changing Meanings of Civil Society

As a theoretical concept and as a manifestation of social relations, civil society has undergone a global renaissance (Keane 1996: 9). The term has also become a favorite of western governments and international institutions in the world of foreign policy. Frequently lauded today as a key ingredient in the consolidation of new postsocialist democracies, the concept of civil society was actually revived in the West in the wake of the nonviolent movements and revolutions against communism in Eastern Europe.[7] It has since been the subject of vigorous debate and widely varying interpretations. For Václav Havel, "the creation of a civil society is the primary task of our time" (Havel and Klaus 1996: 18). George Soros' private philanthropic foundation in Central and Eastern Europe seeks to build momentum for an "open society." Michael Ignatieff (1995) argues that building civil society by supporting non-state actors should be the main western strategy for strengthening reform and democracy in the region. In contrast to economic reform or the making of democratic constitutions building civil society cannot be done by the stroke of a pen. Vibrant civic institutions cannot be created rapidly from above or by western design.[8]

Revival of Czechoslovak Civil Society Before 1989

According to Jenos Szücs, historically, three developmental regions existed in Europe: Western, Eastern, and Eastern-Central. Each region linked state and society in different ways (Szücs 1988: 308). What in the West is seen as the ideal-type of civil society, which structurally and theoretically separates "society" from the "state," arose only in Western Europe. By contrast, civil society in Eastern Central Europe carved out very limited areas of autonomy from the dynastic states, although dynastic rulers were largely immune to those encroachments. It was not until the interwar period, after the breakup of European empires that civil societies more fully emerged in the new states of East-Central Europe. In that period, Czechoslovakia had the most successful and lasting experience with democracy, and was indeed the most bourgeois nation to be formed from the Hapsburg Empire (Szücs 1988: 329). But the postwar 1948 communist coup repressed the democratic development and social differentiation of civil society.

The discourse of civil society was revived in 1970s Czechoslovakia and Eastern Europe during the period of normalization following the failed "Prague Spring" and the Soviet invasion of 1968. At this time, civil society came to represent the struggle for the democratization of state and society in Czechoslovakia as well as other Eastern bloc states. Democratizing society within an authoritarian state depended on the creation of a self-organizing, ethical society "underneath" the party-dominated official structures. Its locus was in the household, among groups of friends, in publishing initiatives, in the workplace, the informal economy, and in the cultural underground (Keane 1996: 86, also 85, 104). These areas of life constituted a public realm that was mobilized against the state. They flourished into a space for society that was illegal and could be coercively repressed by communist regimes.[9]

In nonviolent and gradualist ways, civic movements such as *Charta 77* and other initiatives in the cultural underground opposed the concentration of power in the party-state. They forged a "parallel polis" that challenged the limits of communist power and produced an alternative political discourse, redefining the socialist state as illegitimate (see Benda 1991; Uhl 1985). *Charta 77* literally held the Czechoslovak communist regime to its word, reminding the Czechoslovak public and the regime of its ratification of international treaties and agreements protecting freedom of speech and freedom to associate. It produced a small group of dissidents aware of their oppression and who were prepared for the long struggle for freedom. The Czechoslovak cultural underground had a similar effect. By producing an alternative to socialist consumerism, middle-class attitudes, and hypocritical morality, it anticipated a new generational form of cultural dissent (Uhl 1985: 193–94). The emergence of a revitalized civil society contributed to the weakening of the regime and led to its eventual collapse in a nonviolent revolution. In November and December 1989, the civic movements, which together formed the *Civic Forum*, were able to convince Communist Party officials to minimize acts of sabotage and violence and to relinquish their power. This was an incredible accomplishment, testifying to, in Havel's famous adage, "the power of the powerless" (Havel et al. 1985).

In striking contrast to its development in the West, civil society in East-Central Europe, while opposed to state socialism, was not associated with capitalist social forces (Sakamoto 1997).[10] This oppositional civil society did not emerge out of a bourgeois private sphere, as in Habermas's theory of the invention of the public sphere in the eighteenth century, nor with the rise of a commercial class *for itself*, although once it became the official society after 1989, it quickly moved in that direction. For the first time since the eighteenth century and for the first time in this region, the concept of civil society was differentiated from the market economy (Arato 1982). Civic mobilization against communism needed neither the support of independent economic activities encouraged by capitalism nor the limited pluralism that authoritarian regimes in Latin America tolerated. While in opposition to the state, civil society in East-Central Europe sought "a place for itself by necessarily self-generated, unconventional means" (di Palma 1991–92: 72–73; also Croan 1989: 193). But as Jean L. Cohen and Andrew Arato (1992) have argued, this ideal of a solidaristic civil society can be maintained only while civic movements are united in opposition to the state and outside of government. The transition to democracy, and the opportunity it brings to openly contest government, displaces the former politics of dissidence and serves to break up previously unified social movements.

In the Eastern European dissident experience, family, personal and religious ties played more direct roles in supporting civil society than in the West, where as private and public spheres they are usually constitutionally separated (see Mische 1993).[11] In the Czechoslovak underground, the boundaries of the public and the private were porous and the home was frequently a site of civic resistance as well as family responsibilities and civic action. Consequently, women were not excluded from political participation. Gender roles were not often a source of internal tension in these communities. Solidarity among men and women was forged against a common enemy, the socialist state, and men and women joined the various civic initiatives in roughly equal numbers. However, as we will see, the introduction of democratic competition differentiates the public sphere, allowing gender and ethnic identities to become politicized.

Civil Society as Market Society After 1989

The form and content of civil society changed after the collapse of the Czechoslovak communist regime. One of the first acts passed after the Velvet Revolution was Act No. 83 (1990), allowing citizens to freely form associations. At the same time, in June 1990, new political parties were constituted. By way of these parties, some former dissidents were ushered into positions of power. But along with the dissidents came many individuals from the technical and professional classes who had been neither Communist Party members nor directly opposed to the party-state.[12] The *Civic Forum* (*Občanské Fórum*), which was created from the membership of these two groups, became the government in the first democratic elections in 1990.

Strongly influenced by the global dominance of neoliberal economics in the late 1980s, a "free-market" oriented reform program won over the civic, more elusive but democratically inspired, visions of dissident intellectuals in the Civic Forum. The professional technocratic group rapidly acceded to political power over the former dissidents. The revolutionary Civic Forum party split and contested the 1992 elections as separate political parties. One of the parties, Václav Klaus's Civic Democratic party (ODS), gained the greatest number of seats in the national election and formed a coalition right-of-center government. The 1989 revolution was in many respects a revolution from below, of civil society against the state, but the subsequent transition from communism rapidly became a state-led restoration of capitalism and market-style democracy.

After 1989, "civil society" as conceived in the Eastern European political opposition became associated with a "third way," that is a path between socialism and capitalism, which was discredited around the world in the early 1990s and was quickly marginalized in the Czech transition as well (Arato 1994). The liberation of civil society from the repressive socialist state became inseparable from the liberation of the market economy from the shackles of state ownership (Van der Pijl 1993: 255–6; Holý 1996: 5). Czechoslovakia's civic movements became "vanishing mediators" in the passage from socialism into capitalism (Žižek 1992: 48). Once the communist regime had imploded, the civil society movement was replaced by the rise of new political and technocratic élites. The civic solidarity seen during the Velvet Revolution was overtaken by more powerful neoliberal discourses that stressed individual rather than collective empowerment. Once a site for social struggle, postsocialist "civil society" became increasingly identified with the market economy, private property ownership and individual initiative, and to a lesser extent, human rights.

Between 1992 and 1997 Václav Klaus's ODS-led coalition government actively worked against the development of democratic civil society. Contrary to the government's neoliberal rhetoric of decentralization and individual choice, power was overwhelmingly concentrated in the state under Klaus's leadership. The goal was reform from above, and Klaus promoted his concept of market society based on economic self-interest rather than ethical, collective action.[13] Applying the standard criteria for market stability and democratic consolidation, Klaus stated that the Czech transformation had been successfully completed in 1994 and that the country no longer required foreign assistance.

Relations between the associations and organizations of Czech society and the postsocialist state have not always been mutually supportive during the past decade of transition, and conflicts were particularly visible under the government of Václav Klaus, 1992–1996. Klaus gave the opportunity for civil society to return to its oppositional role, so that much continuity can be found between this transition period and the situation before 1989, with one major exception. While the Czechoslovak communist regime was feared and repressed independent associations during the 1970s and 1980s, the democratically elected Czech government has been indifferent to civic organizations. It has rarely consulted citizens groups outside of electoral campaigns, and has actively opposed support for an independent civic sector that might mediate the relations between citizens and the state.[14] A law allowing associations to register as nonprofit organizations (with certain tax exemptions) and to apply for state grants to carry out public projects was not passed in the Czech Parliament until 1995 (Non-Governmental Non-Profit Sector 1995). This lack of support for civil society was one of the contributing factors that led to the removal of the ODS government in the 1998 elections.

Masculinization of the Public Sphere

Women have never been equal participants in Czech politics. However, under communism, they acquired close to 30 percent of the seats in the National Assembly due to a Party "gender quota" ensuring women's representation. In addition, between 1948 and 1969 there was always at least one woman minister in the Communist Party Presidium. Yet after the Soviet occupation, between 1970 and 1989, there was not a single woman in the communist government. As former Czech émigré and dissident Václav Belohrádský (1999: 247) puts it, "communism was an 'awfully masculine world' to which women belonged only as holders for masculine virtues." Women were very active in the anti-communist opposition movement, however.[15] They made up one-third of the original signatories of *Charta 77*, and were always included among the three spokespersons for that group every year between 1977–89.[16] Things are different now, as Table 6–1 indicates.

Since 1989, and the transition to democracy, women have been hardly visible in formal politics. After the first democratic elections in 1990, only 11 percent of parliamentary deputies were female. This proportion remained virtually unchanged until the 1996 national election when women candidates obtained 15 percent of the seats in the Czech parliament.[17] The proportion of women in the Senate, the Czech upper chamber, was even lower than in the Czech Parliament, at 11 percent after both the 1996 and 1998

TABLE 6.1 The Representation of Men and Women in the Czech Parliament
Before and After 1989

Year	1981	1990	1992	1996		1998	
				Chamber of Dep.	Senate	Chamber of Dep.	Senate
Women	58	22	19	30	9	30	9
Men	142	178	181	170	72	170	72
Women (%)	28	11	9.5	15	11.1	15	11.1

Source: Czech Republic CEDAW Report, www.un.org/womenwatch/daw/cedaw.

TABLE 6.2 Women's Political Representation in the Czech Republic
Based on Election Results

Election Terms	Body	Total No. Elected Persons	No. Women Out of Total	Share of Women (%)
November 1994	Municipal, town, district and local authorities	62,160	11,100	17.9
June 1996	Chamber of Deputies of the Czech Parliament	200	30	15.0
November 1996	Senate of the Czech Parliament	81	9	11.1
November 1996	Municipal, town, district and local authorities	62,412	12,785	20.5

Source: www.volby.cz; 1999 Czech Republic CEDAW Report, www.un.org/womenwatch/daw/cedaw.

elections. After analyzing party lists for the 2002 general election, the Czech daily *Mláda Fronta Dnes* predicted that the Czech parliament will remain an "old boy's club" regardless of the outcome of the election (Radio Free Europe/Radio Liberty 2002). The number of women in the Czech parliament is even likely to decrease from its current 15 percent. Such Czech indifference to the equal representation of men and women contrasts with the "gender quotas," adopted in Latin America, France, Uganda, India and other democratizing parts of the world in the 1990s, which require a certain proportion of party candidates or parliamentary representatives to be women (Klímešová 1996).

Czech women have fared marginally better in local government. As Table 6–2 shows, by 1996 women had 20 percent of the seats on municipal, town, district and local authorities.

As shown in Table 6–3, women's 15 percent share of parliamentary seats in 1996 remained the same following the 1998 election. Table 6–3 also shows that today's democratically elected but largely unreconstructed Communist Party continues to have the highest proportion of women representatives of all the Czech political parties. Indeed, there is some evidence to suggest that the further it is to the left, the more likely a political party is to

TABLE 6.3 Women Parliamentary Representatives in Czech Political Parties following the 1998 National Election

Orientation	Political Parties	No. Seats	No. Women	% Women
Left	Communist Party of Bohemia and Moravia	24	6	25%
	Social Democrats	74	11	15%
	Christian Democrats and Czech People's Party	20	3	15%
	Freedom Union	19	3	16%
	Civic Democratic Alliance	0	–	–
	Civic Democratic Party	63	7	11%
	Republicans	0	–	–
Right	Total	200	30	15%

Source: Czech Electoral Commission; Czech Statistical Office.

have more female deputies.[18] The Social Democratic Party (ČSSD), the current government, has the largest number of women representatives in the Czech Parliament. The Czech Social Democrats are also the only party that applies a 25 percent gender quota for all party bodies. Yet not a single woman has been a cabinet minister during the Social Democratic Government between 1998 and 2002. This situation singles out the Czech Republic as the only country in the Central and Eastern European region without a woman at the ministerial level.[19] It also demonstrates that the masculinist political culture is not limited to the neoliberal Civic Democratic Party.[20]

Only 22 percent of Czechs still regard this low level of women in government as appropriate or natural (Havelková 1999: 147). In a survey conducted by Public Opinion Resarch (IVVM) in August 1996, three-quarters of the Czech population agreed that it is beneficial for the country when women take part in public life, while 60 percent of those polled favored women over men in public office ("Nová elita žen." 1996). Moreover, in her study of five Czech newspapers between 1990 and 1998, Hana Havelková (1999) found that the media had a generally favorable disposition toward women political representatives, viewing them as competent as men but also as potentially more sensible, rational, and moral. Nonetheless, a new gender division within civil society has been manifest in the transition, resulting in the formation of masculine-oriented political parties and a feminized NGO sector.[21]

After the 1989 Velvet Revolution, former communist-dissidents took only a part of their pre-1989 civil society *public.* Together with anti-communists from the profession/technical class, they formed a new, male-dominated "political society." The residue of "civil society" was transformed into a female-dominated "third sector." Although the majority of male dissidents entered the political realm, seeking election after 1989, very few of their female counterparts did so.[22] Most female dissidents carried on the civic initiatives of the pre-1989 opposition. With the breakup of the Civic Forum in 1991–1992 — the movement that became the first democratically elected government in 1990 — political parties rapidly dominated the political space and became the primary vehicles for democratization.

The Czech experience was repeated elsewhere in the former communist region. Men overwhelmingly predominated in the new democratically elected parliaments and governments, causing the term "masculine democracy" to catch on. As Brigitte Young (1999: 224) has noted, "the path of the two sexes parted radically after the Velvet Revolution was over." In Czechoslovakia, men came to the forefront, holding the ministerial and leadership positions, while women receded further into the background of the new public realm. In ČSSD representative Jan Kalvodá's telling, "the year 1989 addressed men in politics." Women find it difficult to get ahead in politics because today's male political élites are a "community that was formed quite accidentally in 1989 or 1990" (Rabenseifnerová 1996). Not only did men dominate the political sphere but a masculinist political culture characterized by arrogance, competitiveness, and corruption, took root as well.[23] People reach the top in politics, the Secretary of the Social Democratic party at the time, Alena Gajdusková observed, not through "concentrated and purposeful work but by a go-ahead style and sharp elbows" ("Strany zakon . . ."1995).

In general, former dissidents were marginalized following the first Czechoslovak democratic elections, to be replaced by their more qualified, professional contemporaries — the technocrats — who were also strong advocates for radical neoliberal reform. The gender dimension of this transformation of political power has been less analyzed. Women involved in the Civic Forum of 1990–1992 were typically the more "contemplative, reflective dissident types, focused on a critical skepticism of the human condition in general," and were less likely to be radically anti-communist or pro-market reform (Pithart 1992: 758–59). It was the "young wild ones" — for the most part men — who formed the Civic Democratic party (under Václav Klaus's leadership) and went on to gain political power.[24] Party politics thus became an arena in the transition for men to assert themselves as men, a channel to promote men's professional advancement that had been inhibited by state socialism (Wagnerová 1999: 84).

During the past decade of transition, politically interested women have predominantly chosen to follow one of two paths. The first involves entry into formal politics where many have either been silently co-opted as helpmates to men or have become non-central players, whose popularity and demonstrable political skills have not been used to advantage by the male political leadership. Women representatives admit that there is no women's agenda or women's perspective in the Czech parliament ("Parlament je čím dál víc mužskou . . ."1995). Without such an agenda, which can be cultivated only with greater support from women and a critical mass of women in parliament, to be taken at all seriously, you must be like a man (Bůzková 1996: 8; Nadace Gender Studies 1996). One Czech journalist writes: "The fact is, that in the [Czech] government, and in the major political parties hardly one woman can be found who speaks out in public. This is not about feminism, or western excess, but about the lack of democracy, which citizens in advanced countries would not allow" (Coudenhové-Kalergiová 1993: 9; Knox 1994: 3). However, implicit in this comment, which resembles state socialist ideology, is a dismissal of western feminism as extremist. Ironically, such socialist-derived, antifeminist attitudes have only served to bolster the masculinist political culture of the new Czech democracy.

Of course, not all Czech women have been co-opted by "masculine politics; some have chosen a second path in politics. These women representatives have had an obvious distaste for the economic agendas of transition politics. Květoslava Kořinková, for example, was the only female minister in the federal government of Czechoslovakia between 1990–1992; she opposed many of the policies of the conservative government and its self-confessed "Thatcherites" (cited in Hauser 1996: 85). Others like Social Democrat deputy, Petra Bůzková, have refused to consent to the prevailing politics of money and power. Bůzková has remarked that, "in a parliament with more women, there would be more concern with areas such as human rights, health and social affairs, which are more familiar to people in their everyday lives" (cited in Vodrážka 1996: 47).

Once nominated as candidates by their parties, Czech women actually perform much better in elections than Czech men (Saxonberg 2000: 148–49). Table 6–4 shows the success rate of women candidates in the most recent local and national elections. But getting nominated by Czech political parties to stand for election is the greatest obstacle for women candidates since their own political parties have often marginalized them.

There is considerable evidence published in the Czech press of male politicians collaborating to keep women out of politics and positions of power.[25] Czech public opinion has not been indifferent to this behavior. In media polls conducted since 1995, people attributed the corrupt and scandalous Czech political scene of the late 1990s to immaturity of male politicians and their greed for power (Havelková 1999: 155). Both the Czech media and public have frequently expressed the opinion that women are more rational, less power seeking and would make better politicians than men ("Vzdy . . ." 1996). According to Havelková (1996: 249), a majority of Czech men and women support the reinstatement of gender quotas in politics.

Despite the favorable disposition of the Czech public toward women representatives, Czech politics has provided many examples of blatant sexism

TABLE 6.4 Women Candidates and Elected Representatives in the Last Elections in 1998

Body	Candidates			Elected Representatives			% Elected Women Candidates
	Total	Women	Women (%)	Total	Women	Women (%)	
Chamber of Deputies	3,631	756	20.1	200	30	15.0	4.0
Senate (27 Districts)	137	12	8.8	27	3	11.1	25.0
Town Councils	163,649	40,774	24.9	59,986	12,257	20.4	30.1
Local District Boards	15,945	5,477	34.3	2.426	528	21.8	9.6

Source: www.volby.cz; 1999 Czech Republic CEDAW Report, www.un.org/womenwatch/daw/cedaw

throughout the past decade. One of my favorites was the statement in 1993 by the Czech Minister of Health, Ludek Rubás, in the major daily. He stated: "I respect women immensely, but their contemporary number in cabinet [one in thirteen] I consider adequate" (Je žen v česke politice dost?" 1993). But the tactics to prevent women from entering the executive level of government and gaining too much power have involved much more than flippant comments. A case in point is the experience of Social Democratic deputy, Petra Bůzková, who single-handedly founded the Czech Social Democratic Women in 1990, the only internal party women's organization in the Czech Republic. In 1996 she was exposed to a public scandal, when *Televize Nova* — the private television network with the largest coverage in the Czech Republic — announced to the public that she was three months pregnant although she had categorically declined to give any personal information. They publicized that her pregnancy would surely influence her political career by reducing the time she had available before the election for politics. ("Ženy mohou dát politice ..." 1996); "Železný se omluvil Bůzkové" 1996).

In the next election year, 1998, Bůzková consistently polled as the most popular Czech politician. A poll taken in February 1998 showed 70 percent of the Czech public supported her candidacy and 65 percent supported Social Democratic deputy (now cabinet minister) Stanislav Gross, both in their thirties. In the same poll only 38 percent supported the Social Democrat Leader, Miloš Zeman and 17 percent supported former Premier and Civic Democratic Party leader Václav Klaus. Bůzková featured more prominently than Zeman himself in the electoral campaign that ushered the Social Democrats into power. She was coined "the beauty queen of the Czech parliament" by the Czech media. (Pitrová 1998). But following the 1998 election, Bůzková distanced herself from the ČSSD party leadership after it signed the opposition agreement with the ODS party allowing it to form a minority government. Considered to be a rival of the new Premier's, her name was floated as a potential successor to President Havel (Dubský and Pitrová 1998).

In August 2000, evidence emerged that advisers to the Premier Miloš Zeman's had plotted to launch a public campaign, "Operation Lead,"[26] to sully Bůzková's reputation.(Radio Free Europe 2000a, b, c). Specifically, officials in Zeman's office drafted a document that listed her weaknesses and laid out ways to discredit and embarrass her in the press. In September 2000, the chief adviser to the Premier acknowledged that he would have to "admit

FIGURE 6.1 Poster-Girl

Czech Social Democratic Party Campaign Poster, 1998.

Courtesy of Czech Social Democratic Party Headquarters, Prague.

some sort of co-responsibility" for these actions in connection with the "Operation Lead" scandal (Radio Free Europe/Radio Liberty 2000e). Yet no wider public discussion has focused on the gender implications of this attempt by the highest-level office in the executive branch of government to destroy the reputation of its most impressive female politician.

The case of the current Social Democratic government is further indicative of the gendered power relations underpinning postsocialist Czech politics. On announcing his all-male cabinet to the public in July 1998, the Premier, Zeman commented patronizingly that the absence of women was, "a sign of respect for female politicians." He explained: "I wouldn't want talented female politicians from the Social Democrats to be needlessly blemished by the decline of their popularity and prestige because of having to deal with immensely difficult and virtually unprecedented tasks."[27] ("Zeman přy nenašel ženu . . ." 2000). Zeman said this would be "government of suicides," but he promised that women would have the chance to work in government positions successfully and "without getting scratched after two years" (Kalenská 1998).

Eighteen months later, in January 2000, Zeman announced that he was replacing five ministers, who had not excelled in their positions, with yet another set of men. "Where expert criteria are concerned," he was quoted as saying "male candidates proved better than women" ("Vláda žen spatřila svetlo sveta . . ." 2000). Challenging Zeman's sexist remarks, Parliamentary deputy, Jana Volfová announced that she would set up a shadow-cabinet composed entirely of women to prove that there were qualified women to fill every single ministerial post. "Female politicians have long been in the shadow of their male colleagues," she said, "so why not take advantage of it and create a shadow government?" ("Czech women take a chisel . . ." 2000).

Jana Volfová's shadow cabinet introduced in March 2000 not only made women visible, it counterposed them to the existing male cabinet which was vulnerable to criticism on performance grounds.[28] Among the list of women shadow ministers, were Eva Kantůrková, the well-known writer and former dissident as Minister of Culture, Kvetoslava Kořinková, the former dissident and parliamentary deputy as Minister of Transportation, Viktoria Čejková, Director of the Law and Economics Faculty at Masarýk University as Minister of Finance, Kateřina Mandovcová, the Trade Unionist as Minister of Labor and Social Affairs, and Michaela Markosová-Tomínová, the then Director of the Prague Gender Studies Center as Minister without Portfolio. No Premier or Defense minister was named because Volfová said, "we already have one Premier and we do not want an army" (Hořejší 2000). As of 2002, four years after Zeman's comments that some women would have the chance to participate in the Social Democratic government, there was still not one woman in the Czech cabinet.

Although some women have taken the conventional path into formal politics in the new Czech democracy, clearly this path has been an uphill battle for them. But some equally active women chose another path after 1989. These women have willingly foregone opportunities to enter formal politics. They have devoted their political energies to building democracy from below in NGOs and citizen initiatives in the new civil society.[29]

Feminization of the Civic Sphere

Although masculine patterns of power and authority have been well established since 1989, postsocialist restructuring has liberated new forms of politics in Czech civil society. An aversion to exclusionary "male" politics has motivated women in the Czech Republic to seek out other forms of social and political action (Marková 1997). The post-1989 careers of women who were active in *Charta 77* are illustrative . Although very active in the opposition before the revolution, almost all of the former dissident women I interviewed in July and August 1996, refused offers to enter politics after 1989 and chose rather to devote their energies to civil society.[30]

A 1996 study found that women headed 84 percent of Czech NGOs.[31] In the early 1990s, with the beginning of shock therapy reforms, some of these organizations mushroomed to fill gaps in under-funded public services. Others contested state policy and legislation for the first time, and provided new social services for women, children, elderly, and disabled people. These civic organizations across Eastern Europe both opened the public space and provided opportunities for the development of women leaders (Hunt 1997).[32] For many Czech women, voluntary associations and NGOs have become schools of empowerment, leadership and management skills needed for the new market environment (Busheikin 1996).

In 1999 more than thirty credible organizations existed in the Czech Republic that were either established for women or that had a women-only membership. Yet just a handful of these organizations directly relate to politics *per se* or to political parties (Nadace Gender Studies 1994).[33] They may lobby politicians but they do not directly seek to place their (women) members in political power. They are more likely to articulate themselves through the language of human rights and citizenship than are western women's groups.[34] Many Czech women's organizations have an affinity for the dissident model of political opposition and share the goals of the former *Charta 77* civic movement to expand the spaces for citizen participation and for independent initiatives.[35] Most, therefore, are not single-issue interest groups. As indicated by table 6–5 the organizations are usually involved in at least two forms of social and political activity. These multiple activities include, providing social services and educational opportunities for women or different groups of citizens in need, giving support to prostitutes and migrant women, and disseminating information and policy ideas. They may also involve activities for self-development of professional career women or women at home (labeled as "traditional" in the table), and that promote ecological values and defend women's human rights.

Table 6–5 emphasizes that while they have little engagement with the formal political power structure, Czech women are very active in the public sphere. One might argue that this civil society is an irrelevant backwater of Czech politics. However, in the postsocialist Czech Republic there is democracy at the macro level but a lack of decentralization of political power. Citizen activism in the nooks and crannies of society therefore has become a more effective way of spreading democracy than the mere adoption of the rules and rituals of western-style political institutions.

Contemporary feminist scholars argue that women and their organizations in civil society strengthen democracy, empowering women and providing a vital mirror to formal politics. Global civil society organizations have recognized the importance of Czech women's initiatives and become a crucial source of support for them. The knowledge, networks, and activism flowing over the boundaries of nation-states and across the East-West divide are now an integral part of Czech women's organizing. There has been a diffusion of women's development projects, gender studies libraries, and university courses and journals devoted to feminist thinking and women's activism more generally.[36] (Ironically, most of these efforts have not been opposed to or been especially threatening to men and male-dominated entities since there is relatively little money to compete for.)[37] Czech women's groups have accepted western assistance and forms, and shaped them according to their own interests (see Havelková 1997; Busheikin 1997). But they are not only net importers of civil society. Women's organizations have uncovered and drawn upon an earlier, interwar feminist tradition in the First

TABLE 6.5 Major Czech Women's Organizations 1999 by Category

Name of Organization	Social Services	Ecological	Traditional	Professional	Education	Information/ Policy	Human Rights
Gender Studies Centre					X	X	X
Rosa Foundation	X						
La Strada	X				X	X	X
Movement for Women's Equal Rights					X	X	X
Association of Businesswomen	X			X			
Prague Mothers		X	X		X		
Czech Women's Union	X		X		X	X	X
Zeleny Kruh		X			X		X
Gaia		X			X		X
Social Democratic Women				X	X	X	
Profem					X	X	
Southern Czech Mothers Ecology Association	X	X	X		X		
Club of Single Mothers	X		X				
Women's Science Technology Club				X	X		
New Humanity		X			X		X
Promluv	X				X		
Bliss without Risk	X				X		
Vesna	X		X				
Elektra	X				X		
White Circle of Safety	X				X		

Source: Table created by author

Czechoslovak Republic, which produced important women leaders and politicians. They have also sought to retrieve and learn from three generations of women's memories of their lives under communism (Feinberg 1998; Frýdlová 1998). Thus, Czech women's organizations have been empowered both by the Velvet Revolution's promise of a free civil society and by global discourses of human rights.

Building Civil Society from Below

Compared with western countries, civil society is relatively weak in the Czech Republic. As a result (and due also to their inexperience with democracy), Czech associations, churches, and NGOs sought outside partners and foreign financial support after 1989. Women's organizations, for example, reached out to western feminist organizations and global networks for resources, ideas, and strategies to combat anti-feminist discourses in Czech society and the state's indifference toward persistent gender inequities. As Gramsci observed, when local progressive forces are scanty and inadequate, a drive for the renewal of civil society may arise if there is "an international situation favorable to their expansion and victory" (1971: 116).

For their part, western states, international institutions, and nongovernmental actors have made "building civil society" a linchpin of their policy toward Central and Eastern Europe. During the cold war, the United States blended anti-communist security policy with efforts to support Eastern European civic opposition movements.[38] Since the end of the cold war, U.S. "low-intensity democracy promotion" abroad has deliberately bypassed state agencies in Central and Eastern Europe, primarily funding the emerging for-profit private sector, and in small doses, "nonprofit" organizations (see Quigley 1996; Wedel 1998).[39] Even the World Bank and International Monetary Fund have preferred the strategy of promoting civil society rather than imposing traditional austerity packages in the region (Burgess 1997: 169). The primary U.S. strategy in the post World War II era was to institutionalize democracy by retraining the old élite and restructuring the branches of the state. The Marshall Plan for Western Europe and the occupation and reconstruction of Japan were informed by this fundamental strategy (Smith 1998; Ikenberry and Kupchan 1990). However, this top-down strategy had been reversed in post-cold war U.S. policy toward Central and Eastern Europe and has been supplemented in European Union policy toward the region by a bottom-up liberal strategy of encouraging civil society and decentralizing power in the market and in nongovernmental initiatives. In the Czech Republic it is estimated that well over half of the funds for the 40,000 registered nonprofit organizations, including more than 4,000 grant-giving foundations, come from foreign sources (Olsen 1997: 161).[40] The open society approach pioneered by George Soros is increasingly prominent. Within this approach, local rather than foreign recruits staff civic initiatives and there is a much more organic relationship to the local society than for instance, in the European Union's enlargement approach, which is focused largely on rebuilding state institutions through the diffusion of foreign rules and norms.

Gender is an important dimension of this liberal approach to building civil society. Empowering women is a means of expanding both markets and democracy. Women's activities are crucial to flourishing civil societies since they are often self-organizing, nonhierarchical and serve practical purposes. By the same token, civil society opens spaces for women's political expression and defends their human rights. To create this civil space, women's organizations in the Czech Republic have turned to western support to facilitate their work. Foreign funding and partnerships with organizations in global civil society enable Czech women to deal with problems, including deeply rooted gender injustices, that either go unacknowledged in the formal political sphere or are put in their "too hard" basket because they involve redistributing power, and resolving conflict. However, importing outside support sometimes has the effect of promoting western agendas and interests at the expense of local needs and priorities.

Four cases of women's projects help to flesh out this global/local relationship in Czech civil society. Two are American-funded projects; one sponsored by the U.S.-based Soros Foundation and another by a smaller organization. The other two are European-funded projects sponsored by the European Union's *Phare* assistance for Central and Eastern Europe program. Together, they represent a cross-section of the everyday life of women's projects in the Czech Republic. Each reveals the successes and problems of building civil society. East-West interaction can serve as a catalyst in the development of an independent civil society, but the process of creating a democratic infrastructure at the grassroots is messy and in the short term the outcomes are often ambiguous. In these respects, the transnational processes contributing to the development of Czech civil society stand in contrast to the interstate process of institutional transfer, such as that between the Czech Republic and the European Union.

American Feminism and NGOization

Consistent with promoting the Soros Foundation's goal of building civil society from below, a regional women's program within Soros' Open Society network was established in 1997 to address gender inequalities in East-Central Europe and the gender dimension of the open society concept. The Russian-American Director, Anastasia Posadskaya-Vanderbeck, believes that liberal societies need the participation and empowerment of women, but that this cannot be achieved by a "laissez-faire" neoliberal approach since it does not allow for the role of civil society in economic and social development and is indifferent to gender inequity.[41] The Soros regional women's program has developed initiatives that exemplify the Soros strategy of building open societies from the bottom-up.

Violence Against Women   The "Women-friendly Response to Violence Against Women project" funded by the Soros Foundation is designed to address domestic violence in Eastern and Central Europe. The project involves conducting multinational training programs (in just two major languages, Russian and English) for women's activists and NGOs in the Czech Republic and other Eastern European countries using as the model, a U.S. domestic violence prevention program pioneered in Duluth, Minnesota (Shepard and Pence 1999). The program is premised on the notion that violence against women was "hidden during communism." With its help, and the publicity efforts of other organizations such as the Czech edition of *Cosmopolitan*, the public and the Czech government are now more aware of or at least less oblivious to domestic violence as a serious problem in their society.

The Soros regional women's program sees domestic violence as one of the key social mechanisms for maintaining gender inequality in former socialist countries. It seeks to contribute to resolving this problem by training local women's organizations to prevent and respond to incidents of domestic violence and to mobilize a broader community response. Women's advocacy groups, independent of the state, are seen as the key agents of social change, capable of transforming attitudes in society and in public agencies toward domestic violence. Thus, the Soros program sees its major role as empowering these local women's groups.

In addition, the regional women's program has helped to develop a culturally sensitive adaptation of the Duluth Domestic Abuse Intervention Project to use across Central and Eastern Europe. Along the way, there have been several difficulties with adapting this model from the United States. First, implicit in the rationale for the Duluth project was the assumption that violence against women in the home has similar causes regardless of specific cultural, material, or historical context. Second, and more importantly, it follows from this assumption that similar responses to episodes of domestic violence are necessary and justifiable. In the case of the Duluth project "the state," its agencies, and male oppressors are identified as the primary perpetrators of domestic violence. But the cases of domestic violence in the Czech Republic and other transition countries are attributed to a range of causes, some of which are unique to the Czech context.

The current violence against women in the Czech Republic has occurred in the specific social and economic context of transition. With the collapse of the repressive socialist state, violence in all its forms was decentralized. Housing shortages (that force divorced couples or others in conflictual relationships to share the same accommodation) as well as high levels of stress and uncertainty have been widespread across Czech society. These conditions suggest the need for a localized response informed by local understandings rather than an imported model. In western countries like the United States where liberal rights and protection are taken for granted, women's advocacy groups were able to change the way state agencies deal with family violence in the community.[42] But an institutionalist perspective should make us skeptical that these transformations could be achieved in the Czech Republic where an authoritarian state existed until recently, and where the family was reified as a site of resistance to this state. The legacy of socialism is such that the desire to protect the family from the repressive state makes it difficult to have legislation that gives the state the right to protect women from domestic violence. Czech women's rights advocates have to take into account women and men's distrust of authorities, especially the police, and their fear of any kind of state intervention into their private lives (Šiklová and Hrádílková 1994: 115). This distrust does not reflect a ideology of autonomy like that of some American feminist groups, for instance, that have developed self-organizing capacities and a critique of the state as male (Ferree and Yaney 1995). Rather, it is the outcome of forty years of the state's domination and control over the lives of Czech citizens.

Although the U.S. model for addressing domestic violence may be inappropriate in the Czech Republic, given that liberal institutions are only in their infancy, the Soros project has facilitated problem-directed East/West dialogue concerning what would constitute an appropriate local response to domestic violence in transition countries. Beyond the traditional western remedies, Czech responses might include a wider public education campaign, NGO challenges to transition reforms, which have had a very negative social impact on families, and fund-raising for an independent support system for battered women. This critical engagement between Central and Eastern European and Western women's groups concerning solutions and problems has allowed for the joint development of a new and better approach to preventing violence against women. In the end what has been imported into transition countries is not simply a program to reduce violence against women, important as that is. Crucially, the dialogue, the *give and take*, between these women's groups has served to educate women in the region in the art of deliberation, problem identification, and local experimentation with creative solutions. Hence, a relatively short-term transnational encounter between women's advocates can have long-term, positive consequences for civil society's development.

East-West Networking   The Network for East-West Women (NEWW) was started in the early 1990s by a group of American feminists. They rallied to the call of Eastern European women, who felt that with the fall of communist regimes western women should do something to facilitate communication among Eastern European women. Given relatively weak civil societies and newly elected male dominated parliaments, these women recognized the need for western assistance to support their organizing in the region. As it has expanded, this East-West Network has encouraged the development of various women's organizations and initiatives, countering the generally negative reception to feminism across the region. Gender Studies centers both in the Czech Republic and other Central and Eastern European countries have mushroomed as a result of the financial support and legitimacy that this transnational network has given to local groups. In addition to providing funding for local women's projects, the East-West network has served as a conduit for the spread of ideas, practical knowledge, political war stories, and so on.[43]

The ties established by the Network for East-West Women have facilitated exchange and learning in the transition from communism. But like many transnational networks, NEWW inadvertently privileges external weak ties over the strong ties at home needed to achieve local social change. In reaching out to women's groups in the Czech Republic and across Eastern Europe, NEWW has tended to bolster existing élite networks of former dissidents and NGOs run by academic, middle-class women rather than to mobilize a broad-based women's movement.[44] This "take me to your leader mentality" has created a small group of women who can be quite powerful local gatekeepers for flows of money from the West (Mortkowitz 1994). It takes time to make strong local connections so western organizations like the NEWW often tend to stick with the same "nodal" person to evaluate grant proposals and approve projects. Those who are not included often view this strategy as favoritism, creating "in-fighting" among Czech women's groups who are resentful of those who have relatively easy access to western support (cf. Penn 1998). In addition, many Czech women's rights activists believe that establishing closer ties among women's organizations within the Czech Republic is a greater priority than transnational networking (see Šiklová 1998b). The lack of consensus among local women's groups makes their advocacy weaker, not stronger, in the Czech Republic. Transnational networks are not always the ties that bind. Indeed, they can sometimes be counter-productive to the flourishing of local civil society.

Take the case of NEWW's project to link up Eastern European women's groups and the Washington/New York headquarters over the Internet for the first time.[45] In 1995 the Network brought several women from Eastern Europe, including the Czech Republic, to the United States for Internet training. These women were then sent back to train women's groups in the region to use the Internet. Flying a select group to Washington DC and sending back trainers who were no more well informed than some locals seemed problematic to many in the Czech Republic. No one asked Czech women's groups what their precise needs were. Nonetheless, there was a lot of excitement about this project, which involved donating computers and software. The Ford, Macarthur, and Eurasia Foundations gladly sponsored the project because it seemed to be achieving a tangible goal; establishing the infrastructure for a more *global*, open society.[46] Closer ties via the Internet, it was presumed, would spontaneously facilitate exchange among the region's women's organizations that would have many subsequent payoffs in the local context. How the links would operate and for what precise purpose were never ascertained in advance. The Board of Directors of the Prague Gender Studies Center all attended the training in order to maintain good relations with their western sister organization.[47]

Although local activists initially scoffed at it, the establishment of the Inter-network had payoffs — just not those payoffs that were foreseen. The East-West women's network has encouraged more regional networking among women from the countries of the former Eastern bloc, which may prove to be of more assistance than the western or U.S. connection in the long run. Regional networking has enabled local Czech groups to coordinate their efforts to address common problems such as the trafficking of women for prostitution and domestic slavery from the former East across Czech borders to the West.

Enlarging European Women's Networks

Europeans have taken a somewhat different approach than Americans in their efforts to support the development of Czech civil society. Rather than dealing exclusively with non-state actors, or creating new externally funded NGOs, they have sought to reform old socialist state institutions and integrate Czech women's networks with European networks.[48] The prospect of European integration is increasingly serving as a driving force in the post-socialist transformation of the Czech Republic. In order to fulfill the prerequisites for European Union (EU) entry, the Czech government and major political parties passed binding agreements in 1999 to ensure equal opportunities for men and women. But within Czech civil society, European integration is more of a reciprocal process. While the EU provides the frameworks for national policy and action,[49] civil society actors such as women's organizations appeal to the EU to support and legitimize their domestic social and political goals. *Phare*, the European Commission's quasi-governmental organization (*quango*), funded from government revenues but administered by nongovernmental actors,[50] has been coordinating this democracy assistance through Central and Eastern European civic organizations such as the former communist, Czech Women's Union and western-based NGOs such as Project Parity.[51]

Project Parity   Project Parity, a UK-based NGO, was contracted by the *Phare* program of the European Union between 1996 and 1998 to train future women leaders in Central and Eastern Europe with the goal of improving the meager political representation of women in that region. In 1998 I attended one of several Project Parity three-day seminars held in several Central and Eastern European countries and in the United Kingdom. More than sixty women from various women's organizations across the Czech Republic were introduced to concepts of gender equality and European integration attended this seminar.[52] It took a foreign partner such as Project

Parity to bring these women's groups together to discuss common problems and strategies in light of the Czech Republic's entry into the European Union. This European NGO deliberately went beyond the "take me to your leader" approach by moving their project out of Prague, seeking to strengthen the network of women's civic organizations within the Czech Republic and to create a domestic constituency of women capable of propelling women into positions of power.

The Project Parity seminar helped shape women's perceptions of their common interests, although at times this did not appear to be the case. In a discussion group on women and politics, which included local government representatives and parliamentary deputies, a number of participants contested the European goal of increasing women's political representation. One group member retorted: "Women in politics do not follow women's interests." Another, with experience, pointed out that, "in politics, as soon as they want to represent or take up a cause, women get into conflict with men, who are selfishly focused on their own careers and power." Following presentations by the British consultants on various aspects of European law and politics, seminar participants also questioned the efficacy of European Union equal opportunities policy in the Czech context, where people reared under socialism habitually ignore the government's "soft" law and policy.

In a workshop on the impact of European integration on the family, participants expressed concerns that, "life will become commercialized and its quality will worsen," and that "women will lose their femininity as they become singularly focused on their careers." The women who participated in the discussion were more interested in discussing informal barriers to equal opportunities than learning how to draw up formal laws in the western, European style. They were also skeptical of legal sanctions and remedies for discrimination against women, when what was needed in their view was a broad public education campaign about gender inequities.[53]

By its own criteria, the Project Parity seminar revealed the crudeness of European efforts to build civil society in a postsocialist setting. But its unintended consequence was to catalyze a critical debate among Czech women about gender equality and European Union. Czech citizens are acutely aware that institutions developed in another cultural and historical context cannot be easily transplanted. In challenging the efficacy of Project Parity, the women used the seminar as a counterpoint to reflect on their own experiences under Soviet tutelage. In so doing, they also educated their European donors about the local history and culture so that they too were led to reflect on European integration in new ways. The Project Parity case suggests that the goal of empowering women and their civic organizations might occasionally be more likely to be reached when the terms of the West, in this instance, the European Union, are contested. Of course, donors might feel uncomfortable with their engagement and question the success of their efforts. But if they take a broader view, they may see success in terms of the greater presence of women in politics and the adjustment of Western European norms to Central and Eastern European experiences.

Czech Women's Union   The Czech Women's Union (ČSŽ — *Český Svaz Žen*) was founded in 1967 (as ČSSŽ — *Český Socialistický Svaz*) in the climate of socialist democratization, associated with the Prague Spring. After 1969, however, when associations and organizations autonomous of the state were banned, it became the official communist organization for the representation of women. Once the regime collapsed in 1989, the Women's Union lost its exclusive identity bestowed by the Party as well as half of its membership. It experienced considerable "social isolation" following the revolution.[54] Women in the *Civic Forum* held the Union in disdain, mocking its traditional activities ("knitting and folk-dancing") as well as its political conformism.[55] However, by 1993, still with approximately 90,000 members and 2,093 local groups, the former communist organization of women had begun to construct a new identity, more appropriate to the concerns of Czech women in a democratizing society.[56] The European Union has helped to transform this organization which existed previously as an appendage of the communist regime into a legitimate interest group, if not yet a women's movement.

With the external assistance of the European Union's *Phare* democracy program, between 1995 and 1998 the Women's Union began to reorient its mission from that of a traditional social network to that of an active, civic organization. This change was primarily registered by the Union's efforts to educate its members in the art of democracy.[57] In 1995 the Women's Union trained 28 women to moderate democracy education seminars for their countrywide membership.[58] These *Phare*-funded projects incorporated discussions of women's rights and equal opportunities, and the European and international communities' approach to both of these principles. In the words of the President of the Union, Zdenka Hajná, "equal opportunities between the sexes is not a social problem but a political problem, fundamental to the building of *parity* democracy" (Český Svaz Žen 1998). Taking up the cause of women's equality, the Women's Union has become active in a number of international women's organizations. As a strong supporter of the Czech Republic's entry into the EU, President Hajná, explains:

> Very often in our society the European Commission, the European Union and the deadline for our possible entry into these organs are criticized. However, let me ask this question: why do we want to enter this Europe? Not the least, to begin to seriously encourage equal opportunities for both sexes (Český Svaz žen 1998: 33).[59]

With *Phare's* help and the considerable social capital accumulated from the communist period, the Women's Union has been able to use its extensive, established network for representing women's interests. Under communism the Women's Union was part of the formal political apparatus and yet was hardly influential, but in the new democracy it is an independent civic organization seeking to have a political impact. It publishes a quarterly magazine and monthly newsletter that contain information on social and political issues of interest to its members and about specific actions they get involved with. These publications also present current research on any number of topics relating to women's interests, for example, the position of rural women on the labor market, the presence of women in politics, and the situation of women in the Czech family.

Also contrary to its role under communism, the new Women's Union has actively lobbied the Czech government on issues of concern to its members. For example, on behalf of the Women's Union in 1997, parliamentary deputy Hana Orgoniková took issue with the then Premier, Václav Klaus, and his government's failure to implement the resolutions of the 1995 United Nations Beijing women's conference ratified by the Parliament two years previously.[60] Klaus dismissed this challenge and expressed a general lack of interest in following through on Beijing's Plan of Action to address gender inequalities. Again representing the Women's Union, Orgoniková initiated a discussion in the Czech Chamber of Deputies. That discussion resulted in a parliamentary resolution (91 representatives for and 61 against) to oppose the Premier's reply. (Five other representatives also spoke on the floor in favor of the resolution.) The story did not end there, however. Giving in to the Parliamentary mandate, Klaus finally agreed to formulate a document detailing government priorities and initiatives for the promotion of gender equality by the end of January 1998. In April 1998, taking credit for its approval, the Women's Union published the government program. The Union's mobilization of its membership and their lobbying of representatives had forced the government to open its eyes to problems of gender discrimination and inequality. With this success, the Women's Union showed itself to be a credible force in civil society, more politically effective in some respects than the newer women's organizations established since the revolution.

The case of the Czech Women's Union shows that European integration represents a strategic opportunity for Czech women and their civic organizations to gain access as "social partners" to governmental actors (Ferge 1997: 167). With the support of the European Union, the previously discredited Czech Women's Union has been able to reform itself, combining traditional women's concerns essentially unchanged from the communist era with a democratic political agenda. Such efforts to revive Czech civil society will likely be more effective in transforming gender inequalities than the Czech Republic's adoption of EU law. Formal laws have been erratically and weakly enforced for forty years or more in the Czech lands so that, individually and nationally, the law is far more often avoided than abided (Sajo 1997).

Summary

Success and failure is a matter of your perspective. In the formal, political sphere emulating western political institutions by instituting "free and fair" elections counts as success. However, in the informal civic sphere, where the goal is to embed democratic practice in the local tradition, success is not guaranteed and when the outcome is favorable, it may take much longer to manifest itself. Thus linkages to actual East-West engagements may be hardly recognizable.

For those Czech women engaged in the difficult work of building civil society at the grassroots, East-West transnational networking has indeed had a catalyzing effect. Projects funded by American and European NGOs have undoubtedly been crucial for helping them to see things in new ways, even if this learning has occasionally occurred in opposition to western organizations' help. Through these encounters with westerners, Czech women's organizations have been able to articulate common, typically neglected, problems in their own language and in terms of their society.

For their part, western donors — NGOs and supra-state organizations such as the EU — are not so naïve as to believe that an unquestioned adoption of their practices could engender a strong civil society in the Czech Republic. What works in the realm of formal institutions (passing laws on equal opportunities, for example) is not likely to work in the social realm where one seeks, for example, to inculcate a respect among individuals for women and men as equally valuable human beings. Political conditionality is not effective here. The best that western organizations can hope for is to develop ongoing partnerships with Czech civil society, and encourage dialogue, trading of ideas, and experiences. By providing some tools, including the very language with which to address critical dilemmas, western partners can help local organizations in their efforts to raise society's consciousness about "parity democracy," "violence against women," and "human rights," and other widely shared liberal and feminist concerns.

Conclusion

Civil society as a realm of social action, autonomous of the government, yet existing parallel to it, was revived in communist Czechoslovakia in the 1970s and 1980s. But this ethical conception of civil society has been undermined during the Czech transition from communism by the rise of a market society that has atomized and differentiated citizens *inter alia* by class, gender, and ethnicity. In formal political terms, women may have had it better under communism. However, one needs to scratch below the surface of politics and look at the flourishing of women's organizations in civil society since 1989 for a more accurate and less pessimistic analysis. Although women have in many ways been pushed out of the formal world of politics during the Czech transition to democracy, they have become increasingly engaged in the informal realm of civil society. To effect real social change, women have gone below, around, and indeed, outside of the state.

The suspicion of the state current among western donors and within the emerging global civil society sphere has played to the advantage of women activists in local civic organizations. Representatives of the United States and the European Union have realized that the transformation of formal power structures will not in itself embed democracy in former socialist societies. Building civil society is considered as important as change in formal political institutions. At some point there has to be a similar realization among male political élites in the Czech Republic. Public demonstrations equal in size to those held during the Velvet Revolution of November 1989 have twice taken place since 1998. In December 1999 more than 150,000 Czechs called for the resignation of Czech Premier, Miloš Zeman, and leader of the opposition, Václav Klaus. Like the communist government before them, the protestors argued, these leaders were indifferent to "ordinary people," and responsible for the economic hardship and corrupt politics of the country. A document signed by 150,000 Czechs called for the renewal of civic values and democracy (Bauerová 1999). It said, among other things:

> We [Czechs] are still burdened by the legacy of 40 years of communism, but most of our current problems are the results of new mistakes and new wrongdoing. The state and the entrepreneurial middle class are not engaged in cooperation but in a fight, which is shot through with distrust, thievery, incompetence, and corruption on the part of public servants.

As the cynicism of Czech citizens toward formal politics grows, and stalemate continues between the major political parties, some concessions must be made both to civil society and those women who have been doing the "hidden" work of importing civil society and building democracy from below. The struggle to expand spaces for citizen participation and rejoin the West was, after all, what the Velvet Revolution of 1989 was all about.

7   Engendering Global Political Economy

The starting point for this study is the view that the transition from socialism in Central and Eastern Europe has been a comprehensive process of economic, social, cultural, and political change; a process often subsumed under the popular term "globalization." Using the case of the Czech transition I have shown how the globalization process might be rethought from the "bottom-up," in terms of changes in social relations upon which other, more macro changes are sustained. To explore these premises, I have analyzed how the family, labor markets, consumer culture, and civil society have been transformed in the Czech Republic from the dissident movement in the 1970s to end of the first decade of transition in 2000. My approach has been informed by Antonio Gramsci's view that international relations follow rather than precede fundamental social relations. In his words, "any organic innovation in the social structure . . . modifies organically absolute and relative relations in the international field too" (1972: 176). But we can go beyond this Gramscian view. The relationship between social relations and international relations is a dialectical one. Global processes modify local social relations. Local social relations modify global processes.

In addition to rethinking transitions as processes of globalization, I have shown how a gendered perspective can provide a captivating lens through which to understand fundamental changes in social relations. I do not explain postsocialist change in terms of patriarchy, Marx's logic of capital, or any other such singular logic. Rather, I suggest that appreciation of the diversity of women's experiences and contexts in the Czech transformation leads to a new understanding of the interrelated character of class and gender exploitation in the globalizing world. Far from being neutral with respect to gender relations, globalization is in fact deeply implicated in the production and reproduction of gender identities and differences. The gendered effects of globalization are closely tied with the liberal capitalist project that is driving globalization itself, but the dynamics of these gendered effects can be understood only in terms of the local forces at work in each country. Mainstream scholarship, both neoliberal and neo-Marxist, has largely ignored both the dialectical quality of the globalization process and the importance of gender relations as a key factor in shaping states and civil societies.

In this final chapter I use the results of the Czech case study to draw out and synthesize the major theoretical implications for our understanding of globalization and its consequences. I then turn to the broader challenge of thinking about how a gender perspective can be "mainstreamed" in international political economy and international relations scholarship; research traditions that have historically either ignored or dismissed the relevance of gender (see Tickner 1997; Whitworth 2000). In my view, efforts to comprehend postsocialist transformations in Central and Eastern Europe without incorporating a gender perspective will inevitably overlook crucial aspects of social change and change in world order.

Perspectives on Contemporary Globalization

As this study has sought to show, the interaction between global and local forces in the Czech transition has been complex, dynamic, and often ambiguous in its outcomes. None of the four interpretations of postsocialist transformations presented in the first chapter — neoliberalism, neo-Marxism, institutionalism and feminism — adequately comprehends or explains globalization as such a *dialectical* process.

Neoliberals predict the continued global expansion of markets and homogenization of global culture, and support the values of individualism and democracy. They view globalization as a one-way process in which market models for economic change are applied universally irrespective of local, cultural context. Ironically, neoliberals, like Marxists, see capitalist markets as dissolving all institutions that are incompatible with capitalist ends. Contemporary Marxists argue that the globalization process is shaped — if not determined — by the overwhelming penetration of international capital.

Neo-Gramscian Marxists, for their part, see globalization not only as increasing inequality and exploitation, but also as leading to the formation of a *transnational* capitalist class (sometimes called a "globalizing élite," or a "business civilization") with global ideological and cultural power.[1] Institutionalists worry that economic globalization undermines and constrains the power of nation-states to self-govern, and fear the power of the hegemon, the United States, to impose its worldview on all other states, denying local differences and repressing alternative national economic models. But many institutionalists nonetheless think that states ultimately control capital and are the main agents of social and economic development. Finally, feminists tend to interpret globalization in terms of its negative impact on women, the environment, and subjugated peoples. They tend to view the processes of expanding markets and liberal democracy as consolidating rather than transforming existing social hierarchies, in particular, the hierarchy of men over women.

It is my contention that a gendered analysis provides a better and more comprehensive understanding of globalization than any single theoretical perspective — neoliberalism, neo-Marxism, institutionalism, or feminism. The gendered approach advanced here has drawn on aspects of both institutionalist and neo-Gramscian perspectives. Gramscian theory provides an entry point for gender analysis with its focus on bottom-up, systemic change and the cultural fractions that make up the current capitalist world order. In the case of postsocialist transitions, the cultural and symbolic aspects of capitalism conveyed through gender identities and differences (advertising and marketing, consumer goods, status-symbols, and new identities) played a central role in initially persuading former socialist subjects of the benefits of global markets, while obscuring the forthcoming costs (growing unemployment, poverty, exploitation, and crime). Institutionalist theory also contributes to this analysis by highlighting the structuring role of historically embedded institutions and relationships in periods of radical change. The institutional legacy of state socialism and its gender regime, has powerfully shaped the postsocialist transition. Consequently, liberal democratic and capitalist institutions that have been imported into the region need to be more fully supported locally by culturally appropriate institutions. In short, the synthetic, dialectical approach developed here interprets the power of global trade, financial flows, and production networks not merely as economic transactions, but as fundamentally *constitutive* processes that promote competing models of gendered social relations on a global scale.

These global processes are extremely visible in the Czech transition from

socialism, where the contestation over old and new ways of organizing political economy play out in a competition for men and women's souls and
bodies. An advertisement used by *Czechinvest*, the state agency for foreign
investment, to market the Czech Republic abroad illustrates this point. The
advertisement, which appeared in the *Economist* twice in November 2000,
reads:

> What makes the Czech Republic a *Model Location* for foreign inves-
> tors? No, it's not the Czech Republic's top international models like
> Eva Herzigová. Rather, it's the country's proven ability to satisfy the
> needs of foreign investors seeking to better serve their customers while
> enhancing profitability."

It is impossible to analyze this document and ignore gender relations, and
their part in the constitution of globalization.

A number of interpretations of *Czechinvest's* advertisement might apply,
but the assumption underlying that organization's marketing strategy to seduce western foreign investors is that globalization is essentially a pact among
men. In this model investment climate, women's bodies are used symbolically as bait for big financial fish, just as in reality many men grubby their
hands in the Eastern European sex trade, where women are frequently ex-
pended for a couple of cars, a pile of illegal arms or drugs. Another, equally
plausible reading of the advertisement might be that Czech male élites, like
those East European women who surrender to western male fantasy in the
prostitution market, are willing to be feminized as handmaidens to global
capital in order to attract foreign investors. Certainly, this book provides
evidence that élite men in the Czech Republic have wanted to prove that
they are "man" enough to rejoin the capitalist West.

Theory out of Particulars

While global forces have clearly influenced the transition from socialism
in the Czech Republic and other former socialist states, much of what is
politically interesting about this process has eluded scholars of international
relations and international political economy, who typically do not closely
study domestic politics in a given country or region. In addition to their
similarly one-sided analysis of globalization, both neoliberal economics and

FIGURE 7.1 CzechInvest Advertisement

What makes the Czech Republic the MODEL LOCATION for foreign investors?

Top international model Miss Eva Herzigova, from the Czech Republic

FDI in the Czech Republic (millions $US)

1997 1998 1999 2000
1300 2770 5108

No, it's not the Czech Republic's top international models like Eva Herzigova. Rather, its the country's proven ability to satisfy the needs of foreign investors seeking to better serve their customers while enhancing profitability.

The Czech Government's commitment to further enhance the **investment climate model** through the provision of tailored incentives and development of property options, has helped double the flow of foreign direct investment over two consecutive years.

Over 1,200 foreign investors manufacturing in the Czech Republic are already benefiting from significant cost efficiencies, strategic location and the ability to source locally from the Czech Republic's world class supply base. And it's the combination of these advantages with the intellectual capital of the workforce, now and in the future, along with CzechInvest's ability to satisfy the needs of the foreign investors that makes the Czech Republic the **model location**.

To find out how your company will benefit from establishing a service, manufacturing or sourcing operation in the Czech Republic, take a look at **www.czechinvest.org** or contact the office nearest you.

CZECHINVEST
The Investment Promotion Arm of the Ministry of Industry and Trade

Chief Executive Officer: Mr. Martin Jahn
Headquarters: Stepanska 15, 120 00 Prague, Czech Republic
phone: +420 2 9634 2530, fax: +420 2 9634 2502, marketing@czechinvest.org

LONDON
Ms. Vladimíra Rysankova
london@czechinvest.org

CHICAGO
Ms. Hana Lasslerova
chicago@czechinvest.org

SILICON VALLEY
Mr. Radomil Novak
siliconvalley@czechinvest.org

DÜSSELDORF
Ms. Daniela Johannsen
dusseldorf@czechinvest.org

PARIS
Mr. Vladimir Kubes
paris@czechinvest.org

YOKOHAMA
Mr. Jan Kubicek
yokohama@czechinvest.org

This ad appeared in *The Economist*, November 2000.

Courtesy of CzechInvest, Prague.

neo-Marxism rely on a global, aggregate method (for Marx, there are no exceptions to the "laws of social change"). But as Bourdieu (1998: 2) writes, "the deepest logic of the social world can be grasped only if one lunges into the particularity of an empirical reality, historically-located and dated, but with the objective of constructing it as a 'special case of what is possible.' " In this sense the Czech case presented here is historically specific and yet not unique, since aspects of the processes of transformation that have occurred there could feasibly be occurring elsewhere, especially in light of globalization.

When I began my research in the Czech Republic I did not expect to encounter a political discourse of social and economic change that was so explicitly sexist. This overt sexism revealed, among other things, how little state socialism had achieved with respect to women's emancipation. I did not expect to find potentials for feminist politics on the pages of *Cosmopolitan*, nor that the promotion of democracy in the postsocialist context would produce such stark gendering of formal and informal politics. The dialectical research approach I have used has generated knowledge, which is meaningful both for understanding politics in a given context and for the purpose of theory building.

This book has examined four areas of the Czech transition in detail: the family, the labor market, consumer culture, and civil society. First, I explored changes in the family before and after 1989. Czech postsocialist political parties have hailed the heterosexual, nuclear family as the fundamental unit of the new market democracy. However, despite their rhetorical support of the family, divorce rates rose and marriage and birth rates fell dramatically after 1989. If anything, the nuclear family has been one of the "losers" of market reform. The demographic revolution has been an overlooked element of the Czech economic and political transition. The decline in the population and in new family formation has serious implications for the future social and economic viability of the Czech Republic.

The second area I explored was the establishment of the labor market in the Czech Republic. I argued that the new labor market has produced new forms of gender and class inequality and segregation. A three-tiered hierarchical labor force has emerged, where workers in the nascent private and foreign-owned sectors are privileged relative to those working in the public and domestic sectors and in the informal, underground economy, which is increasingly transnationalized. In spite of efforts by employers and politicians to send them home, however, women have remained strong participants in the labor force, making up nearly half of the economically active population as they had during socialism. But the introduction of "market forces" has commodified labor in ways that systematically discriminate against women workers. The new sexual freedom brought by the transition has allowed sexual harassment to run rife in the workplace. An even more dire consequence of the new labor market is the emergence of a "market in women." The low wages paid to women in the official economy have frequently resulted in women being lured into the sex industry and sold on the global market as bonded prostitutes. Local political leaders have essentially turned a blind eye to this illegal trade. Displaying the extent to which ideology can trump even a sense of irony, pro-market politicians have allowed the global sex market to flourish in the Czech Republic, alongside their public embrace of "family values."

The third area investigated in the book was the expansion of the consumer market. Global capitalism spreads by stimulating the domestic demand for new goods and services. In the Czech transition, marketing gender-specific products and playing up sexual identities and differences in advertising has expanded consumerism in spite of declining national wealth and production. In the transition from communism, global media have not only served to extend markets, they have also responded to non-consumer needs. Foreign women's publications in particular, have provided forums for local discussions about social change, even feminist change.

Finally and fourth, I looked closely at the reemergence of civil society, questioning why many Czech women retreated from formal politics after 1989. Democratic transitions in other regions of the world have provided opportunities for articulating women's interests and furthering feminist legislative agendas, but this has not been the case by and large in postsocialist Central and Eastern Europe. The Czech Republic has disassociated itself from communist-tainted projects of "emancipation" and adopted explicitly anti-feminist policies in its democratic transition. However, women have not given up on democracy altogether. Rather than struggling to be heard in male-dominated political parties, many women have put their energies into building democratic institutions from below in the nascent Czech civil society. Here women have capitalized on the process of globalization, and the possibilities it opens up for transcending national politics in an emerging global civil society.

The Czech transition provides new insight into the gendered nature of capitalist democracy and its globalization. Postsocialist economic institutions and the masculinism of politics have marginalized many women and men, even those who were visible and active in the dissident movement that helped to overthrow communism. The simultaneous transitions in the economy and the social, cultural and political realms have sometimes compounded the effects of this marginalization. But empowerment in one realm, for instance, in the cultural realm, has often alleviated the negative effects in another realm, for instance, in the economy. It is often argued that gender bias in the processes of economic and political restructuring is inadvertent.[2] The argument goes, if only policymakers, managers and other decisionmaking elites were made more aware of the differential impact of their policies and behavior on women and men, they would attempt to put things right. But this line of argument ignores the powerful institutional and individual reaction to the socialist "equality." More importantly, it underestimates the competition for power that occurs in conditions of rapid structural change.

While most theoretical approaches to postsocialist transformations have been blind to gendered power relations, those who have been actively constructing market democracy and living the transition in the Czech Republic certainly have not been. There is ample evidence of the consciousness of gender among key actors in the Czech transformation. Collectively the behavior of a range of local and global actors in the Czech transition has restructured the new capitalist marketplace and democratic institutions in explicitly gendered ways.

In 1990 policymakers in Czechoslovakia believed that sending women workers home would solve the problem of structural unemployment in the transition to capitalism, (although women have often ended up choosing to relegate family considerations and children rather than give up their jobs). Union leaders were prepared to sacrifice women's jobs in order to save the jobs of men. Employers preferred to hire men, in the hope of avoiding any of the social costs associated with the social reproduction of labor and foreign-owned firms adopted the non-western practice of using gender-specific linguistic forms in job advertising. Turning to the cultural realm we find western managers were quick to recognize the "market-pull" of gender-specific products and sexually explicit advertising images, while global media corporations saw a gap in the local market for selling "women's" content. In national politics, patterns of sexism reveal a degree of gender consciousness among élites as well. The Czech Premier and leader of the Social Democratic political party decided to appoint all men to the cabinet in 1996 and 1998, ostensibly on the grounds that women are inexperienced for such high-level political posts. The policymaking that has harmed women was often done with full knowledge that such harm would occur. Ironically, and tragically, many of those policy calculations have had — and will continue to have — adverse effects for many Czech men as well as for Czech women.

Yet the news here is not all bad. Globalization is a dialectical, negotiated process, involving local and global agents. Contemporary gender relations in the Czech Republic are not simply the product of globalization. Rather, they emerge out of a specific historical context and the interaction of former socialist subjects in that context with the forces of globalization. As such, women have resisted the public policies and ideological pressures accompanying the introduction of capitalism. Shaped in part by the socialist legacy, women have remained active participants in the labor force and in what has amounted to a "fertility strike," they have deferred or foregone marriage and children in increasing numbers. Countering the anti-feminism in the local media and politics, the editors of Czech-*Harlequin* and *Cosmopolitan* have deliberately used the global medium to cultivate a liberal, public space and to market feminist ideas to the Czech public. In this way, the so-called western cultural invasion since 1989 has been turned locally to the advantage of women. For their part, international organizations and western governments have sought to extend and deepen democratization by financing and supporting women's organizations. This support has served not merely to consolidate neoliberal reforms, but to enhance Czech women's activism in civil society, when they have been excluded from the formal political sphere.

If those involved in the Czech transition have been conscious of the dialectical, gendered dimensions of change, then why have mainstream approaches ignored them? First, these approaches have tended to view the transition from a planned to a market economy as the primary process of change, as if (as in theory), the economy were bracketed off from transitions in society, politics, and culture. Neoliberalism — where this theoretical abstraction of economic relations is most stark — has been the guiding philosophy of the Czech transition. Neoliberalism promised the new Czech power élite a "road from serfdom" to be followed in five or more easy steps not unlike a neo-Stalinist five year plan (see Mlčoch 1998).[3]

Observers of postsocialist developments have also typically worked with the neoliberal approach, or some derivation of it. Striking regional phenomena such as the pervasive employment discrimination against women and the sex trafficking of more than half a million Central and Eastern European women have been viewed by such observers as mere outcomes of the return to the "natural" law of supply and demand. Other significant social and political trends in the Czech transition analyzed here, such as the plummeting of birth and marriage rates after 1989 and the relative paucity of women in the new Czech parliament (not to mention the executive of the government) have escaped the notice of most mainstream analysts, who view male political behavior as representative of citizen political behavior in general. A narrow preoccupation with macro-economic and formal institutional criteria has led these analysts to ignore the crisis in social reproduction and the deficit in democratic participation in the Czech Republic and other postsocialist countries.

A second reason why mainstream analysts have ignored the dialectical aspects of change is that they focus primarily on the official political and economic spheres. Like neoliberal perspectives, contemporary Marxist theories provide incomplete accounts of social change. Even the neo-Gramscian perspective, with its emphasis on cultural hegemony, lacks the gendered focus on everyday life. A gendered perspective brings into view sexual practices and the intimate, family lives of human beings, it makes visible the often invisible "care economy," it draws attention to politics at the grassroots and in the so-called private sphere, and it reveals, in new ways, the political significance of culture and identities. Making explicit use of a gender lens opens up a range of fresh questions about the differential impact of globalization and the processes that lead to these diverse outcomes for differently situated social groups. We see global and local capitalisms together creating a spectrum of forms of economic exploitation and empowerment. In such a context, it is unlikely that fast privatization, liberal trade, and European citizenship will create security for all women and men. Even an institutionalist political and economic strategy attuned to the local context will leave women marginalized within the Czech lands and the global economy if institutional reforms do not include mechanisms designed to create equal participation and employment opportunities for women and men in their economy and society.

The approach of this book provides an important critique of existing theoretical approaches to the study of postsocialist transformations and global political economy. Hard-and-fast expectations about the outcomes of economic and democratic transitions are disrupted when a gender perspective is brought to bear. For example, evidence of the high level of participation by women in the underground Czech politics of the 1970s and 1980s might lead us to expect women to play a key role in the contemporary Czech parliament, as is the case for their male counterparts. This has not been the case. But this does not mean that women are playing no role in contemporary Czech politics. A fairly convincing argument could be made that, through their pivotal efforts to build a new civil society, Czech women are engaging in political actions that will have far-reaching effects. More importantly, these women are engaging in forms of political action that they feel comfortable with. They are forging new political identities on their own terms and, it could be argued, in so doing they are exhibiting more political efficacy than many of their male counterparts.

Mainstreaming Gender

A first generation of feminist scholarship demonstrated the need for an agenda in international studies that takes gender seriously. A second generation of feminist scholarship in that field now looks for — and experiments with — ways to do that empirically. This study contributes to that second collective body of scholarship by analyzing the impact of globalization on the Czech Republic in a way that empirically and theoretically integrates gender. It has sought to merge a feminist perspective with a broader critical analysis of social change. Specifically, once we recognize the tight connections between cultural and social forms and aspects of political economy, integrating a gender perspective into the analysis of international political economy becomes a relatively straightforward exercise that can generate new insights.

In order to advance feminist perspectives today, we need to get better at showing *where* and *how* gender matters, combining theory with close empirical study of global processes. In addition, we need to get better at articulating and empirically demonstrating the ways that gender relations interact — and are mutually constructed — with other social relations. We can gain a lot of analytical leverage through the careful investigation of specific cases. Ultimately, feminist contributions to international studies will depend not only on theoretical discussions of their promise but also on empirical demonstrations of the range of possibilities opened up by gendered analyses.

Feminist scholars need to engage in more self-conscious dialogue with a variety of other perspectives on social change and global political economy. Integrating gender perspectives with institutionalist and neo-Gramscian approaches represents one important strategy for engaging with other scholars of international relations and alerting proponents of "mainstream" international relations to the illuminating effects that can come from viewing social and political processes from a gender perspective. When such integration results in dialogue with those who work from other perspectives, then opportunities for the sharing of knowledge and methodologies are more likely to arise.

Reprise

The transformations that have occurred in Central and Eastern Europe since 1989 cannot be fully understood without an understanding of the extent to which gender has infused their every aspect. Mainstream efforts to interpret the transitions have missed key economic and political processes precisely because they have failed to view the transitions in gendered terms. Until recently. Consider the case of the World Bank. This institution has been heavily invested in a variety of ways in the transitions in Eastern Europe. Aside from having prescribed the blueprint for privatization and liberalization, this international organization has routinely reported on developments in the region. If you go back and look at these World Bank reports, you will find no direct discussion of the gender dimensions of change. But, maybe things are starting to change.

In 2000, the World Bank produced a regional report titled, "Making the Transition Work for Everyone" (World Bank 2000). Although the World Bank was among the first to analyze the transitions in Eastern Europe, it is interesting that it took more than a decade for one of its reports to notice the gendered aspects of labor markets and social policy in the region. The Bank report states:

> Policies that foster the labour market participation of women may reduce poverty as well as having other beneficial effects, including reducing women's vulnerability to violence and increasing investments in children. The link between women's labour force participation, affordable childcare programs, and higher household incomes justifies a renewed focus on childcare — especially if it can be tied to early childhood education programs that improve the life chances of poor children (World Bank 2000: 26).

The report goes on to conclude, "[E]ffective poverty reduction strategies will entail removing the barriers to equal participation in the market and in political life" (World Bank 2000: 27).

If you did not know that this was a quote from a World Bank report, you could be forgiven for reading it as a good *socialist* argument for economic development through women's emancipation. It could also be read as an admission that the western, neoliberal strategy of transformation in the region up until this point has been extremely lacking. The good news is that even mainstream international institutions are coming to realize that the institutional, gendered aspects of transitions cannot be ignored. But it is only a beginning — gender analysis has much more to offer.

This work constitutes more than an empirical study of the Czech Republic in transition. It demonstrates that globalization and gendering processes are inextricably bound. It also suggests that an analysis of globalization that stops at the macro level is untenable. Macro approaches be they neoliberal or neo-Marxist tell us more about the victimization than the agency of people, and mask much of the picture of gender dynamics. They often ignore micro-level factors that produce locally differentiated outcomes.

When gender and culture are taken into account, globalization is a two-way street, negotiated between a myriad of local and global actors. In the Czech case, as elsewhere, the sites of power and transformation are not just the domains of political and economic élites; such sites also exist in the nooks and crannies of civil society. A gender perspective illuminates the social transformations and power shifts that occur within states and civil societies, but that have global ramifications.

A number of scholars have asked where the resistance to neoliberal globalization might be found.[4] This study shows that resistance does not always occur in conventional places or in the conventional political forms. The view from below as opposed to the bird's-eye view of the macro theorist helps us to see the linkages between global processes and everyday relationships. As scholars of international relations and international political economy, we must be prepared to go into the traditional territory of the comparativist. Here at the local level, and informed by our theorizations of globalization, we can investigate how broader, macro processes play out at the micro level; how they interact with different histories, cultures, and identities. After all, it is in this *localization* process that the possibilities for social change lie.

Notes

1. Gender, Globalization, and Postsocialism

1. See Tickner (1997, 2001) for a discussion of the methodological and substantive differences between feminist and mainstream approaches to international relations.
2. See also Enloe (1989; 1994), Pettman (1996); Prügl (1999).
3. See Hooper (2000) and Marchand and Runyan (2000).
4. See Feinberg (1999), also Garver (1985).
5. See also Scott (1974).
6. The Czechoslovak regime denounced Stalin in October 1962, demolishing the monumental statue of Stalin, erected on Letná Park in Prague (and clearly visible from all parts of the city). The statue took three dynamite explosions to destroy, and was watched by cheering crowds.
7. Originally published in *Rudé právo*, 10 April 1968, see the English translation in Remington (1969).
8. See Kosík (1995); Kůsin (1971); Satterwhite (1992); Shore (1998).
9. In addition to the Communist Party, the Czechoslovak National Front in 1968 consisted of four minor parties, fifteen social organizations (mostly trade unions), and nine issue groups. For a thorough description, see Skilling (1976). To join these organizations Czechoslovaks did not have to be members of the Communist Party.
10. Soviet troops remained stationed in Czechoslovakia for more than twenty years until their withdrawal in 1990–91.
11. Ironically, Gustav Husák had spent the Stalinist 1950s in a Slovak prison as a "bourgeois nationalist" class enemy.

12. Dubček was expelled from the Communist Party in January 1970 and was quickly relegated to obscurity. He spent the 1970s and 80s working in a lowly job with the state forestry administration in Bratislava (Slovakia).

13. For a discussion of the countrywide "normalization" process, see Šimečka (1984).

14. See Skilling (1981); Chilton (1995). For a further analysis of the importance of the Helsinki Final Act of 1975 in the Czech context see Thomas (1999).

15. Communist police used force on occasion and the threat of Soviet force was ever present in Eastern Europe in 1988–89. The use of Soviet military against independence movements in the Baltic states in early 1991 is evidence that Gorbachev was not beyond the use of force when Soviet interests were clearly at stake.

16. The G-7 is made up of the United States, Canada, Great Britain, France, Italy, Germany and Japan. (It is now the G-8, including Russia).

17. For an analysis of Latin American political transitions as precursors to the transitions in Eastern and Central Europe see O'Donnell, Schmitter and Whitehead (1986); Linz and Stepan (1996).

18. See Pedziwol (1997); Earle, et al. (1994).

19. Central and Eastern Eurobarometer No. 8, 1997 reveals a marked decline in Czech public support for the creation of a market economy since the first survey of 1,000 households in 1990. Probably due to the economic and political turmoil in 1997, 50 percent of Czechs opposed the statement that "the creation of a market economy is right for the future of my country" and thus compared with their counterparts in other East-Central European countries, gave it the most negative evaluation.

20. The gains of privatization deals were invested outside of the Czech Republic in high-return, global money markets. In March 1997, 1.3. billion Czech crowns was said to have been embezzled from one of the country's largest investment funds, *CS Fondy*, and deposited in banks abroad (Perlez 1997). Victor Koženy's *Harvard Capital Fund* is infamous for tunneling Czech companies and sending millions of dollars in profits out of the country.

21. This information is taken from a poll conducted by STEM in June, 2001 see Radio Free Europe/Radio Liberty (2001b).

22. This December 1999 protest culminated in a document signed by 150,000 Czechs, including former students leaders from the 1989 Velvet Revolution, see Bauerová (1999).

23. Among other reports see the editorial, "The Battle for Czech TV" (2001); Erlanger (2001).

24. Hayek invoked Marx by arguing that "free" markets were preconditions for democratic freedoms rather than the other way around (1994 [1944]: 116).

25. Valtr Komárek was previously Klaus's boss at the Economic Prognosis Institute and Deputy Prime Minister in the post-revolution government at the time. For

a discussion of gradualist versus shock therapy approaches to economic transition see Murrell (1992); Pickel and Weisenthal (1997).

26. See Klaus (1991a), (1997); Husák (1997); and Greskovits (1998) for an argument that neoliberal reforms in Central and Eastern Europe were "homegrown" to the extent that they involved mutual collaboration between local élites and international organizations such as the IMF and World Bank.

27. For an overview of these arguments see O. Williamson (1985); J. Williamson (1994). For a review of the justification for radical reform in postsocialist transitions see Prybyla (1991); Brada (1993).

28. See for example, Sachs (1989), (1994); Aslund (1994); Balcerowicz (1996); Sachs and Warner (1996).

29. The open society vision was inspired by Karl Popper's (1966) anti-communist philosophy. See George Soros' interpretation (1995), (2000).

30. Contributing to building these foundations for a revived civil society, soon after the revolutions against communism, Soros established the Central European University, which is dedicated to educating students from the region and to researching the transition underway there, and has sponsored many other, independent education, publishing, media and cultural initiatives. For example, Soros has funded education in neoclassical economics and even one particular neoclassical economist, the former Swedish diplomat Anders Aslund.

31. Recently, Soros himself (1997, 1998–1999, 1999) has begun to vigorously criticize neoliberal reform. He has argued that unfettered capitalism rather than communism is the greatest threat to the flourishing of open societies today, and their prerequisites; human development, social stability and democracy.

32. See, for example, Van der Pijl (1998); Cox (1987); Gill ed. (1993).

33. Increased income inequality is indicated by the nearly 50 percent rise in the decile ratio of wage earnings in the Czech Republic between 1989 and 1997 from 2.45 to 2.80. All income groups saw decreases in their earnings with the exception of the tenth decile group, who saw a large increase in income (Večerník and Matejů 1999: 118–20).

34. See Gill (1994: 181); Gowan (1995); Radice (1999); Van Der Pijl (1993).

35. Poznanski (1999a: 344) argues further that foreign majority-owned capitalism is the specific form of capitalism emerging across Eastern Europe. The case of Hungary where foreigners control 70 percent of industry and banking provides particularly strong support for his claim.

36. See Cox (1987; 1991); also Gill (1990; 1993) for a discussion of Cox's neo-Gramscian perspective on international political economy compared with the Realist perspective of Robert Gilpin.

37. For applications of Gramsci's concepts of hegemony and common sense in civil society and popular culture, see Hann and Dunn (1996); Jackson Lears (1985).

38. See for example Robinson (1996) and Burgess (1997).

39. Evoking parallels with the original bourgeois revolutions across Europe, little force was needed to bring down communism in 1989 and 1990: "The bayonets of Napoleon's armies found their road already smoothed by an invisible army of books and pamphlets that had swarmed Paris from the first half of the eighteenth century and had prepared both men and institutions for their necessary renewal." (Gramsci 1977: 12). On the spread of western ideas and norms in communist Eastern Europe through transnational networks see Skilling (1989); Jancar-Webster (1993); Chilton (1995); Evangelista (1999); and especially Day (1999) for an account of the Oxford professors who visited Czechoslovakia to teach conservative philosophy underground under the auspices of the *Jan Hus Foundation* in London

40. See for example some of the essays in Bönker, Pickel and Müller (2002).

41. According to W. Richard Scott (2001) there are three pillars that make up institutions, the regulative, the normative and the cognitive. Economists typically focus on the regulative rule-making or instrumental aspects of institutions, political scientists often analyze institutions in light of their normative, value-laden, and obligatory dimensions, while sociologists and anthropologists go even deeper to study the taken for granted cultural dispositions and frameworks that underlie institutions. See also North (1990).

42. See Crawford and Lijphart (1995); Elster, Offe and Preuss (1997); Grabher and Stark (1997); Nelson, Tilly and Walker (1997).

43. See Berger and Dore (1996); Hollingsworth and Boyer (1997); Whitley (1999).

44. As Polanyi noted with reference to the nineteenth-century expansion of the self-regulating market system in Great Britain: "For upon this rate, mainly, depended whether the dispossessed could adjust themselves to changed conditions without fatally damaging their substance, human and economic, physical and moral; whether they would find new employment in the fields of opportunity indirectly connected with the change; and whether the effect of increased imports induced by increased exports would enable those who lost employment through the change to find new sources of sustenance. The answer depended in every case on the relative rates of change and adjustment. (1957 [1944]: 36–7).

45. See Burawoy and Krotov (1992); Mlčoch (1996); Stark and Bruszt (1998).

46. In the early 1990s, Prime Minister Klaus continually invoked the Prague Spring's slogan "socialism with a human face," when he pronounced to western audiences "we want capitalism without adjectives." In his January 2000 New Year's address President Havel criticized Czech politicians and parties for their complicity with a form of "globalization without a conscience."

47. Václav Klaus frequently spoke of post-communism as "a return to the natural order of things" in 1990–1, and is still one of the most articulate proponents of this view in the Czech Republic. See Klaus (1991b); also Lagerspetz (1999).

48. See Funk and Mueller Eds. (1993); Mies and Shiva (1993); Moghadam Ed. (1994) Rueschmeyer Ed. (1994).

49. Corrin Ed. (1992); Watson (1993); Matynia (1995).
50. My notion that postsocialist transitions involve a contest between dominant western masculinities and *aspiring* western, Eastern and Central European masculinities can be compared with Charlotte Hooper's (2000: 75) discussion of subordinate and hegemonic masculinities. These concepts convey that there are multiple masculinities, while, at the same time, stressing the power relations between between different groups of men as well as between men and women.
51. For example, see Jones (1996) and Hinde (1996).
52. The West's identity was destabilized by the collapse of the Soviet Union. However, in Eastern Europe, Slavoj Žižek argues, "the West found a sucker still having faith in its values" (1992: 25). As pupils of capitalist democracy, Eastern European countries provide "an object with which the [western] subject can identify even as it differentiates itself" (Norton 1990: 53).
53. For critiques of the masculine bias of these political economy perspectives see Tickner (1992): 67–96; Steans (1999).
54. Social reproduction can be defined as "the activities, attitudes, behaviors and emotions as well as responsibilities and relationships directly involved in maintaining a life on a daily basis and intergenerationally" (Brenner and Laslett 1991: 313-316). For a discussion of the concept of social reproduction as it relates to the feminist critique of political economy and to the analysis of actual political economies see Picchio (1992); Folbre (1994); also Pearson (1998); "The invisible heart — care and the global economy." (UNDP 1999: 77–83).
55. This conception of gender relations draws on Sandra Whitworth's (1994) location of gender at the core of the analysis of social relations at the state and global levels. It also shares her notion of gender as both an *agent* and a *structure*, simultaneously informing social practice and being reproduced by and through the practices of social actors.
56. My analysis here follows Joan Scott's (1996) study of the paradoxical nature of feminist thought in the context of the French revolution.

2. Gendering State Socialism

1. The terms, "really existing socialism" or "real socialism," are used to distinguish state socialist regimes in Eastern Europe from the ideals of socialism as espoused by social and political theorists such as Karl Marx. See Skilling (1981); Cox (1991).
2. For example, see Jancar (1978); Lapidus (1978); Heitlinger (1979); Wolchik, (1981a), (1981b); Wolchik and Meyer (1985).
3. This hierarchy existed "in spite of the fact that the primary sphere is of no use without the secondary and tertiary spheres" (Scott 1974: 25).
4. For a discussion, see Szalai, (1991: 159).

5. See Katherine Verdery's (1996: 20–23) discussion of the political economy of state socialism.

6. Personal interview with Helena Klímová, Prague, August 8, 1996.

7. These terms are intentionally literal translations from the Czech: *zamestnané matky, neuplné rodiny, mateřské dovolené.*

8. Personal interview with Czech psychologist, Helena Klímová, Prague, August 8, 1996.

9. By the end of the 1960s 26–35 weeks of paid maternity leave were available and up to two years of unpaid leave after which a woman could return to her former job (Heitlinger 1979: 180–83). However, only in the GDR, with a fully paid "baby" year of maternity leave were women given a real choice over whether and when to have children and when to reenter the workforce after childbirth. See Einhorn (1993).

10. According to Heitlinger (1979: 184) 20 percent of the increase in fertility after 1970 is explained by the increase in the population of "baby-boomer" women of childbearing age, leaving 80 percent of the increase to be explained by the state's policy incentives.

11. Možný and Rabušic (1999: 102). See also Havelková 1993; Mische 1993.

12. Personal interview with Dr. Kateřina Mandocová, ČMKOS, Prague, October 5, 1998.

13. The editorial collective of *Vlasta* (the women's magazine published by The Central Committee of the Czechoslovak Socialist Union of Women) expressed their view about the leadership of the ČSSŽ Central Committee: "Helena Leflerová's silence did not surprise us. We knew her function as President was a formality, and about her disinterest in solving women's questions in Parliament, her cold attitude toward our magazine. . . . The committee during the Plenary accused the editorship of *Vlasta* of non-Marxist and anti-Party views towards the question of women's equality. . . . We believe that comrades Leflerová, Karlovaská, Besserová, and Machacová had to leave their functions in ČSSŽ" ("Stanovisko" 1968).

14. *Rudé Právo*, the Communist Party daily was the largest news publication in Czechoslovakia at the time.

15. The publication of *Literární Listy* was voluntarily halted on August 28, 1968 at Dubček's request, one week after the Warsaw pact invasion. Brezhnev was infuriated by what he saw as the efforts of the intelligentsia to create a real political opposition to communism. *Literární Listy* was seen as a symbol of this "anti-socialist" and "counter-revolutionary" scourge.

16. "Women work full time — from eight to six with two hours for lunch — and spend at least five hours each day on household duties, thus relative to men they lack free time" (Koželkova 1968).

17. Jiřina Šiklová (1998a: 34–35) argues that this cohesion between Czech men and women was first established during the national revival under the Austro-

Hungarian Empire in the late nineteenth century. During World War II men and women also had a common enemy. In Šiklová's view it was not until the communists took power in 1948 that "real" patriarchy developed in Czechoslovakia. Following an anti-communist historical narrative, Šiklová contends that it was natural that men and women would ally together to oppose the arbitrary, manipulative power of communists and struggle for human and civil rights, see also Šiklová (1998b).

18. In Prague in July and August 1996, I interviewed ten of these dissident women about their experiences in *Charta 77* between 1977–89. Their views are reflected in this section. Markéta Fiáklová, Dagmar Battková, Dana Nemcová, Jiřina Šiklová, Petruška Šustrová, Libuše Šilhánová, Eva Kantůrková, Helena Klímová.

19. Calculated from Prečan (1990: 477–86).

20. Personal interview with Dr. Libuše Šilhánová, Prague, July 27, 1996; also Šilhánová (1997). In some respects, the activities of women dissidents in Czechoslovakia resemble those of Parisian women in the salons of prerevolutionary France. In both instances, a public sphere of debate and discussion emerged from below, out of a so-called private sphere. Of course, the counter public sphere that arose in communist Czechoslovakia was not rooted in bourgeois society and class relations, but rather in resistance to the homogenizing, repressive project of socialist modernity. See Landes (1988); also Habermas (1989).

21. See Document 7, translated in *White Paper on Czechoslovakia* (1977: 88–89).

3. Refashioning the Family

1. On average, Czechoslovak families had 2.5 children in the 1970s and 2.0 children in the 1980s compared with 1.2–1.8 in western European countries (Večerník and Mateju 1999: 104).

2. Večerník and Mateju (1999: 110) observe that this proportion of mothers in the Czech population is extremely high, given that four percent of the female population is generally barren, and that before socialism fifteen percent of Czech women remained childless.

3. Differences in family forms and the allocation of labor within the family may account for important differences in the outcomes of economic transitions. For example, Kazimierz Poznanski (1998: 198) suggests that the differences in family structures may account for "the striking contrast between China and Russia's growth pattern."

4. See also Castle-Kanerová (1992); Rueschmeyer and Wolchik (1999).

5. In *Global Social Policy* (1998), Bob Deacon and his co-authors discuss the conflict among different international organizations over the restructuring of social policy in the former socialist countries in Eastern Europe. The ILO

located in Geneva has advocated maintaining the universal aspects of the welfare state and adopting a European social market model, whereas the Americans who dominate the World Bank and IMF located in Washington DC have favored neoliberal social policies targeted at the deserving poor and especially needy. However, Deacon also notes the struggles within the World Bank among European and American policy analysts over the appropriate social policy prescriptions for transition countries.

6. When the official was asked whether this meant some decline in the role of women, the answer was: "No, no. Women especially, don't consider it a decline in their role. Their role is in the family and in the education of children. This is their natural and primary role" (quoted in Moghadam 1990: 27). Orenstein (1996) also discusses the role of incentives to encourage women to retreat to the home in the active labor market strategy of the first democratic government.

7. Personal interview with the Director of the Research Institute for Labor and Social Affairs, Martin Mácha, Ministry of Labor and Social Affairs, Prague, April 1998.

8. When I asked two prominent sociologists involved in this strategy in the Civic Forum manifesto in April and May 1998, *they denied ever pursuing it*. Now that the Czech Republic must approximate European Union standards of equal opportunities it is clearly not *au fait* to admit to this earlier discriminatory thinking.

9. Although men have generally not taken up their right to parental leave, they have formed a small association to lobby for child custody rights since Czech family law and the Czech courts traditionally privilege the rights of mothers to custody (Legge 1998a). In 1996, fathers were given the right to claim paternity without the consent of the biological mother. Previously only the wishes of mothers were considered in adoption cases (McClune 1996).

10. In 1997 the Czech Republic's main children's crisis center reported a 100 percent increase in the number of calls from abused children, including sexually abused children. The United Nations called on the Czech government to strengthen its protection of children's rights and state-coordinated assistance to children. General Secretary of the Czech Society of Pediatricians, Lubomír Kukla, links the explosion in the number of child abuse cases to the steep rise in new family stresses resulting from the introduction of the market economy (Legge 1997).

11. In 1990, the total abortion rate for the Czech Republic was 1.773. In 2000, it was 0.630.

12. In 1994, during the midst of the economic transition when materialistic values were on the rise, 86 percent of women and 74 percent of men considered the family to be the highest life value (Večerník and Matejů 1999: 100).

13. Figure cited in *The Prague Post*, March 12, 1997

14. Personal interview, Dr. Vera Kuchařová, Researcher on Family Issues at Ministry of Labor and Social Affairs, Prague, April 16, 1998.
15. Personal interview, Helena Klímová, Prague, August 8 1996.

4. Establishing Labor Markets

1. Personal interview with Dr. Jiřina Šiklová, Prague, August 3, 1996.
2. In 1995, housewives represented only 9 percent of the "non-active" female population in the Czech Republic (Paukert 1995b: 6).
3. For a critique of Cox's (1995, 1999) typology of the different forms of labor in globalization, see Ackerly and True (2001).
4. Foreign investors also own approximately 50 percent of the state assets sold by the Ministry of Privatization and National Property Fund under their large-scale privatization program. The proceeds from these sales amounted to a total of $4.6 billion (Zemplínerová 1997: 19).
5. Personal interview with the Deputy-Secretary of the Combined Czech and Moravian Trade Union, Kateřina Mandovcová, Prague, October 1, 1998.
6. The Czech government was reluctant to privatize major steel works, such as Nová Huť and Vitkovice in Ostrava, for fear of mass redundancies. Poldní Kládno steel mill was sold (and went bankrupt in 1998), while some brown coal mines were closed in Northern Bohemia for environmental reasons and others are now in the process of being privatized. However, in contrast to Hungary, where nearly 60,000 steel workers were sacked leaving only a rump industry employing 17,000, the Czech steel industry still employed 60,000 workers in 1997 (Kapoor 1996/7). The current Czech Social Democratic government has spent billions to renationalize strategic industries on the verge of bankruptcy ("Czech renationalization." 1999). During socialism, women were the majority of low-skilled workers in light industries such as footwear, glass, food processing and textiles.
7. Senator Richard Falbr, President of the Czech and Moravian Combined Trade Unions as cited in (Cook 1996).
8. This is an area where the Czech Republic cannot compete due to lower cost, female-intensive, production in East Asia. In the female labor-intensive glass and ceramic industry employment fell from 69,000 to 34,000 with near complete privatisation ("The Glass and Ceramic Industry . . ." 1998).
9. Interview, Kateřina Mandovcová, October 1, 1998. Rutland (1993: 103) tells the story of the thousands of Czech miners who protested the closure of Northern Bohemian coalmines in Prague in 1992. When informed by the Minister of Economics that the mines had to be closed for environmental reasons but that the government would be compensating them by creating new jobs, the

miners "politely applauded and then dispersed for an hour shopping in the new K-Mart . . . before returning to their buses and the trip home."

10. Education and health expenditures as a proportion of GDP have hardly changed since 1989. In 1989 government spending on education was equal to 4 per cent of GDP, in 1999 it was 4.3 percent of GDP. Data for government spending on health in 1989 is not available, however, in 1995 it was equal to 5.7 percent of GDP and in 1999 it was 6.2 percent of GDP (UNICEF 2001).

11. At the end of 1996 average unit labor costs compared at purchasing power parity in the Czech Republic amounted to only 28 percent of the Austrian level; in Slovenia they were 60 percent. For much of the 1990s, Czech labor costs were as much as 50 percent lower than in Poland and Hungary. In western Germany the average male worker earned $33.21 an hour, in Poland $2.36, and in the Czech Republic $1.76 (Lyons 1996).

12. The Czech Republic has received the greatest amount of FDI per capita of the countries in the Central and Eastern European region since 1990. While this amount of FDI is still relatively small in global terms (in 1996 FDI = 2.6 percent GDP) it represents a windfall in contrast to pre-1990s nil FDI. (World Development Indicators CD ROM 1999).

13. The Ministry of Labor and Social Affairs official wage charts contains a post-script to the chart that shows a disproportionate increase in *male* managers wages between 1995 and 1998. It reads: "Beware. These figures do not indicate discrimination in real terms. The difference is mostly because women are usu-ally put into less difficult jobs with lower salaries. Even in the same job, the woman is usually in charge of less-qualified work within the same job category as men" (McClune 1998).

14. Personal interview with Karin Genton-L'Epée, L'Epée Consulting, Prague, 8 April 1998; also McClune (1998).

15. The Czech Helsinki Foundation in Prague has compiled a file of discrimina-tory job advertisements according to job titles, the specified age and sex re-quired for the position. (Personal interview with the Vice-Chair of the Czech Helsinki Committee, Dr. Libuše Šilhánová, July 25, 1996.)

16. Looking good is believed to be essential to gaining employment in western corporations (where particular personal features are often a job specification), and being successful generally. A 1995 *Wall Street Journal* article reports the increase in plastic surgery and personal makeovers in the Czech Republic. The owner of a Medical Cosmetics Institute in Prague commented: "It's good to look young, to look successful, to look active. Companies want that image. They want young people. A man or woman who enters here can leave after a couple of days, completely new" (Newman 1995).

17. Some of the most visible foreigners in Central and Eastern Europe are busi-nesswomen. Just one recent example is an American businesswoman and single mother, Barbara Lundberg. She restructured the Polish-American Enterprise

fund, a venture capital fund financed by the U.S. government to support Poland's nascent private sector. In 1999 she became CEO of *Electrim*, a conglomeration of former Polish state enterprises and has since transformed it into a major telecommunications multinational (Andrews 1999).

18. Klaus Nielsen (1995) argues that foreign influence in East-Central European transitions results in institutional isomorphism with western formal and informal institutions. He distinguishes three ways in which this process occurs: Through 1) coercive isomorphism, such as international financial conditionality; 2) normative isomorphism, as local actors engage in transnational (i.e. EU) networks that diffuse knowledge and practices; and 3) by mimetic isomorphism, where western norms and institutions are adopted due to an all-pervasive global ideology, neoliberalism for example.

19. Catherine MacKinnon (1989: 3) wrote that, sexuality is to feminism, what work is to Marxism. Both are dialectical, "socially constructed yet constructing, universal as activity yet historically specific, jointly comprised of matter and mind. As the organized expropriation of the work of some for the benefit of others defines a class, workers, the organized expropriation of the sexuality of some for the use of others defines the sex, woman."

20. This study of the opinion of women on the problem of sexual harassment at work in the Czech Republic was commissioned by the major Czech liberal daily newspaper, *Lidové Noviny,* and was conducted by Sofres-Factum Prague, a Czech social marketing agency and division of the multinational firm Taylor Nelson Sofres. The study was based on focus group interviews of a nationally representative sample of 522 women workers in the Czech Republic between the ages of 18 and 50 years (controlling for salary, age, region, and size of workplace); see also Kučera (1999b).

21. During communism the private sphere and the business sphere were not strictly separated. There was a strong wish to make friends and less distinction between public and private affairs than in the West. In addition, the private sphere had to take on all the needs, which could not be otherwise met in the public sphere of inefficient large organizations. Under these circumstances, a shift of all kinds of resources (labor, materials, time and so on) from the "shop" to the "home" was unavoidable. The effects of these transfers were numerous: dilapidated public property, tolerance of fraud, avoidance of conflict, and an ability to improvise, a population that owned second homes, valued informal networks and extended family above all, and lacked interest in public concerns. In the postsocialist context, aspects of socialist organization and behavioral routine may undermine efforts at reform in Central and Eastern Europe (Feitlinger and Fink 1998).

22. Škvorecký (1992a) writes: "The worst thing that can happen to a good idea is to have some fanatic, a la Lenin make it the basis of an ideology. What happens is this: the avant-garde of the educated elite teach the stupid but well-meaning

masses how to hate and thus transform social awareness and attempt to create social justice into a perversion of feelings and social hatred, which results in the exact opposite of any kind of justice. The newest example of this process, which we have experienced is the basic adventure of American feminism." See also Škvorecký (1992b, 1992c).

23. This English translation of Josef Škvorecký's article in the liberal weekly, *Respekt*, quoted above, according to Czechs, lacks the irony of the original article in Czech. See also Laura Busheikin's (1993) response to Škvorecký.

24. Personal interview with Barbel Butterweck, Director of *La Strada*, Prague, 4 May 1998; see also Havelková (1997).

25. The 79 page CIA report was titled "International Trafficking in Women to the United States: A Contemporary Manifestation of Slavery," see Brinkley (2000).

26. In October 2001 the European Union reached an agreement among its member states to coordinate their efforts to clamp down on trafficking in the European sex industry. The agreement was based on negotiations among the 15 member states to harmonize their definition of human trafficking and their minimum sentences for the crime. According to their common definition a trafficker is someone who uses "coercion, force and deceit to exploit women and children sexually and in other ways" (BBC 2001).

27. There is already also a Project Management Unit (PMU) for coordinating European integration and international relations managed by the *Phare* program of the EU inside the Czech Ministry of Labor and Social Affairs.

28. The mandate of the Department for the Equal Status of Men and Women in the Czech Ministry of Labor and Social Affairs is to report to both the European Union and the United Nations as to how the Czech Republic will approximate EU equal opportunities standards and fulfill international treaty obligations under CEDAW and the ILO (Convention 156, "Equal Opportunities and Equal Treatment for Men and Women Workers with Family Duties").

29. The International Women's Network held a roundtable on women and part-time, flexible work in February 1998 with prominent researchers, government and nongovernmental officials as participants.

30. Personal interviews, Pavel Černoch, Pre-Accession Section, Delegation of the European Commission, Prague, April 2, 1998 and September 24, 1998.

31. This seminar was held as part of a European Commission sub-contracted evaluation of equal opportunities in the Czech Republic.

32. In this seminar Project Parity consultants from the UK introduced Czech women community leaders from outside Prague to the development of European Union's (EU) gender equality directives and problems of discrimination against women in EU member states.

33. Radio Free Europe/Radio Liberty *Newsline*, Volume 2, August 8, 2000.

5. *Expanding Consumer Markets*

1. An earlier version of this chapter was published as, Jacqui True, "Expanding markets and marketing gender: the integration of the Czech Republic." *Review of International Political Economy* 6, no. 3 (1999), pp. 360–89. I would like to acknowledge Taylor & Francis Ltd, P.O. Box 25, Abingdon, Oxfordshire, OX14 3UE England, http://www.tandf.co.uk/journals for granting me permission to reproduce parts of this article here.
2. See for example, Wade (2001a, 2001b); Rodrik (2001, 1999).
3. For a burgeoning literature that applies the concept of culture to the study of international change, see, Alker and Shapiro, eds. (1996); Rosow, Inyatullah and Rupert, eds. (1994); Weldes, et al. (1999).
4. See Bunce (1999); Evangelista (1999); Thomas (1999).
5. See Cagatay, Elson and Grown (1995, 2000); Chumlee-Wright (1997); Kofman and Youngs (1996); Marchand and Runyan, eds. (2000).
6. There are several feminist works that do successfully integrate political-economic analysis with the cultural study of gender and consumption. Studies by Kowaleski-Wallace (1997) and Lury (1997) look at the construction of the female as subject and object of consumption in market society but without seriously differentiating women in terms of their class inequalities and access to consumption. However, Angela McRobbie (1997) provides an argument for bridging feminist analysis across the production and consumption divide with her study of women in the global garment/fashion industry. In a similar way, Judith Williamson (1986) explores the reinforcing processes of objectification, images of colonized women and imperialism, and Stuart Ewen and Elizabeth Ewen (1992) trace the expansion of American capitalist consumerism through the commericalization of gender and sexuality.
7. See for an example the article by Pamela Hansford Johnson (1963), which argues that a new femininity is softening the post-Stalinist Soviet Union by encouraging the growth of the consumer economy. The same argument has also been made in contemporary Mainland China, see for example, "The Feminist . . ."(1999); "Soap Operas, Frozen Food . . ." (1997).
8. In recent years the Czech political and economic transition has become less of a transition "showcase." Between 1997 and 2000 the Czech Republic endured a deep economic depression and considerable governmental instability that many analysts contended that this downturn was the result of an almost exclusive transition focus on macroeconomics and rapid privatization, rather than institution-building and industrial restructuring, that allowed "crony capitalism," including widespread corruption and insider trading, to develop.
9. Explanations for the massive contraction of output (as much as 50–60 percent) after 1989 are the subject of considerable debate among scholars of post-

socialist transitions. However, typical explanations attribute this contraction to demand shifts as a result of market liberalization, the collapse of CMEA trading bloc, and supply disruptions due to vanishing socialist institutions that had distorted production incentives, see World Bank (1996).

10. Between 1990 and 1999 household final consumption expenditure grew on average 2.5 percent each year, while general government final consumption expenditure contracted on average by more than one percent a year (World Bank 2001).

11. Personal interview with Dagmar Degrínová, Harlequin Enterprises Headquarters, Prague, April 28, 1998.

12. *His* and *her* cigarettes are distinguished both by their length and width — hers are long, thin and elegant, his are more regular — as well as their gender-specific packaging.

13. The original Czech slogan read: "Maličký telefon, velká pokrýti" and later "Malický telefon, velká láska." Mobile phones have become a status symbol in East-Central Europe. Although they perform a very practical function in the Czech Republic where the basic telecommunications infrastructure is poor and only three or four people out of ten on average had home telephones in the early 1990s. The ownership of mobile phones is now very high — more than 1 in 10 (Fronk 1999; see table 5–2).

14. The use of sexual imagery, more frequently of male prowess is a common formula for global marketing of alcohol see (Jernigan 1997).

15. Advertising is an important source of consumer information in the Czech Republic where there have not been independent consumer associations that monitor the production, sale, and quality of products.

16. "Management and Marketing for Success." Presentation by Marcela Speert, Director of *Mary Kay*, Czech Republic at the International Women's Network Meeting, Prague, April 9, 1998.

17. Interestingly, Mr. Magurean was not only present at the meetings of the International Network of Women but was also the most vocal member at the meetings I attended. The International Women's Network is a group of Czech and expatriate business executives whose goal is to have social and political influence on key contemporary policy issues. The network was formed by a Czech-Canadian expatriate, Jana Outratová.

18. Women-friendly multinational companies like Mary Kay have even given rise to women's political activism in Eastern Europe. In Plyussa, Russia, Anya Vanina found the Mary Kay motto of financial independence, international sisterhood and lifestyle so appealing that she turned her Mary Kay beauty salon into a women's center. Later, when mold formed on the ceiling of her sauna and she could not find an affordable place to move, she started a civil liberties organization (Tavernise 2002).

19. This is only half the market in romance novels however! (Strauník 1997:10–11). *The Prague Business Journal* estimates that Czech-*Harlequin* revenues were approximately 156 million crowns per annum in 1996. *Harlequin* was ranked the fourth largest publisher in the Czech Republic on the basis of the number of titles released per annum. In 1994, Degrínová was awarded the prestigious Advertising Age International Marketing Superstar Award for her promotional and entrepreneurial efforts.

20. State and ceremonial holidays have undergone various metamorphoses since 1989. "May Day" established in Eastern Europe after the war represented the recurring utopia of communism every year. "International Women's Day" too, introduced by the Communist International before World War I had the effect in socialist countries of marking women's emancipation yearly, without requiring the participation or initiative of women themselves. After falling out of favor in 1989, it was not until 1998 that International Women's Day was again celebrated in the Prague, this time more authentically with the opening of a new women's center, the first such center in the Czech lands since the communist takeover, see Garkisch (1998).

21. Personal interview with Dagmar Degrínová, Harlequin Enterprises Headquarters, Prague, April 28, 1998.

22. During an interview, *Harlequin* Director, Degrínová discussed her strategy of using a menstrual calendar for marketing the schedule for Harlequin book releases.

23. Latin American television soap operas are similar to the Harlequin phenomena and very popular with women in Central and Eastern European countries. These passionate, steamy "telenovelas" have provoked the creation of "femme" TV channels in Romania, Poland, Bulgaria and even Kazhakstan, although not yet the Czech Republic, see Meils (1998).

24. A number of American feminist scholars have sought to legitimate women's interpretations of Harlequin romances, while also locating their reading within the context of the power relations between men and women. When women read romances novels they express their cultural resistance to patriarchal domination, and reconfigure it as romantic love. However, Tania Modelski (1998; also 1982) argues that reading *Harlequin* is a limited political strategy for raising women's consciousness. Likewise, Janice Radway (1984) contends that reading romances only allows the female reader to make her present situation tolerable without any substantive reordering of its patriarchal structure. See also (Snitow 1983).

25. For Hauserová (1997), the most "shining example of 'hidden feminism' is to be found in books from Motto publishers, which feed women huge doses of self-confidence, a desire to become independent, self-reliant and to stand up to the competition of men." In her view "they do so in a simple way, so that it

would hardly occur to anyone that women infected by this propaganda would perhaps one day get hold of Czech capital and business and snatch away men's property and attractive positions." Motto self-help books are very popular in the Czech Republic, where there are many women who have professional ambitions that they are not willing to compromise on behalf of the family.

26. For a discussion of the liberties taken by Czech translator of romance novels, see Strauník (1997). Many of the readers of Czech-*Harlequin* are adolescent girls and young women, as opposed to older women as in western countries.

27. In a recent survey of 6,200 women in 21 countries by *Harlequin* entitled "Time for Romance" the majority of women in most countries were satisfied with the amount of time they have for their partners, families, friends, and even for themselves. Discontent however, was registered in Hungary and the Czech Republic where women were most likely to feel a lack of sufficient (quality) time for themselves and for their loved ones. www.romance.net and <loveletters@romance.net.> Harlequin Enterprises and Torstar Electronic Publishing, March 24, 1998.

28. In response to Mr. Gahr, *Ms Magazine* (October 1997) wrote: "When the subject is feminism, a guy with a teeny-weeny problem lurks behind many a *Wall Street Journal* column."

29. China's 168 page trial issue contained 30 advertising pages. Russia's September 1997 issue "ran an arm-breaking 850 pages in honor of Moscow's 850th birthday and included approximately 620 pages of ads." The monthly Czech edition comes with copious samples of beauty products and numerous three-dimensional advertisements to seduce consumers (Greenberg 1998).

30. According to Danielle Crittendon and Gloria Steinem, compared with today's magazine, American *Cosmopolitan* in the 1960s and 1970s was both more intelligent and more social change than sex-oriented, see Kuczynski (1999).

31. Barbara Osvaldová (1998: 15) notes that 3,049,250 weekly and monthly magazines are published in the Czech Republic each week, for a population of approximately 10 million and around 3.5 million women over the age of 15 years.

32. Examples are Cosmo Žena series, Dočekal (1998); "Cosmo Kariera" (1998); "Mezinárodní Soutež Cosmpolitanu" (1998).

33. Personal interview with Eva Hauserová, Prague, April 7, 1998.

34. See Putnová (1998) and "Evropské Unie: Co Každému." (1998).

35. See for example, the magazines *Betty, Vlasta, Mlády Svet, Businesswoman*. Earlier in the1990s, multinational magazines such as *Elle* and *Playboy* had short-lived experiences with feminist journalism in the first year of their Czech publication.

36. This is in contrast to the US-based journal, *Pravdivé Romance* ("True Story"), which is literally translated from English with only the personal and place names indigenized in the Czech language.

37. See Kuczynski (2000: C16); "Romania." (2000); Nistorescu (2000).
38. Two recent dissertations on *Harlequin* in Sweden and *Cosmopolitan* magazine in Denmark respectively make similar arguments to that presented here. Eva Wirten Hemmungs (1998) argues that the actual content of *Harlequin* romance novels gets altered in the process of translation for a Swedish audience. Ula Outtrup and Birgitte Ramsoe Thomsen (1994) argue that *Cosmopolitan* does not perpetuate oppressive gender norms and values but rather, reading *Cosmopolitan* is a meaning-making, everyday experience that can be pleasurable and empowering for Danish women (and as such should be studied).
39. See Central and Eastern Eurobarometer No. 8. This was the most negative evaluation in the East-Central European region. 50 percent of Czechs opposed the statement "the creation of a market economy is right for the future of my country."

6. Importing Civil Society

1. For an application of Gramsci's theory of hegemony to Eastern Europe, in particular to the Polish Solidarity movement vis-à-vis the communist state see Beem (1998).
2. A number of authors have used the term "male democracy" to describe Eastern and Central European postsocialist states. See for example Heinen (1992); Eisenstein (1994), chapter 1, "Eastern European Male Democracies: A Problem of Unequal Equality," pp. 15–36.
3. For a discussion of the structural exclusion of women in modern liberal states see Pateman (1989).
4. In contrast to postsocialist Central and Eastern European states, transitional, democratizing states in Latin America and Africa have embraced electoral gender quotas to promote women's political representation, see, for example, Waylen (1994); Jaquette and Wolchik (1998); Karam (1998); and Htun and Jones (2002).
5. There is much debate over global civil society in the field of International Relations. Many scholars are skeptical about the existence of a global civil society since there are no actually existing institutions that democratically represent "global citizens." Among these scholars, whether or not there are citizens whose loyalties transcend nation-state citizenship is a subject for debate. For an entrée to this debate, see Schechter (2000); Lipschutz (1992), and for an analysis of the actors and movements claiming to represent global civil society see, Clark, Friedman and Hochstetler (1998); Price (1998); Keck and Sikkink (1998).
6. Voter turnout in the Czech Republic has declined considerably since the first two democratic elections in June 1990 and 1992 respectively. In 1990, 96. 7 percent of registered voters participated in the election of the lower house of

the federal parliament. In 1998 only 73.86 percent of voters turned out (Rose et al 1998). In the Senate elections in November 1996 and 1998, 39 percent and 46 percent of voters participated. At the local level, the decline in voter turnout was even greater. In 1994 62 percent of registered voters participated in municipal elections, in 1998 just 42 percent voted (Naegle 1998).

7. The renewal of the language of civil society, John Keane (1996, 1999) points out actually began in Japan in the 1960s, see also Sakamoto (1997).

8. Ralf Dahrendorf (1990) goes as far to say that creating civil societies in eastern Europe will take at least sixty years, compared with the approximately six months needed to institute market reforms and six years needed to consolidate a democracy.

9. The politics of Central and Eastern European independent initiatives and civil society were termed "anti-politics" by Václav Havel and Gyorgy Konrad. John Keane (1996) prefers the revised term "anti-party politics." However, both these terms are often misinterpreted as meaning apolitical when anti-political really conveys opposition only to the particular brand of politics represented by the Communist Party.

10. Andrew Arato (1982) suggests there are three possible sources of civil society: 1) the capitalist logic of industrialization, 2) the etatist logic of modernization, and 3) a public sphere from below.

11. Theories of civil society typically exclude the family, see Colas (1995).

12. Jiřina Šiklová (1990) had called this group of individuals even before the collapse of the communist regime, "the grey zone."

13. Václav Klaus summed up his view of "civil society" in this statement: "For me the term democratic society is enough. Instead of civil society I would rather say "society of free citizens, who cooperate, assemble and organize however they wish" (cited in Havel and Klaus 1996: 18); see also Klaus (1997).

14. For example, an initiative by the Czech Parliament in 1995–96 to establish an Ombudsperson office was successfully squashed by the ODS government, although there was considerable public support for the office. Under the Social Democratic government, the Ombudsperson office was finally approved by the Czech Parliament in December 2000. The former Justice Minister, Otakár Motějl was elected by the Czech parliament to fill the office, which is located in Brno, the second-largest city in the Czech Republic and the capital of the provinceof Moravia.

15. Women members of *Charta 77* did most of the re-typing of *samizdat* documents, *feuilliton*, and novels for other dissidents; they arranged the distribution and spread of carbon copies, and were often involved in the risky transportation of materials abroad, to and from Czechoslovakia. They were the clerical and support staff that kept the underground movement going (Šiklová 1996: 17). Also personal interview, Jiřina Šiklová, Prague, 17 August 1996; For an account

of those Czechoslovak and foreign women involved in the transportation of clandestine materials through the Palach Press Agency from Great Britain to Czechoslovakia see Weschler (1992).

16. See chapter 2 note 19; also Ort (1993: 63).

17. The 1999 USAID (1999: 13–14) report to the United States Congress stated that women's participation in formal decisionmaking across Eastern Europe has plummeted from roughly one-third of all elected officials to between three percent and twenty percent, and that the new political parties typically marginalize women candidates' concerns.

18. Interestingly, and in addition to the greater presence of women in center and left-oriented political parties, Czech women voters have almost never voted for right wing extremists. As a constituency, women have helped to marginalize the far right in the Czech Republic, in contrast to other transition countries in Central and Eastern Europe where far right parties have a stronger elected presence (Petraček 1996).

19. Women have rarely been present in the executive arm of democratic government since 1989. Between 1990 and 1998 there were only five women present in the governments of the Czechoslovak Federal Republic and the Czech Republic. In the provisional Czechoslovak government between January and June 1990, only two women were cabinet ministers.

20. Hana Marvanová became the first woman to head a Czech political party in 2001, when she was elected leader of the minor party, *Freedom Union* (SU) (Radio Free Europe/Radio Liberty 2001a).

21. Czech social democrat, Petra Bůzková, likens discussions about men and women, or questions of gender and politics to a "secret service": "neither officially exist, but both are unofficially carried on underneath and outside the formal institutions of state and society." Interviewed by Mírek Vodrážka in Vodrážka (1996: 8).

22. Former Chartists, Dagmar Burešová, Eva Kantůrková, Hana Marvanová, Dana Nemcová and Kvetoslava Kořinková were elected to Parliament as members of the Civic Forum in 1990–1992. Alena Hromádková led the Democratic Union (DEU), which did not gain any seats in the Czech parliament (Gomez 1994). Chartists, Rita Klímová and Markéta Fiáklová appointed as Czech ambassadors to the USA and Poland respectively.

23. See, for example, Bělohrádský (1999); Zelený Krůh (1996).

24. Dr. Libuše Šilhánová, Personal interview, Prague, 26 July, 1996.

25. See, for example, "Je žen v české politice dost?" (1993: 5); Brdečková (1994); Radio Free Europe (2000a).

26. The campaign against Bůzková was named "Operation Lead" because her initials PB symbolize lead on the periodic table of elements.

27. Miloš Zeman quoted in *Mláda Fronta Dnes*, July 20, 1998.

28. Interestingly, the four minor centrist Czech political parties in Parliament later decided to emulate Volfová's strategy and set up their own shadow cabinet, in informal opposition to the government, see Radio Free Europe/Radio Liberty (2000d).

29. At several conferences on women and politics I attended in the Czech Republic during 1996 and 1998 prior to the national elections in those years, many of the women who attended stated that they were "emancipated" and didn't need feminism or women's rights movements. But they also admitted that they didn't have the self-confidence to enter the public realm and shape the new politics, see Zelený Krůh (1996); Nadace Gender Studies (1996); Český svaz žen (1998).

30. Hana Marvanová, an activist in the Velvet Revolution, and now leader of the Freedom Union (SU) party is one of the few exceptions to the general rule that women dissidents have not pursued political careers.

31. Data taken from "Odpovědí Na Otázky Neziskový Sektor" (1997). The 1999 USAID (1999: 13) report to the United States Congress notes that women comprise the overwhelming majority of those working on civil society issues across Eastern Europe.

32. For a discussion of the feminization of civil society in Poland, the former GDR and Russia see Kozinska-Baldyga (1996); Miethe (1999); Liborakina (1998) respectively. In Poland 80 percent of NGO members are women and, as in the Czech Republic, women have generally preferred to participate in civic associations rather than political parties. Alena Kozinska-Baldyga (1996) argues that Polish women's civic participation provides an opening for Polish feminism and the transformation of the state. In the Russian context, Marina Liborakina (1998: 62) notes that women are one of the main agents of social change, and their contribution to volunteerism and public relief is of major proportions. However, she argues that "women's lack of visibility threatens to make civic organization a female ghetto of underpaid jobs and little power" and a mere expression of "maternal" natures.

33. In 1997 approximately 40,000 civic associations were registered in the Czech Republic, as well as 4,000 foundations, with an average growth rate of 5,000 new associations per year. Most foundations are of foreign origin, see "Odpovědí Na Otázky Neziskový Sektor" (1997).

34. See, for example, Šiklová (1993); Šmejkalová-Strickland (1993); Heitlinger (1996, 1999); True (1999).

35. The majority of Czech women's NGOs defend their autonomy from the state, seeking their funding from non-state sources and promoting a self-regulating, nonhierarchical organizational structure. In that way they distinguish themselves from socialist era associations coopted by the state.

36. For example, gender studies courses are now offered across disciplines at

Charles University in Prague, Masaryk University in Brno, Palacký University in Olomouc and the Pedagogical Institute in Prague. A regular university program in gender studies began at Charles University in 1994, and in 1999 a Center for Gender Studies was established in the School of Arts and Department of Social-Work to coordinate courses. In the 1999–2000 academic year fifteen core and specialized courses in gender studies were offered. For a discussion of the development of women's studies in the Czech Republic see (Grunell 1995, Šmejkalová-Strickland 1995). In terms of local publishing the feminist journal *Aspekt* is published in Bratislava, and in Prague, *inter alia*, a bilingual Czech-English journal *Jedním Okem/One Eye Open* has been devoted to women's issues in the East-Central European region, albeit irregularly published. See also Havelková and Vodrážka (1998).

37. See Burton (1996); also my own participant observations at a meeting of the committee to establish a Women's Studies Center and Specialization at the Charles University, Prague, May 1998. The meager funding of women's and gender-based projects is changing now that the Czech Republic seems likely to join the European Union. In order to be eligible for EU Structural Funds, projects from any country, region or, locale must show that they have taken account considerations of gender equity, and that they do not adversely affect any one group, either men or women for instance (see Woodward 2001).

38. For example, this was the approach of The National Endowment of Democracy under the Reagan administration.

39. The Czech Republic adopted the American term "nonprofit," to refer to nongovernmental, public or civic-spirited organizations after the law regarding not for profit legal entities was instituted in 1995.

40. The Czech Republic received significantly less assistance than Poland and Hungary for their economic and political transition; 16.4 percent of the aid to Central and Eastern Europe from international financial institutions, 20.7 percent of aid to the region from the European Union, and 9.7 percent from independent foundations. Eighty percent of this assistance (125 million between 1990–94) was directed at economic restructuring and 4 percent (5.1 million) at building democracy (Quigley 1996: 17–18).

41. Personal interview, Kate Blumenreich, women's program officer, the Open Society Foundation, New York City, December 17, 1997.

42. Claire Reinelt (1995) discusses how the U.S. state became a partner to activist women in the establishment of shelters for battered women.

43. For example, see Ann Snitow's (1994; also 2000) list of the difficulties faced by often isolated and beleaguered feminists in Central and Eastern Europe against the background of her personal experiences as a feminist activist in the US. This article has been much discussed among women's rights activists in the region.

44. For a similar criticism of western feminism, see Sabine Lang (1997: 101). For a discussion of feminist NGOization in Latin America see Alvarez (1999).
45. Valerie Sperling (1999, chapter 7) discusses this NEWW project among other western-funded women's initiatives in the context of her study of the postsocialist Russian women's movement.
46. The Eurasia Foundation's support of the Internet project was indirectly funded by USAID. *The Network for East-West Women Newsletter* Summer (1995): 1.
47. During March–August 1995, I was a participant observer and volunteer at the Prague Gender Studies Centre.
48. Personal interview, Pavel Černoch, Pre-Accession Section, Delegation of the European Union, Prague, April 8 and September 29 1998.
49. In addition to the binding European gender directives on equal opportunities, policy guidelines are provided by a whole package of EU "soft law" proposals, resolutions and recommendations that have developed the concepts of equal treatment, direct and indirect discrimination and equal opportunities. These legal mechanisms include recommendations on part-time work, vocational training for women and their reintegration into the workforce, protection from sexual harassment, the employment of migrant women, the sharing of family and work responsibilities, childcare and minimum parental leave, see European Parliament (1998); also European Commission (1997a,b, 1998).
50. *Quangos* were an innovation of the Thatcher government in Great Britain. They are common throughout Europe and are similar to state-owned enterprises — where the state is the owner but not the manager of a business enterprise that operates according to market principles or of a service-based organization — in the nonprofit sector.
51. By 1997 the *Phare* program had spent $565 million in the Czech Republic since 1990, nearly three times the amount of all other donors put together, and 1.5 billion in the region annually. Some have argued that Phare manages its programs in Central and Eastern Europe like European countries used to administer their colonial empires (Werbowski 1998). In a recent report on the Phare program by the European Union's own Court of Auditors, it was confirmed that much of the tens of millions spent on Central and Eastern European projects have actually been eaten up by contracts to highly paid Western consultants. However, Phare was not seen as so corrupt as the European Bank for Reconstruction and Development which spent twice as much on its running costs and offices as on loans and investments to Eastern Europe in 1990–93 (see Evaluation Unit of the European Commission 1997).
52. *Project Parity* Seminar "Postávení žen v legislative EU," Čelakovice, Czech Republic, April 17–20, 1998.
53. Similar views were expressed at a government seminar held as part of a European Commission evaluation of equal opportunities in the Czech Republic (see Castle-Kanerová 1996).

54. See the Česky svaz žen quarterly journal, *Prestiž* 1 (1997: 2).
55. See Kriséova (1993: 254–5); Nadace Gender Studies (1994: 36–37); Hauser (1996).
56. See the Czech Women's Union reflections on its own transformation in the interview with its President, Zdenka Hajná, "Ženám chýbí společna (1996); "Uloha českého svažu žen (the role of the Czech Women's Union is changing") (1997); and also "Ke sjezdu českého svažu žen (the Congress of the Czech Women's Union) (1997).
57. Personal interview, Zdenka Hajná, ČSŽ Headquarters, Prague, October 3, 1998.
58. See Projekt Phare-Democracy 1995–6 report by Český svaž žen (1997).
59. Czech Women's Union President, Dr. Zdenka Hajná also makes the instrumental argument that it is necessary for the Czech Republic to design a range of political institutions and initiatives for improving the position of women and ensuring equal opportunities since they are a precondition of entry in to the EU.
60. See *Prestižní Žena* (November 1997): 4–7.

7. Engendering Global Political Economy

1. See, for example, Cox (1987); Gill (1993). Although not a neo-Marxist, Susan Strange (1994) has contributed to the analysis of structural power in the global political economy, and coined the term "business civilization."
2. Even the 1999 UNICEF-ICDC report, *Women in Transition*, distorts the empirical data by interpreting the market transition as more positive in its impacts on women than it actually has been and by suggesting that the negative impacts can be easily rectified. The report summarizes its findings by stating that things have not gotten considerably worse since 1989 since the gap between men and women's wages is unaltered. However, this summary overlooks other indications that many of the gains of gender equality achieved under socialism have been lost.
3. The similarity between neoliberalism and neo-Stalinism has not been lost on the Czech public. The comparison was probably helped by the appearance in November 1998 of a 10 by 20 meter billboard of the neoliberal, former Premier, Václav Klaus and in September 1996 a monumental statue of Michael Jackson, poster-boy for American cultural capitalism, on the very spot where the largest statue of Stalin in the world once stood (in Letná Park overlooking the city of Prague), see Morrison (1996); *Pravo*, November 4, 1998.
4. For a discussion of local resistances to globalization see Chin and Mittleman (1999); Cox (1999); Marchand and Runyan (2000); Mittleman (2000).

References

"5x5x5: Demokratice." 1968. *Vlasta* 31, 31 July: 10–11.

"5x5x5: Povoláni." 1968. *Vlasta* 32, 7 August: 14–15.

"5x5x5: Vztah k partnerovi." 1968. *Vlasta* 33, 14 August: 14.

"5x5x5: Rodina." 1968. *Vlasta* 34, 21 August: 11.

"5x5x5: Móda." 1968. *Vlasta* 35, 11 September: 10–11.

"A New Course: Elektrim's new boss makes a splash." 1999. *Business Central Europe*, May: 22.

Ackerly, Brooke and Jacqui True. 2001. "Transnational Justice: A Feminist Development of Critical International Relations Theory." Center for International Studies working paper, Los Angeles, University of Southern California.

Alker, Hayward. R and Michael J. Shapiro, Eds. 1996. *Challenging Boundaries: Global Flows, Territorial Identities*. Minneapolis: University of Minnesota Press.

Alvarez, Sonia. 1999. "Advocating Feminism: The Latin American Feminist NGO 'Boom.' " *International Feminist Journal of Politics* 1 (2): 181–209.

Andrews, Edmund L. 1999. "An American in Warsaw: U.S. Businesswoman challenges old phone monopoly." *The New York Times*, June 12.

Anyz, Daniel and Tomas Vrba. 1998. "The Unbearable Lightness of Best Sellers: The Czech literary scene grapples with market conditions and how-to books." *Transitions* 7, no. 2 (February): 75–77.

Appadurai, Arjan. 1996. *Modernity at Large: the Cultural Dimensions of Globalization*. Minneapolis: University of Minnesota Press.

Appel, Hilary and John Gould. "Identity Politics and Economic Reform: Examining Industry-State Relations in the Czech and Slovak Republics." *Europe-Asia Studies* 52: 111–131.

Arato, Andrew. 1982. "Civil Society against the State: Poland 1980–81." *Telos* 47: 23–47.

———. 1994. "Revolution, Restoration, and Legitimization: Ideological Problems of the Transition from State Socialism." In *Envisioning Eastern Europe: Post-communist Cultural Studies*. Ed. Michael A. Kennedy. Ann Arbor: University of Michigan Press.

Ascoly, Nina. 1994. "Abroad with Iron Jan." Z *Magazine*, November: 21–22.

Aslund, Anders. 1994. "The Case for Radical Reform." *Journal of Democracy* 5, no. 4: 63–74.

Balcerowicz, Leszek. 1996. *Socialism, Capitalism and Transformation*. Budapest: Central European University Press.

"The Battle for Czech Television." 2001. *The New York Times Editorial*, January 5: A20.

Bauerová, Ladíslava. 1998. "Who is the Czech Consumer?" *The Prague Tribune*, May.

———. 1998. "Embassy Tied to Sex Raids in New York: Czech visa clerk greased path to US exploitation." *The Prague Post*, March 21–8: 1, 9.

Bauerová, Ladka. 1999. "Citing Revolution, Czechs Again Demand Leaders' Ouster." *The New York Times*, December 4: A4.

———. 2000. "Czech Poll: Harassment of Women is Common." *The New York Times*, January 9: A3.

Bednáček, Vladimír and Alena Zemplínerová. 1997. "Foreign Direct Investment in the Czech Manufacturing Sector." *Prague Economic Papers* 2: 141–155.

Beem, Christopher. 1998. "Civil Society in the Polish Solidarity Movement: Eastern European Neo-Gramscianism." Presented to the Annual Meeting of the Midwest Political Science Association, April.

Belk, Russell W. 1997. "Romanian Consumer Desires and Feelings of Deservingness." In *Romania in Transition*. Ed. Lavinia Stan. Aldershot, UK: Dartmouth Press.

Bělohrádský, Václav. 1999. "Pohlaví rozumu." In *Nové čtení sveta feminismus devadesátých let českýma očima*. Ed. Marie Chřibková, Josef Chuchma and Eva Klimentová. Praha: Marie Chřibková.

Benda, Václav. 1991. "The Parallel 'Polis'." In *Civic Freedom in Central Europe: Voices from Czechoslovakia*. Eds. H. Gordon Skilling and Paul Wilson. London: Macmillan.

Berger, Suzanne and Ronald Dore, Eds. 1996. *National Diversity and Global Capitalism*. Ithaca, NY: Cornell University Press.

"Bohemia's Fading Rhapsody." 1997. *The Economist*, May 31: 66.

Bönker, Frank, Andreas Pickel, and Klaus Muller, Eds. 2002. *Post-Communist Transformations and the Social Sciences: Cross-Disciplinary Approaches*. Lanham, MD: Rowman and Littlefield.

Borneman, John and Nick Fowler. 1997. "Europeanization." *Annual Review of Anthropology* 26: 487–514.

Borocz, Josef. 1999. "From Comprador State to Auctioneer State: Property Change, Realignment, and Peripheralization in Post-State Socialist Central and Eastern Europe" In *States and Sovereignty in the Global Economy*. Eds. David A. Smith, Dorothy J. Solinger and Steven C. Topik. New York: Routledge.

Bourdieu, Pierre. 1984. *Distinctions: A Social Critique of the Judgement of Taste*. Trans. Richard Nice. Cambridge, MA: Harvard University Press.

———. 1998. *Practical Reason: On the Theory of Action*. Stanford: Stanford University Press.

Brada, Josef. 1993. "The Transformation from Communism to Capitalism: How Far? How Fast?" *Post-Soviet Affairs* 9, 1: 87–110

Bransten, Jeremy. 2000. "Fewer Babies Spell Trouble for Czech Republic's Future." *Radio Free Europe/Radio Liberty Newsline*, October 24.

Brdečkova, Tereza. 1994. "Čekání na Libuši: Příštích sto let by měly světu vládnout ženy." *Respekt* 41, October 10: 7–10.

Brenner, Johanna and Barbara Laslett. 1991. "Gender, Social Reproduction, and Women's Self-Organization: Considering the US Welfare State." *Gender and Society* 5: 311–33.

Brent, John. 1998. "The Innocent Girl and the Experienced Child." *Nová Přítomnost*, May.

"Březen — Nezapomenutelný měsíc plný vzruchu, očekávání, nadějí a důvery v tvořivé a demokratické síly našich národu." 1968. *Vlasta* 27 March: 2

Brinkley, Joel. 2000. "C.I.A. Depicts a Vast Trade in Forced Labor, A New Slavery is Growing in the US, CIA Report finds." *The New York Times*, April 2: A1, 18.

British Broadcasting Corporation. 2001. "EU Nations Act on Women Trafficking." *World Service*, September 28.

Brodie, Janine. 1994. "Shifting the Boundaries: Gender and Politics of Restructuring." In *The Strategic Silence: Gender and Economic Policy*. Ed. Isabella Bakker. London: Zed Books.

Brussa, Licia. Ed. 1999. *Health, Migration and Sex Work: The Experience of TAMPEP*. European Commission.

Budde, Michael L. 1998. "Embracing Pop Culture: The Catholic Church in the World Market." *World Policy Journal* (Spring): 77–87.

Bunce, Valerie. 1999. *Subversive Institutions: The Design and Destruction of Socialism and the State*. New York: Cambridge University Press.

Burawoy, Michael. nd. "Dwelling in Capitalism, Traveling Through Socialism." Unpublished paper, University of California — Berkeley.

——— and Pavel Krotov. 1992. "The Soviet Transition from Socialism to Capitalism." *American Sociological Review* 57, no. 1: 16–38.

Burgess, Adam. 1997. *Divided Europe: The New Domination of the East*. London: Pluto.

Burgess, Radha and Petr Tůma. 1997. "Česká reklama devadesátých let na šikmé ploše?/ Prone to Shock: Czech Advertising in the 90s?" *The Prague Tribune*, January: 16–22.

Burton, Bollag. 1996. "Women's Studies Programs Gain a Foothold in Eastern Europe." *The Chronicle of Higher Education* 43: 16, December 13: A 14.

Busheikin, Laura et al, 1992. "Can There Be Sex Without Rape?" *The Prague Post*, November 25–December 1: 17.

Busheikin, Laura. 1993. "Sex and the Czechs." *This Magazine*, 26: 28–9.

———. 1997. "Is Sisterhood Really Global? Western Feminism in Eastern Europe." In *Ana's Land: Sisterhood in Eastern Europe*. Ed. Tanya Renne. Boulder, CO: Westview Press.

Busheikin, Laura and Dana Potočková. 1996. *Kabelky Plný Prachů: průvodce fondy ženské projeky v neziskovém sektoru*. Praha: ProFem.

Busheikin, Laura. 1996. "Ženy, finanční zdroje a třetí sector." In *Kabelky plný prachu provodce fondy pro ženské projekty v neziskovém sektoru*. Eds. L. Busheikin and Dana Potočková. Praha: Profem.

Butora, Daniel. 1998. "Meciar and the Velvet Divorce." *Transitions* 5, no. 8 (August).

Butler, Judith. 1990. *Gender Trouble: Feminist Subversions of Identity*. New York: Routledge.

Bůzková, Petra 1996. "Jsou u nás ženy v postávení minority." *Lidové Noviny*, March 20: 8.

Çağatay, Nilufer, Diane Elson, Caren Grown. 1995. "Gender, adjustment and macroeconomics." Special Issue of *World Development* 23, no. 11.

Çağatay, Nilufer, Diane Elson, Caren Grown. 2000. "Growth, Trade, Finance and Gender Inequality." Special Issue of *World Development* 28, no. 7.

Čapek, Karel. 1991. "O Ženách a Politice." In *Karel Čapek kritika slov o večech obecných čili Zoon Politikon*. Praha: Československy Spisovatel.

Čapová, Helena. 1998. "Být na ženou." *Respekt* 38, September.

Castells, Manuel. 1996. *The Rise of the Network Society*. Volume II. Berkeley: University of California Press.

Castle, Mita. 1990. "Our Woman in Prague." *Catalyst* 4, July-September.

Castle-Kanerová, Mita. 1992. "Social Policy in Czechoslovakia," In *The New Eastern Europe: Social Policy Past, Present, and Future*. Ed. Bob Deacon. London: Sage Publications.

———. 1996. "Výhodnočení stejných příležitostí pro muže a ženy v České Republice" [Evaluating Equal Opportunities for Men and Women in the Czech Republic] (Phare: European Commission.

———. 1999. "Equal Opportunities in the Czech Republic and other East-Central

European countries as part of the requirement for accession into the European Union." *Czech Sociological Review* 7, no. 2: 236–241.

Center for Democracy and USAID. 1992. "The Role of Women and Transition to Democracy in Central and Eastern Europe." An International Conference cosponsored by The Palais de L'Europe, Strasbourg, France, October.

Čermáková, Maria. 1996. "Processes of Developing Pro-women Policies in the Czech Republic." Paper presented at "Women, Gender and the Transition." Lucca, Italy, June.

Český Svaz Žen, 1997. *Postávení Žen v České Republice a demokrátizační procesy v ženském hnutí*. Praha.

Český Svaz Žen. 1998. *Postavení žen v České Republice* (The position of women in the Czech Republic) Report from the Seminar held at Čelakovice, May.

"Československý svaz žen má svůj akční program." 1968. *Vlasta* 28, 10 July: 2.

Český statistický úřad. 1993–2001. *Statistická ročenka České Republiky*. Praha.

Chase, R. S. 1997a. "Baby Boom or Bust? Changing Fertility in the Post-Communist Czech and Slovak Republic." Yale Economic Growth Center Papers No. 768.

———. 1997b. "Women's Labor Force Participation During and After Communism: A Case Study of the Czech Republic and Slovakia." Yale Economic Growth Center Papers 769.

———. 1998. "Markets for Communist Human Capital: Returns to Education and Experience in the Czech Republic and Slovakia." *Industrial and Labor Relations Review* 51, no. 3: 401–24.

Chilton, Patricia. 1995. Mechanics of Change: social movements, transnational coalitions, and the transformation processes in Eastern Europe. In *Bringing transnational relations back in: Non-state actors, domestic structures and international institutions*. Ed. Thomas Risse Kappen. Cambridge: Cambridge University Press.

Chin, Christine B. N. and James H. Mittleman. 1997. "Conceptualising Resistance to Globalization." *New Political Economy* 2, no. 1: 25–37.

Chin, Christine B. N. 1998. *In Service and In Servitude: Foreign Female Domestic Workers and the Malaysian "Modernity" Project*. New York: Columbia University Press.

Chumlee-Wright, Emily. 1997. *The Cultural Foundations of the Market*. New York: Routledge.

Clark, Ann-Marie, Elisabeth Friedman, and Kathryn Hochstetler. 1998. "The Sovereign Limits of Global Civil Society: A Comparison of NGO Participation in UN World Conferences on the Environment, Human Rights, and Women." *World Politics* 51: 1–35.

"Co říkájí významní české ženy na sexuální obtežování." 1998. *Lidové Noviny*, February 4: 3.

Cohen, Jean L. and Andrew Arato. 1992. *Civil Society and Political Theory*. Cambridge, MA: MIT Press.

Cohen, Karen. 1997. "Needle and Thread: Kanafas find a niche in the dying textile industry." *The Prague Business Journal*, November 21–28.

Cohen, Roger. 2000. "The Oldest Profession Seeks New Market in West Europe." *The New York Times*, September 19: A1, 10.

Colas, Dominque. 1995. "Civil Society: From Utopia to Management, from Marxism to Anti-Marxism." *The South Atlantic Quarterly* 94, no. 4: 1009–23.

Cook, Joe, with Ronan Lyons and Ana Nicholls. 1997. "Survey: How Consumerism Transformed Central Europe." *Business Central Europe*, June.

Cook, Joe. 1996. "The Czech Republic," *Business Central Europe*, July/August.

Cook, Tanya. 1993. "Remember Nothing's Impossible: An Outsider's Look at Access to Abortion in the Czech Republic." *Jedním Okem/One Eye Open* 1, no. 2: 65–71.

Cooper, Charlie and Nigel Morpeth. 1998. "The Impact of Tourism on Residential Experience in Central-Eastern Europe: The Development of a New Legitimation Crisis in the Czech Republic." *Urban Studies* 35, no. 12: 2253–76.

Corrin, Chris. Ed. 1992. *Superwomen and the Double Burden: Women's Experience of Change in Central and Eastern Europe*. Toronto: Second Story Press.

"Cosmo gains toehold behind Bamboo Curtain." 1998. *Associated Press*, April 4.

"Cosmo Kariéra: "Co je to firemní kultura?" *Cosmopolitan*, February 1998.

Coudenhové-Kalergiová, Barbara. 1993. "Očima Západu." *Respekt* 52, December 27: 9.

Cox, Robert W. 1987. *Production, Power, and World Order*. New York: Columbia University Press.

———. 1991. "Real Socialism in Historical Perspective." In *Socialist Register 1991*. Ed. Leo Panitch. New York: Monthly Review Press.

———. 1995. "Critical Political Economy." In *International Political Economy: Under Global Disorder*, ed. Bjorn Hettne. London: Zed Books.

———. 1996. "A Perspective on Globalization." In *Globalization: Critical Perspectives*. Ed. James H. Mittleman. Boulder, CO: Lynne Rienner.

———. 1999. "Civil Society at the Turn of the Millennium: Prospects for an Alternative World Order." *Review of International Studies* 25, 1: 3–28.

Crawford, Beverley and Arend Lijphart. 1995. "Explaining Political and Economic Change in Post-Communist Eastern Europe." *Comparative Political Studies* 28, 2: 171–199.

Cresswellová, Jasmine. 1998. *Svatby De Wilde, Porušené sliby*. January.

Croan, Melvin. 1989. "Lands In-Between: The Politics of Cultural Identity in Contemporary Eastern Europe." *Eastern European Politics and Societies* 3, no. 2: 176–97.

Cruisieová, Jennifer. 1998. *Chci Jen Tebe*. January.

Čtk, J. 1996. "Osamelé matky nejchudší." *Lidové Noviny*, March 23: 3.

"Czech renationalisation." 1999. *The Economist*, February 6: 65–66.

"The Czech Republic, The New Bohemians." 1994. *The Economist*, 22–28 October.

"Czech women take chisel to stone wall of politics." 2000. *The New York Times*, February 27: A14.

"Czech youth; wicked really." 1999. *The Economist*, February 20: 47–8.

Dahrendorf, Ralf. 1990. *Reflections on the Revolution in Europe: in a letter intended to have been sent to a gentleman in Warsaw.* New York: Random House.

Day, Barbara. 1999. *The Velvet Philosophers.* London: Claridge.

Deacon, Bob with Michelle Hulse and Paul Stubbs. 1998. *Global Social Policy.* New York: Sage.

di Palma, Giuseppe. 1991–92. "Legitimation from the Top to Civil Society: Politico-Cultural Change in Eastern Europe." *World Politics* 44: 49–80.

Dočekal, Boris. 1998. "Barbel Butterwecková, Chci být svobodná." *Cosmopolitan*, April.

Donovan, Jeffrey. 2000. "Love for Sale — and it's tax-free." The *Prague Post*, January 5–12: 1.

Drakulic, Slavenka. 1993. *How We Survived Communism and Even Laughed.* New York: Harper Perennial.

Dubský, Vladimír and Zuzana Pitrová. 1998. "Havlem zmínená jména maji možná jen symbolický význam." *Lidové Noviny*, September 24: 3.

Dvořák, Josef and Iva Solčová. 1998. *Vademecům: moderní manažerky.* Praha: Management Press.

Earle, John S., Frydman, Roman, Andrzej Rapaczynski and Joel Turkewitz. 1994. *Small Privatization: The Transformation of Retail Trade and Consumer Services in the Czech Republic, Hungary and Poland.* Budapest: Central European University Press.

"Eastern Europe Recasts Itself: A Survey of Business in Eastern Europe." 1997. *The Economist*, November 22: 20–22.

Eichengreen, Barry and Richard Kohl. 1998. The External Sector, the State and Development in Eastern Europe." *Working Paper 125.* The Berkeley Roundtable on the International Economy.

Einhorn, Barbara. 1993. *Cinderella Goes to Market: Women's Movements in East-Central Europe.* London: Verso.

———. 1995. "Ironies of History: Citizenship Issues in the New Market Economies of East-Central Europe." In *Women and Market Societies: Crisis and Opportunity.* Eds. B. Einhorn and E. Janes. Aldershot: Edward Elgar.

Eisenstein, Zillah R. 1994. *The Color of Gender: Re-imaging Democracy.* Berkeley: University of California Press.

Elshtain, Jean Bethke. 1995. "Exporting Feminism." *Journal of International Affairs* 48, no. 2: 541–58.

Elster, Jon, Claus Offe and Ulrich Preuss. 1997. *Institutional Design in Post-Communist Societies: Rebuilding the Ship at Sea*. Cambridge: Cambridge University Press.

Engels, Friedrich with Karl Marx. 1972 [1884].*The Origin of the Family, Private Property, and the State*. New York: International Publishers.

Enloe, Cynthia. 1989. *Bananas, Beaches and Bases: Making Feminist Sense of International Politics*. London: Pandora.

————. 1994. *The Morning After: Sexual Politics at the End of the Cold War*. Berkeley: University of California Press.

————. 1997. "Margins, Silences, and Bottom-rungs: How to Overcome the Underestimation of Power in the Study of International Relations." In *International Theory: Positivism and Beyond*. Eds. Steve Smith, Ken Booth, Marysia Zalewski. Cambridge: Cambridge University Press.

Erlanger, Steven. 2000. "Birthrate Dips in Ex-Communist Countries: Why so few babies? For some mothers, fear; for others, jobs." *The New York Times*, May 4: A3.

————. 2001. "50,000 Demonstrate for Dissident Journalists in Prague." *International Herald Tribune*, January 4: 5.

Estrin, Saul, Kirsty Hughes and Sarah Todd. 1997. *Foreign Direct Investment in Central and Eastern Europe: Multinationals in Transition*. London and Washington: Pinter and The Royal Institute of International Affairs.

European Commission. 1997. *Central and Eastern Eurobarometer No. 8*. Brussels: EC.

————. 1997. *Accession Partnerships: Czech Republic*. Directorate General for External Relations. Brussels.

————. 1998. *Regular Report from the Commission on the Czech Republic' Progress Towards Accession*. Brussels.

European Parliament. 1998. "The Social Dimension of Enlargement: Social Law and Policy in the Czech Republic, Estonia, Hungary, Poland and Slovenia," *Social Affairs Working Paper Series* SOCI 100, no. 4. Luxembourg: Directorate General for Research.

Evaluation Unit of the European Commission. 1997. *Phare: An interim evaluation*. Brussels: European Commission.

Evangelista, Matthew. 1999. *Unarmed Forces: The Transnational Movements to End the Cold War*. Ithaca, Cornell University Press.

"Evropské Unie: co každému z nás přineše clenství v Evropské unii?" 1998. *Respekt*, August.

Ewen, Stuart and Elizabeth Ewen. 1992. *Channels of Desire: Mass Images and the Shaping of the American Consciousness*. Minneapolis: University of Minnesota Press.

Eyal, G., I. Szelenyi and E.R. Townsley. 1999. *Making Capitalism Without Capi-*

talists: Class Formation and Elite Struggles in Post-Communist Central Europe. London: Verso.

"Facing a Rush from Poland, Czechs Limit Abortion Rights." 1993. *The New York Times*, April 14.

Feinberg, Melissa. 1999. "Masarýk, Democracy and the Making of a Czech Feminist Identity." Paper presented at the American Association for the Advancement of Slavic Studies Annual Meeting, St. Louis, November.

Feitlinger, Claudia and Gerhard Fink. 1998. "Post-Communist Management: Towards a Theory of Collective Culture Shock." *Journal of Cross-Cultural Competence and Management* 1: 36–60.

"The Feminist: TV Producer is from New Breed of Woman." 1999. *The New York Times*, September 28: A1.

Ferge, Zsusa. 1997. "Women and Social Transformation in Central-Eastern Europe. The 'Old Left' and the 'New Right'." *Czech Sociological Review* 5, no. 2: 159–78.

Fialová, Ludmila, Pavla Horská, Milan Kučera. 1995. "Současné a perspektivní promeny rodiny, manželství a rodičovství." *Vyzkumné studie 11.* Nadace pro vyzkum sociální transformace.

Folbre, Nancy. 1994. *Who Pays for the Kids? Gender and the structures of constraint.* New York: Routledge.

Fodor, Eva. 1997. "Gender in Transition: Unemployment in Hungary, Poland and Slovakia." *East European Politics and Societies.* 11, no. 3: 470–500.

Fodor, Eva and Tanja Van der Lippe. 1998. "Changes in gender inequality in six eastern European countries." *Acta Sociologica* 41, no. 2: 131–49.

Fong, Monica and Gillian Paull. 1993. "Women's Economic Status in the Restructuring of Eastern Europe." In *Democratic Reform and the Position of Women in Transitional Economies.* Ed. Valentine M. Moghadam. Oxford: Clarendon Press.

Fraser, Nancy. 1992. "Rethinking the Public Sphere: A Contribution to the Critique of Actually Existing Democracy." In *Habermas and the Public Sphere.* Ed. Craig Calhoun. Cambridge: MIT Press.

"Free at Last." 1998. *The Economist*, June 13.

Friedman, Bruce Jay. 1993. "My Prague (Czechoslovakia)." *Playboy*, 40, no. 1 (January): 114–116.

Friedman, Milton. 1982 [1962] *Capitalism and Freedom.* Chicago: University of Chicago Press.

Fronk, Katka. 1998. "St. Valentine brings big business." *The Prague Post*, February: 11–17.

———. 1999. "Mobile mega-marketing." *The Prague Post*, February 17: 10.

Frýdlová, Pavla, Ed. 1998. *The memory of women/Pamet' žen.* Prague: The Foundation for Gender Studies.

Fuchs, Miroslav. 1998. "Připrávujéme se ke vstupu do EU: Rovné přiležitostí pro muže a ženy." *Sociální Politika*, 24, no. 9: 3–6.

Fukuyama, Francis. 1989. "The End of History." *The National Interest* 17: 3–18.

Funk, Nanette and Magda Mueller, Eds. 1993. *Gender and the Politics of Post-Communism*. New York: Routledge.

Gahr, Evan. 1997. "Uncovering the Politics of Women's Magazines," *The Wall Street Journal*, August 21: A: 14.

Gal, Susan. 1997. "Feminism and Civil Society." In Joan W. Scott, Cora Kaplan, Debra Keates, eds. *Transitions, Environments, Translations: Feminisms in International Politics*. New York: Routledge.

———— and Gail Kligman. 2000. *The Politics of Gender After Socialism*. Princeton: Princeton University Press.

Garkisch, David. 1998. "Ženy chtěji obnovít tradici svátku žen." *Mládá Fronta Dnes*. March 7: 1.

Garton-Ash, Timothy. 1990. *The Magic Lantern: The Revolutions of '89 Witnessed in Warsaw, Budapest, Berlin and Prague*. New York: Random House.

Garver, Bruce. 1985. "Women in the First Czechoslovak Republic. "In *Women, State and Party in Eastern Europe*. Eds. Sharon L. Wolchik and Alfred G. Meyer. Durham: Duke University Press

Grabher, Gernot and David Stark, Eds. 1997. *Restructuring Networks in Post-socialism. Legacies, Linkages and Localities*. Oxford: Oxford University Press.

Gibbs, Helena Sedlačková. 2000. "Debts to Olga: Identity, Gender and Writing in Václav Havel's Letters from Prison." *Jedním Okém/One Eye Open* 7.

Gill, Stephen. 1990. "Two Concepts of International Political Economy." *Review of International Studies* 16: 369–381.

————. Ed. 1993. *Gramsci, Historical Materialism and International Relations*. Cambridge: Cambridge University Press.

————. 1994. "Structural Change and Global Political Economy: Globalising Elites in the Emerging World Order." In *Global Transformation: Challenges to the State System*. Ed. Y. Sakamoto. Tokyo: United Nations University Press.

Giordano, J. M. 1998. "Too sexy for the recession." *The Prague Post*, September 16–22: A9.

"The Glass and Ceramic Industry in the Czech Republic." 1998. *Czech Business and Trade Journal*, 3.

Global Survival Network. 1997. *Crime and Servitude: An Expose of the Traffic in Women for Prostitution from the Newly Independent States*. In collaboration with the International League for Human Rights. Washington DC.

Gomez, Victor. 1994."Dark Horse Leader and Academic: Alena Hromádková." *The Prague Post*, December 14–29.

Goven, Joanna. 1993. "The Gendered Foundations of Hungarian Socialism: State,

Society, and the Anti-Politics of Anti-Feminism, 1948–1990. Ph.D dissertation, University of California — Berkeley.

Gowan, Peter. 1995. "Neo-Liberal Theory and Practice for Eastern Europe." *New Left Review* 213: 3–60

Gramsci, Antonio. 1971. *Selections from the Prison Notebooks.* Trans. Gregory Noare. Ed. Quintin Hoare. New York: International Books.

————. 1977. *Selections from Political Writings, 1910–1920: with additional texts by Bordiga and Tasca.* Trans. John Mathews. Ed. Quintin Hoare. New York: International Publishers.

Greenberg, Susan H. 1998. "Cosmo goes Global: Your Very Own Cosmo." *Newsweek.* May 11.

Greskovits, Bela. 1998. *The Political Economy of Protest and Patience. East European and Latin American Transformations Compared.* Budapest: Central European University Press.

Grunell, Marianne. 1995. "State of the Art: Feminism Meets Scepticism: Women's Studies in the Czech Republic." *European Journal of Women's Studies* 2: 101–111.

Gurley Brown, Helen. 1998. "Women are the Same." *Newsweek.* May 11.

Habermas, Jurgen. 1989. *The Structural Transformation of the Public Sphere: an inquiry into a category of bourgeois society.* Cambridge, Mass: MIT Press.

Hajék, Igor. 1994. "Czech Culture in the Cauldron." *Europe-Asia Studies* 46, no. 1: 127–142.

Haková, Libuše. 1965. "Ženach na radě." *Kulturní tvorba,* August 26: 76.

————. 1968. "Čas uhlavní ne přítel." *Vlasta* 3, 17 January.

Hanley, Sean. 1999. "The new right in the new Europe? Unravelling the ideology of 'Czech Thatcherism'." *Journal of Political Ideologies* 4, no. 2: 163–90.

Hann, Chris and Elizabeth Dunn, Eds. 1996. *Civil Society: Challenging Western Models,* New York: Routledge.

Hansford Johnson, Pamela. 1963. "Moscow: The Feminine Touch." *The Sunday Times,* February 3: 1–8.

Harvey, David. 1989. *The Condition of Postmodernity.* Oxford: Blackwell.

————. 1996. *Justice, Nature and the Geography of Difference.* Cambridge, MA: Blackwell

Hauser, Eva. 1996. "How and why do Czech women organise? Altos, sopranos, and a few discordant voices." *Canadian Journal of Women's Studies* 16, no. 1: 85–89.

Hauserová, Eva. 1995. *Na košteti se dá i lítat/Broomsticks can also be used for flying.* Praha: Lidové Noviny.

————. 1997. "Cosmopolitan a Harlequinky: plíživá emancipace ze Západu/ Cosmopolitan and Harlequin Books: Sneaky Emancipation from the West." *Jedním Okem/One Eye Open* 5: 9–12.

————. 1998. *Jsi přece ženska nebolí malý feministický rádce/You're a Woman After All or, A Little Feminist Guidebook.* Praha: Grada.

Havel, Václav et al. 1985. *The Power of the Powerless: Citizens Against the State in Central Eastern Europe.* Ed. John Keane and trans. Paul Wilson. Armonk, NY: M.E.Sharpe Inc.

————. 1991. *Open Letters: Selected Prose, 1965–90.* Trans. Paul Wilson. London: Faber.

————. 1997. *The Art of the Impossible: Politics as Morality in Practice: Speeches and Writing, 1990–96.* Trans. Paul Wilson and others. New York: Knopf.

————. 1998. "New Year's Day Speech." Lony, Czech Republic.

Havel, Václav and Václav Klaus with commentary by Petr Pithart. 1996. "Rival Visions: Civil Society after Communism." *Journal of Democracy* 7, no. 1: 12–23.

Havelková, Hana. 1993. "Patriarchy in Czech Society." *Hypatia* 8, no. 4: 89–96.

————. 1996. "Abstract Citizenship? Women and Power in the Czech Republic." *Social Politics* 3, 2–3: 243–60.

————. 1997. "Transitory and Persistent Differences: Feminism East and West." In *Transitions, Environments, Translations: Feminisms in International Politics.* Eds. Joan Scott, Cora Kaplan and Debra Keates. New York: Routledge.

————. 1999. "The Political Representation of Women in Mass Media Discourse in the Czech Republic 1990–1998." *Czech Sociological Review* 7, no. 2: 145–165.

Havelková, Hana and Mirek Vodrážka. 1998. *Žena a muž v médiích.* Praha: Cerná Kočka.

Havlik, Petr. 1983. "A Comparison Of Purchasing Power Parity And Consumption Levels In Austria And Czechoslovakia." Vienna: Institute for Comparative Economic Studies.

Hayek von, F.A. 1944. *The Road from Serfdom.* Chicago: University of Chicago Press.

Heinen, Jacqueline. 1990. "Inequalities at Work: The Gender Division of Labour in the Soviet Union and Eastern Europe" *Studies of Political Economy* 33, no. 3.

————. 1992. "Polish Democracy is a Masculine Democracy?" *Women's Studies International Forum* 15, no. 1: 129–40.

Heinrich Boll Foundation. 1996. *Conference: Sex Work, Sex Tourism, and Trafficking in Women: A New Reality in Eastern Europe?* Prague.

Heitlinger, Alena. 1979. *Women and State Socialism: Sex Inequality in the Soviet Union and Czechoslovakia.* Montreal: McGill-Queens University Press.

————. 1993. "The Impact of the Transition from Communism on the Status of Women in the Czech and Slovak Republics." In *Gender Politics and Post-Communism.* Eds. Nanette Funk and Magda Mueller. New York: Routledge.

————. 1996. "Framing feminism in post-communist Czech Republic." *Communist and Post-Communist Studies* 29, no. 1: 77–93.

————. Ed. 1999. *Emigre Feminisms*: Transnational Perspectives. Toronto: University of Toronto Press.

———— and Susanna Trnka. 1998. *Young Women of Prague*. London: Macmillan.

Hell, Julia. 1997. "History as Trauma, or, Turning to the Past, Once Again: Germany 1949/1989." *South Atlantic Quarterly* 96, no. 4: 911–948.

Hellman, J. "Winners Take All: The Politics of Partial Reform in Postcommunist Transitions." *World Politics* 50, no. 2: 203–234.

Hinde, S. 1996. "Scroders." *Sunday Express*, June 6.

Hobsbawm, Eric. 1982. "Man and woman: Images on the Left." In *Workers: Worlds of Labour*. New York: Pantheon Books.

Hollingsworth, Roger and Robert Boyer, eds. 1997. *Contemporary Capitalism: The Embeddedness of Institutions*. Cambridge: Cambridge University Press.

Holý, Ladislav. 1996. *The Little Czech and the Great Czech Nation*. Cambridge: Cambridge University Press.

Hooper, Charlotte. 2000. "Masculinities in Transition: the Case of Globalization." In *Gender and Global Restructuring*. Eds. Marianne Marchand and Anne Sisson Runyan. New York: Routledge.

Hořejší, Tomáš. 2000. "Jana Volfová představila stínový kabinet žen." *Lidové Noviny*, March 16: 2.

Hradílková, Jana. 1993. "The Discipline of Gender Studies." *Jedním Okem/One Eye Open* 1, no. 1: 39–45.

Hruby, Peter. 1980. *Fools and Heroes*. Oxford: Pergamon Press.

Htun, Mala N. and Mark P. Jones. 2002. "Engendering the Right to Participate in Decision-making: Electoral Quotas and Women's Leadership in Latin America." In *Gender and the Politics of Rights and Democracy in Latin America*. Eds. Maxine Molyneux and Nikki Craske. New York: Palgrave.

Hudsonová, Jan. 1997. *Svatba Na Pokračování*. August.

Humphrey, Caroline. 1995. "Creating a culture of disillusionment: Consumption in Moscow a chronicle of changing times." In *Worlds Apart: Modernity Through the Prism of the Local*. Ed. Daniel Miller. London: Routledge.

Hunt, Swanee. 1997. "Women's Vital Voices: The Costs of Exclusion in Eastern Europe." *Foreign Affairs* 76, no. 4: 2–9.

Husák, Petr. 1997. *Budování kapitalismu v Čechách: Rozhovory s Tomášem Ježkem*. Praha: Volvox Globator.

Igger, Wilma A. 1996. *Women in Prague: Ethnic Diversity and Social Change from the Eighteenth Century to the Present*. Berghahn Books.

Ignatieff, Michael. 1995. "On Civil Society: Why Eastern Europe's revolutions could succeed." *Foreign Affairs* 74, no. 2: 128–136.

Ikenberry, John and Charles Kupchan. 1990. "Socialization and Hegemonic Power." *International Organization* 44, 3: 292–314.

Imrých, Robert. 1998."Přišel čas na premiérku." *Cosmopolitan*, January: 30.

International Labor Office. 1997. *Maternity Protection at Work: Revision of the Maternity Protection Convention (Revised)* 1952 (No. 103) and Recommendation, 1952 (No. 95), Geneva: ILO Publications. Geneva: ILO Publications.

ILO-Central East European Team. 2000. *Women in the World of Work: Women Workers" Rights in Hungary*. Budapest: ILO Publications.

Indruchová, Libora. 1995. "Žena na ulici: stereotypizace ženy v současné velkoplošné reklame v České Republice/Women on the Street: Stereotypes of Women in Billboard Advertising in the Czech Republic." *Sociologický časopis* 31, no. 1: 85–104.

International Committee for the Support of Charter 77 in Czechoslovakia. 1977. *White Paper on Czechoslovakia*. Paris.

Jackson Lears, T. J. 1985. "The Concept of Cultural Hegemony: Problems and Possibilities." *American Historical Review* 90, no. 3: 567–593.

Jaquette, Jane S. and Sharon L. Wolchik. Eds. 1998. *Women and Democracy: Latin America and Central and Eastern Europe*. Baltimore: Johns Hopkins University Press.

"Jak trnitá je cesta žen k postum nejvzšším." 1998. *The Prague Tribune*, March: 13.

"Jaké chtejí být a jaká je skutečnost?" 1968. *Vlasta* 4, 31 January: 6–7.

Jancar-Webster, Barbara. 1978. *Women Under Communism*. Baltimore: Johns Hopkins University Press.

———. 1985. "Women in the Opposition in Poland and Czechoslovakia in the 1970s." In *Women, State, and Party in Eastern Europe*. Eds. Sharon L. Wolchik and Alfred G. Meyer. Durham: Duke University Press

———. 1993. *Environmental Action in Eastern Europe*. New York: M.E. Sharpe.

"Je žen v České politice dost?" 1993. *Lidové Noviny*, August 7: 5.

Jedličková, Petra. 1996a. "Hledáme atraktivní asistenku ředitelé do 25-ti let: Discriminace podle veku a pohlaví v inžeratech naších zamestnávatelu." *Žen sen* 1, no. 2.

———. 1996b. "Discriminace na pracovním trhu, žena a zamestnání, sexuální obtežovaní." *Žen sen* 1, no. 2.

Jernigan, David H. 1997. "Thirsting for Markets: Corporate Alcohol Goes Global," *Economics* 18: 7–8.

Jones, Adam. 1996. "Time to invest in foreign adventure." *Sunday Times*, June 9.

"Jsou čest zamestnáncí v zahraničních firmach diskriminovani?" 1998. *Ekonom*, No. 35: 34.

Jung, Nora. 1994. "Eastern European Women with Western Eyes." In *Stirring It: Challenges for Feminism*. Eds. G. Griffin et al. London: Taylor & Francis.

Kabat, Marcel. 1998. "Obchod s láskou aned Čokoli chcete." *Lidové Noviny*, September 12: 1–3.

Kantůrková, Eva. 1980. *Sešly jsme se v této knize*. Cologne: Index.

————. 1981. *Douze Femmes á Prague*. [In French] Trans. Catherine Fournier. Paris: Francois Maspero.

————. 1984. *Přitelkyně z domu smutku*. Cologne: Index.

————. 1987. *My Companions from the Bleak House*. Woodstock, New York: Overlook Press.

Kapoor, Michael with Ronan Lyons. 1996/7. "Labor Pains." *Business Central Europe*, December/January.

Karam, Azza ed. 1998. *Women in Parliament: Beyond Numbers*. Handbook Series 2. Stockholm: International Institute for Democracy and Electoral Assistance.

Karat Coalition for Regional Action. 1998. Platforma pro Akcí Shrnutí závěrů 4. světové konference o ženach v Pekingu 1995 Česká situace strategie 1998, překažky kroky vedoucí ke změnám. Praha: Nadace Gender Studies.

Karat Coalition. 1999. "Regional Report on Institutional Mechanisms for the Advancement of Women in the countries of Central and Eastern Europe." Report of the Regional Network of Women's NGOS in Central and Eastern Europe prepared for the 43rd session of the Committee on the Status of Women, the United Nations, Warsaw.

"Ke sjezdu Českého svažu Žen." 1997. *Prestiž*, Zvlástní číslo, November 15.

Keane, John. 1996. *Reflections on Violence*. London: Verso.

————. 1999. *Civil Society: Old Images, New Visions*, Stanford: Stanford University Press.

Keck, Margaret and Kathryn Sikkink. 1997. *Activists Beyond Borders: Advocacy Networks in International Politics*. Cornell: Cornell University Press.

Kempadoo, Kamala and Jo Doezema. 1998. *Global Sex Workers: Rights, Resistances, and Redefinitions*. New York: Routledge.

Kirss, Tiina. 2000. "Kantůrková's *My Companions from the Bleak House*: A Gendered Map of Prison." In *Gender and Historical Memory, Special Issue of Jedním Okem* 6. Eds. Jacqueline True, Marci Shore, and Eva Vešínová (Prague).

Klaus, Václav . 1991a. *Cesta k tržní ekonomice výber z članku, projevu a přednášek v zahráničí /A Road to Market Economy selected articles, speeches and lectures held abroad*. Praha: Top Agency.

————. 1991b. *Nemám rád katastrofické scénaře*. Ostrava: Sagit.

————. 1997. *Renaissance: The Birth of Liberty in the Heart of Europe*. Washington DC: Cato Institute.

Klauserová, Eva. 1968. "Emancipace od deti." *Literární Listy* I (11): 1 April: 7.

Klein, Naomi. 1999. *No Logo: Taking Aim at the Brand Bullies*. New York: Picador.

Klimešova, Hana. 1996. "Kvóty — uplneni v praxi v různých zemich světa, názory a doporučeni meziparlamentni komise." In *Politika s ženámi ci bez žen?* Nadace Gender Studies. Documentací z Semináře 17 April, Praha.

Klímová, Helena. 1969. "Co si myslíme u nás doma." *Literární Listy* II (6), 13 February: 3.

Knight, Robin. 1994. "Sewing up Central Europe's work force: Western companies hire cheap labor in former communist countries." *US News and World Report*, August 24: 46.

Knox, Kathleen. 1994. "Czech Women in Politics: Only few at the top." *The Prague Post*, September 9–16: 3.

Kobešová, Jana and Dvořáková, Markéta. 1998. "Muží často mivají přednost: České ženy si připadají v zamestnání diskriminovány." *Lidové Noviny*, April 15: 5.

Kofman, Eleonore and Gillian Youngs. eds. 1996. *Globalization: Theory and Practice*. London: Pinter.

Kohák, Erazim. 1997. "Consolidating Freedom in Central Europe." *Dissent*, Spring: 21–27.

Kollonay, Csilla. 2000. "What's Good is Wrong? Women's Rights in Labour Legislation" In *Women in the World of Work: Women Workers' Rights in Hungary*. Ed. ILO, Central and Eastern European Team. Budapest: ILO Publications.

Komínek, Jiří. 1998. "Czechs falling behind in R&D spending." *The Prague Post*, 15–22 July.

"Komuniké ze zasedání předsednictva UV ČS. Svazu Žen." 1968. *Vlasta*, 27 March: 2.

Kornai, Janos. 1992. *The Socialist System: The Political Economy of Communism*. Princeton, NJ: Princeton Univesity Press.

Kosík, Karel. 1995. *The Crisis of Modernity: Essays and Observations from the 1968 Era*. Ed. James Satterwhite. Lanham: Rowman & Littlefield.

Kowaleski-Wallace, Eva. 1997. *Consuming Subjects: Women, Shopping, and Business in the Eighteenth Century*. New York: Columbia University Press.

Kozinska-Baldyga, Alina. 1996. "Women, Democracy and Civil Society: The Case of Poland." Paper presented at "A World in Transition: Feminist Perspectives on International Relations," Lund University, Sweden, June.

Koželkova, Soňa. 1968 . "Proč máme dělat za ne?" *Vlasta* 2, 10 January: 3

Kriséová, Eda. 1968. "A-Sociálni-Ismus." *Literární Listy* 1, no. 10. (April 2).

————. 1993. *Václav Havel: The Authorized Biography*. New York.

Křižková, Alena. "The Division of Labour in Czech Households in the 1990s." *Czech Sociological Review* 7, no. 2: 205–214.

Kučera, Petr. 1999a. "Sexuální obtežování bude protizákonné." *Lidové Noviny*, December 4: 1.

Kučera, Petr. 1999b. "Nepříjemní sexuální návrhy nuť české ženy mnohdy řike zmnení místa." *Lidové Noviny*, December 9: 1.

Kučerová-Turková, Markéta and Terezie Jungrová. 1998. "Chcete práci? Dobehnete si pro potvrženi od gynekologa." *Cosmopolitan*, January: 72–73.

Kuchařova, Věra. 1996. "Stable and New Features of Family Formation in the Czech Republic." Unpublished manuscript. Prague: Research Institute for Labour and Social Affairs, October.

————. 1999. "Women and Employment." *Czech Sociological Review* 7, no. 2: 179–194.

Kuczynski, Alex. 1999. "Enough about feminism: Should I wear lipstick?" *The New York Times*, Sunday March 28: WK 4.

Kuczynski, Alex. 2000. "Romanian Playboy article draws protests: Satire on wife-beating also brings reprimand from US offices." *The New York Times*, Monday April 24: C16.

Kurczewski, Jacek. 1996. "The Family as an Institution of Polish Civil Society: Church, Parties and a Constitution in the Making." *Polish Sociological Review* 116, no. 4: 323–336.

Kusín, Vladimir V. 1971. *The Intellectual Origins of the Prague Spring*. Cambridge: Cambridge University Press.

Lagerspetz, Mikko. 1999. "Postsocialism as a Return: Notes on a Discursive Strategy." *East European Politics and Societies* 13, no. 2: 377–91.

Lampland, Martha. 1990. "Unthinkable Subjects: Women and Labor in Socialist Hungary." *East European Quarterly* 23: 4: 389–98.

————. 1995. *Objects of Labor*. Chicago: University of Chicago Press.

Landes, Joan. 1988. *Women and the Public Sphere in the Age of the French Revolution*. Ithaca: Cornell University Press.

Lang, Sabine. 1997. "The NGOization of Feminism." In *Transitions, Environments, Translations: Feminisms in International Politics*. Eds. Joan Scott, Cora Kaplan, Debra Keates. New York: Routledge.

Lapidus, Gail. 1978. *Women in Soviet Society*. Berkeley: University of California Press.

Laux, Jeanne Kirk. 2000. "Return to Europe: The Future Political Economy of Eastern Europe." In Richard Stubbs and Geoffrey R. D. Underhill, eds. *Political Economy and the Changing Global Order*. New York: Oxford University Press.

Legge, Michele. 1997. "State Urged To Protect Children." *The Prague Post*, October 29–November 4: A3.

————. 1998a. "Father's Fight for Child-Custody Rights." *The Prague Post*, February 11–17: A3.

————. 1998b. "Czech Life-Spans Grow Longer." *The Prague Post*, April 22–28: A1, 11.

Lhotska, Vera. 1995. "Past Trends in Differentiation of Family Patterns according to Census Data." In *Past and Present trends in Differentiation of Family Patterns in the Czech Republic*. Research Institute for Labour and Social Affairs, Prague, October.

Liborakina, Marina. 1998. "The Unappreciated Mothers of Civil Society." *Transitions* 5, no. 1: 52–57

Linz, Juan and Alfred Stepan. 1996. *Problems of Democratic Transition and Consol-*

idation: Southern Europe, South America and Post-Communist Europe. Baltimore: Johns Hopkins Press.

Lipschutz, Ronnie D. 1992. "Reconstructing World Politics: The Emergence of Global Civil Society." *Millennium: Journal of International Studies* 21, no. 3: 389–420.

Lury, Celia. 1997. *Consumer Culture.* News Brunswick: Rutgers University Press.

Lyons, Ronan. 1996. "Economic Focus: Labor Costs." *Business Central Europe*, November.

MacKinnon, Catherine A. 1979. *Sexual Harassment of Working Women: A Case of Sex Discrimination.* New Haven: Yale University Press.

———. 1989. *Toward a Feminist Theory of the State.* Cambridge, MA: Harvard University Press.

Madden, Normandy. 1996a. "TV Advertising Leads a Marketing Revolution Throughout East-Central Europe." *Transitions* 3, no. 4: 6–8.

———. 1996b. "Cross-Cultural Miscommunications Can Mar Western Advertising Campaigns." *Transitions* 3, no. 4: 9.

Marchand, Marianne and Anne Sisson Runyan, Eds. 2000. *Gender and Global Restructuring: Sightings, Sites and Resistances.* New York: Routledge.

Marková, Marta. 1997. *Olga Havlová a ty druhé: Ženy ve vnitřní emigraci.* Brno: Barrister and Principla.

Márová, Zdenka. 1968 . "Před pultem za pultem." *Vlasta* 31, 31 July: 4–5.

Matynia, Elzbieta. 1995. "Finding a Voice: Women in Central Europe." In *The Challenge of Local Feminisms: Women' Movements in Global Perspective.* Ed. A. Basu. Boulder, CO: Westview Press.

McClune, Emma and Jan Stojaspol. 1996. "Banker is Country's First Fired for Sexual Harassment." *The Prague Post*, August 21–27: Al.

McClune, Emma. 1996. "Adoption reforms Could Leave Kids Languishing: The State of the Czech Family Part Two." *The Prague Post*, February 14–20: A3.

———. 1998. "So, How Far Have You Really Come Baby." *The Prague Tribune*, March.

McDowell, Linda. 1991. "Life Without Father And Ford: The New Gender Order Of Post-Fordism." *Transaction: the Journal of British Geographers* 16, no. 4: 403–19.

McRobbie, Angela. 1997. "Bridging the Gap: Feminism, Fashion and Consumption." *Feminist Review* 55: 73–89.

Menon, Rita. 1996. "Beijing's Lessons": Book Review of "The Challenge of Local Feminisms: Women's Movements in Global Perspective." *The Women's Review of Books* XIII, no. 12: 15–16.

Merkel, Ina. 1994. "From a Socialist Society of Labor into a Consumer Society? The Transformation of East German Identities and Systems." In *Envisioning Eastern Europe.* Ed. M. Kennedy. Ann Arbor: University of Michigan Press.

Meils, Cathy. 1998. "East Europeans soak in soaps: femme channels pant for steamy telenovelas (television for women in Eastern Europe) *Variety* 371, July 13: 33.

"Mezinárodní Soutež Cosmpolitanu: Ne všechny fun, fearless, female jsou slavné." *Cosmopolitan*, March 1998.

Miethe, Ingrid. 1999. "From Mothers of the Revolution to Fathers of Unification." *Social Politics* 6, no. 1: 1–22.

Mikolášová, Jarmila. 1968. "Emancipace ženy v dneším slova smyslu je uplnou degradací ženství." *Vlasta* 19, 8 May: 15

Mieczkowski, Bogdan. 1975. *Personal and Social Consumption: Poland, Czechoslovakia, Hungary, and East Germany.* New York: Praeger Publishers.

Mies, Maria and Vandana Shiva. 1993. *Ecofeminism.* London: Zed Books.

Millic-Czerniak, Roza, Ed. 1998. *Households in Central Europe: The Impact of Transformations 1990–1995.* Warsawa: Polish Academy of Sciences.

Mische, Ann. 1993. "Post-Communism's Lost Treasure: Subjectivity and Gender in a Shifting Public Sphere." *Praxis International* 13, no. 3: 242–267.

Mittleman, James. 2000. *The Globalization Syndrome.* Princeton, NJ: Princeton University Press.

Mlčoch, Lubomír. 1996. *Institucionální Ekonomie.* Univerzita Karlova. Praha.

———. 1998. "Introducing Czech-style Capitalism." *Nová Přítomnost*, January.

Modelski, Tania. 1998. "Questioning scholars' torrid romance with popular culture." *The Chronicle of Higher Education* 45, no. 2, November 13: B8.

Modelski, Tania. 1982. *Loving with a Vengeance: Mass-produced fantasies for women.* New York: Routledge.

Mogdaham, Valentine M. 1990. "Gender and Restructuring: Perestroika, the 1989 Revolutions and Women." Helsinki: UNU/WIDER Working Paper No. 87.

———. ed. 1992. *Privatization and Democratization in Central and Eastern Europe and the Soviet Union: The Gender Dimension.* World Institute for Development Economics Research of the United Nations University.

———. ed. 1993. *Democratic Reform and the Position of Women in Transitional Economies.* New York: Oxford University Press.

Mohanty, Chandra T. 1991. "Under Western Eyes: Feminist Scholarship and Colonial Discourses." In *Third World Women and the Politics of Feminism.* Eds. Chandra T. Mohanty, Ann Russo, and Lourdes Torres. Bloomington: Indiana University Press.

Moon, Katherine S. 1997. *Sex Among Allies: Military Prostitution in US-Korea Relations.* New York: Columbia University Press.

Morrison, Melissa. 1996. "Tanks for the Memories: Michael Jackson Imposes HIStory on the Czech Republic." *Rolling Stone*, October.

Mortkowitz, Siegfried. 1994. "Foreign Funding Still Needed for Women's 'Nerve Center'." *The Prague Post*, September 9–16: 1, 3.

Mortkowitz, Siegfried and Jan Stojaspal. 1996. "Prostitution is Tip of the Vice-Berg on Czech Highway of Sleaze, E 55." *The Prague Post*, September 11–17: 4.

Možný, Ivo. 1991. *Proč tak snado — nekteré rodinné důvody sametové revoluce/*Why so easy — some family reasons for the Velvet Revolution. Praha: Slon

————. 1994. "The Czech Family in Transition: From Social to Economic Capital." In *Social Reform in the Czech Republic, Prague Papers on Social Responses to Transformation*, Volume II. Eds. Steve Ringen and Claire Wallace. Praha.

———— and Ladislav Rabušic. 1999. "The Czech Family, the Marriage Market, and the Reproductive Climate." In *Ten years of Rebuilding Capitalism: Czech Society after 1989*. Eds. Jiří Večerník and Petr Matějů Praha: Academia, pp. 94–112.

Murphy, Craig N. and Cristina Rojas de Ferro. 1995. "The Power of Representation in International Political Economy." *Review of International Political Economy* 2, no. 1: 63–183.

Murray, S. 1995. "In Czech Republic's Move to Capitalism, High Unemployment is Notably Absent." *The Wall Street Journal*, August 24, 1995.

Murrell, Peter. 1992. "Evolutionary and Radical Approaches to Economic Reform." *Economics of Planning* 25, no. 1: 79–95.

————. 1995. "The Transition According to Cambridge, Mass." *Journal of Economic Literature* 33, no. 1: 164–9.

Musilová, Martina. 1999. "Equal Opportunity as a Matter of Public Interest." *Czech Sociological Review* 7, no. 2: 195–204.

"Nad 32 stránkami." 1968. *Vlasta* 17, 24 April: 25.

Nadace Gender Studies. 1994. *Alty a soprány: Kapesní atlas ženských iniciatic.* Praha.

————. 1996. *Politika s ženámi ci bez žen?* Documentací z semináře April 17. Praha.

Naegle, Jolyon. 1998. "Czech Republic: most voters stay home in elections." *Radio Free Europe/Radio Liberty Newsline*, November 17.

Nagle, John D. 1994. "Political Generation Theory and Post-Communist Youth in East-Central Europe." *Research in Social Movements, Conflicts and Change* 17: 25–52.

"Názory, diskuse, úvahy: k tomu Potřebujeme svou organizaci." 1968. *Vlasta* 30, July 24: 7.

Nelson, Joan M, Charles Tilly and L. Walker Eds. 1997. *Transforming Post-Communist Political Economies*. Washington, D.C.: National Academy Press.

"Nesmíme promarnit příležitost: musíme důsledne jednat v zájmu všech žen." 1968. *Vlasta* 18, May 1: 3.

Neunerová, Pavla. 1999. "Sexuální obtežování se netýká jen žen." *Lidové Noviny*, December 10: 10.

Newman, B. 1995. "Dip and Snip: Czechs Take to the Waters, Go Under the Knife: New Post-Communist Values Include Health and Beauty: Radon Baths, Face Lifts." *The Wall Street Journal*, March 20.

Nicholls, Ana. 1999. "Welcome to Silicon Valley." *Business, Central Europe.* February.

Nielsen, Klaus. 1995. "Institutional Dynamics in Post-Communist Economic Transformation: Choice and Redirection of Strategy." In *Europe: Central and East.* Eds. Marguerite Mendell and Klaus Nielsen. Montreal: Black Rose Books.

Nistorescu, Cornel. 2000. "With Playboy and with the Wooden Spoon." *Evenimentul zilei,* March 25.

Non-Governmental Non-Profit Sector. 1995. *Material from the Fourth Conference of Non-Governmental, Non-Profit Organizations in the Czech Republic,* November 10–11, Prague: ICN.

North, Douglass. 1990. *Institutions, Institutional Change and Economic Performance.* Cambridge: Cambridge University Press.

Norton, Ann. 1990. *Reflections on Political Identity.* Baltimore: Johns Hopkins University Press.

"Nová elita žen." 1996. *The Prague Tribune.* February/March: 9–15.

Nove, Alex. 1991. *The Economics of Feasible Socialism Revisited.* Second edition. London: Harper Collins.

"Nové perspectivy pro ženské hnutí: dopis vláde." 1968. *Vlasta* 17, April 24: 2.

"O ženách pro ženy." 1968. *Vlasta* 1, January 3: 3.

O'Donnell, G, P. C. Schmitter and L. Whitehead, eds. 1986. *Transition from Authoritarianism: Prospects for Democracy.* Baltimore: Johns Hopkins Press.

"Odpovědí Na Otázky Neziskový Sektor" v České Republice/Responses to Questions about the Non-Profit Sector in the Czech Republic." 1997. Material from the Sixth Conference of Non-Profit organizations in the Czech Republic, Prague, November 28–29.

Olsen, David. 1997. "Democratization and Political Participation: The Experience of the Czech Republic." In *The Consolidation of Democracy in East-Central Europe.* Eds. K. Dawisha and B. Parrott. Cambridge: Cambridge University Press.

Orenstein, Mitchell. 1996. Out of the Red: Building Capitalism and Democracy in Post-Communist Europe. Ph. D dissertation, Yale University.

———. 1998. "Václav Klaus: Revolutionary and Parliamentarian." *East European Constitutional Review* 7, no. 1: 46–55.

———. 2001. *Out of the Red: Building Capitalism and Democracy in Post-Communist Europe.* Ann Arbor: University of Michigan Press.

Organization for Economic Co-operation and Development (OECD). 1995. *Review of the Labour Market in the Czech Republic.* Paris: OECD Publications.

———. 1999a. *Financial Market Trends,* No. 73, June, Paris.

———. 1999b. *Measuring Globalisation: The Role of Multinationals in OECD economies.* Paris: OECD Publications.

Orol, Ron. 1998. "Foreign Women Enjoy Advantage." *The Prague Post*, March 18–24: A8.

Ort, Suzy. 1993. "East-West Feminism: An Interview with Rita Klímová." *Jedním Okem/One Eye Open* 1, no. 2: 59–64.

Ostner, Ilona and Jane Lewis. 1995. "Gender and the Evolution of European Social Policies." In *European Social Policy: Between Fragmentation and Integration*. Eds. Stephan Leibfried and Paul Pierson. Washington DC: Brookings Institution.

Osvaldová. Barbara. 1998. "Současný český tisk pro ženy." In *Žena a muž v médiích*. Eds. Hana Havelková and Mirek Vodrážka. Praha: Cerná Kočka.

"Otevřený list všem Československém ženám." 1968. *Vlasta* 19, May 8: 2.

Outtrup, Ula and Birgitte Ramsoe Thomsen. 1994. Mixed Messages — Mixed Feelings: Women Reading Cosmopolitan. M.A. disseration, Roskilde University, Denmark.

Oxley, A. 1973. *Czechoslovakia: The Party and the People*. London: Penguin.

Palumbo-Liu, David and Hans Ulrich Gumbrecht. 1997. *Streams of Cultural Capital*. Stanford: Stanford University Press.

Paraschiv, Roxana Tesiu, ed. 2002. *Monitoring the EU Accession Process: Equal Opportunities for Women and Men*. The Network Women's Program: Open Society Institute/EU Accession Program.

"Parlament je čím dál víc mužskou záležitostí." 1995. *Mláda Fronta Dnes*, February 23: 7.

Pateman, Carole. 1989. *The Disorder of Women: Democracy, Feminism and Political Theory*. Stanford: Stanford University Press.

Paul, Ellen Frankel. 1999. "Strangers in a Strange Land: The Mitsubishi Sexual Harassment Case." In *Business Ethics in the Global Market*. Ed. Tibor R Machan. Stanford: Hoover Institution Press.

Paukert, Liba. 1991. "The Economic Status of Women in the Transition to a Market System: The Case of Czechoslovakia." *International Labor Review* 130.

———. 1995. "Economic Transition and women's employment in four Central European countries, 1989–1994." *Labour Market Papers* 7. Geneva: ILO.

———. 1995. "Privatization and Employment: Labour Transfer Policies and Practices in the Czech Republic." *Labour Market Papers No. 4*, Geneva: International Labour Organization.

Pearson, Ruth. 1997. "Renegotiating the Reproductive Bargain: Gender Analysis of Economic Transition in Cuba in the 1990s." *Development and Change* 28: 671–705.

———. 1998."The Political Economy Of Social Reproduction: The Case Of Cuba In The 1990s." *New Political Economy* 3, no. 2: 241–59.

Pedziwol, A. 1997. "The Great Game of Privatization." *Transitions* 4, no. 1 (January).

Pehe, Jiří. 1997. "Czech Government Braces Itself For Vote Of Confidence." *Newsline*, June 10.

———. 1998. "The Czechs Fall from their Ivory Tower." *Transitions* 7, no. 1.

Penn, Shana. 1994. "The National Secret." *Journal of Women's History* 5, no. 3: 55–69.

———. 1998. "Looking East, Looking West." *Transitions* 7, January: 48–51.

Perlez, Jane. 1996. "Central Europe Learns About Sexual Harassment." *The New York Times*, October 3: A3.

Perlez, Jane. 1997. "Fenced In At Home, Marlboro Man Looks Abroad: Marlboro Man's Call Is 'Go East'." *The New York Times*, June 24: A1.

Perlez, Jane. 1998. "Ban on [Amway] Film has Poland Debating Censorship." *The New York Times*, June 14: A4.

Petraček, Z. 1996. "Kdyby nebylo žen . . ." *Respekt* 10–16 June: 2.

Petrová, Věra. 1968. "Pokrok a demokracie. *Vlasta* 25, 19 June: 14

Pettman, Jan Jindy. 1996. *Worlding Women: A Feminist International Politics.* New York: Routledge.

Picchio, Antonella. 1992. *Social Reproduction: The Political Economy of the Labour Market.* Cambridge: Cambridge University Press.

Pickel, Andreas and Helmut Wiesthenthal. 1997. *The Grand Experiment?: Debating Shock Therapy, Transition Theory and the East German Experience.* Boulder, CO: Westview Press.

Pithart, Petr. 1993. "Intellectuals in Politics: Double Dissent in the Past, Double Disappointment Today." *Social Research* 60, no. 4: 751–761.

"Plenty Of Muck, Not Much Money, Prague." 1999. *The Economist*, May 8: 52.

Plotová, Alena. 1999. "Soud potřestal užitelé za sexuální obtežování." Mláda Fronta Dnes, February 19: 1.

"Poland's Market In Goods And Ideas." 1999. *The Economist*, April 10,: 52

Polanyi, Karl. 1957 [1944]. *The Great Transformation: The Social and Political Origins Of Our Time.* Boston: Beacon Press.

Popper, Karl R. 1966. *The Open Society and its Enemies* (Two Volumes) Fifth revised edition. Princeton: Princeton University Press.

Potůček, Martin. 1993. "Current Social Policy Developments in the Czech and Slovak Republics." *Journal of European Public Policy* 3, no. 3.

Poznanski, Kazimierz Z. 1996. *Poland's Protracted Transition: Economic Growth and Institutional Change in 1970–1994.* Cambridge: Cambridge University Press.

———. 1998. "Rethinking Comparative Economics: From Organizational Simplicity to Institutional Complexity." *East European Politics and Societies* 12, no. 1: 171–199.

———. 1999a. "Recounting Transition." *East European Politics and Societies* 13, no. 2: 328–345.

———. 1999b. "The Morals of Transition: Decline of Public Interest and Runaway

Reforms in Eastern Europe." Seattle: University of Washington, unpublished manuscript.

———. 2000. "The Crisis of Modernity: Capitalism and Communism Reexamined." *East European Politics and Societies* 14, no. 3: 676–692.

Prague Post, The. 1998. *The 1998 Book of Business Lists.* Prague: Prague Post Foundation.

Prečan, Vilém, ed. 1990. *Charta 77 1977–1989: Od morální k demokratické revoluci.* Scheinfeld, Germany: Československé středisko nezávislé literátury and Bratislava: Archa.

Price, Richard. 1998. "Reversing The Gun Sights: Transnational Civil Society Targets Land Mines." *International Organization* 52, no. 3: 613–644.

Pringle, Rosemary and Sophie Watson. 1992. 'Women's Interests and the Post-Structuralist State', in *Destabilizing Theory: Contemporary Feminist Debates.* Eds. Michele Barrett and Anne Phillips. London: Polity, pp. 53–73.

Prügl, Elisabeth. 1999. *The Global Construction of Gender: Home-Based Work in the Political Economy of the Twentieth Century.* New York: Columbia University Press.

Prybyla, Jan. 1991. "The Road from Socialism: Why, Where, What and How?" *Problems of Communism*, January-April: 1–17.

Putnová, Anna. 1998. "Rýchlík do Evropy nečeká." *Cosmopolitan*, July: 64–5.

Quigley, Kevin F. F. 1996. *For Democracy's Sake: Foundations and Democracy Assistance in Central Europe.* Woodrow Wilson Centre and Johns Hopkins University Press.

Radice, Hugo. 1999. "Capitalism Restored in East-Central Europe." Leeds Business School, unpublished manuscript.

Radio Free Europe/Radio Liberty. 1999. "Czech government approves amendment to labor code." *Newsline*, December 23.

———. 2000a. "Adviser to Czech Premier Named as Author of 'Operation Lead'." *Newsline*, August 18.

———. 2000b. "Czech Premier Blames Outsiders for 'Operation Lead' but Suspends Advisers." *Newsline*, August 25.

———. 2000c. "Charges Brought in Czech Operation Lead Scandal." 2000. *Newsline* September 28.

———. 2000d. "Czech four party coalition set up Shadow Cabinet." *Newsline* September 29.

———. 2000e. "Czech Premier's Chief Aid Admits 'Co-Responsibility' in 'Operation Lead' Scandal." 2000. *Newsline* October 2.

———. 2000f. "European Parliament Approves Report on Czech Progress to Accession." *Newsline*, October 5.

———. 2001a. "First Woman Elected to Head Party in Czech Republic." *Newsline*, June 25.

———. 2001b. "One in Four Czechs is Nostalgic About Communism." *Newsline*, August 20.

———. 2002. "Czech Parliament Will Remain An Old-Boy's Club." *Newsline*, April 17.

Radway, Janice. 1984. *Reading The Romance: Women, Patriarchy, And Popular Culture*. Chapel Hill: University of North Carolina Press.

Reinelt, Claire. 1995. "Moving onto the Terrain of the State: The Battered Women's Movement and the Politics of Engagement." In *Feminist Organizations: Harvest of the New Women's Movement*. Eds. Myra Marx Ferree and Patricia Yaney Martin. Philadelphia: Temple University Press.

Remington, Robin. 1969. *Winter in Prague*. Cambridge, MA: MIT Press.

Renne, Tanya, Ed. 1997. *Sisterhood in Eastern Europe*. Boulder, CO: Westview Press.

Research Institute for Labour and Social Affairs. 1998. *Main Economic and Social Indicators of the Czech Republic, 1990–98*, No. 11, Praha.

"Retailing revolution reshapes Eastern Europe." 1996. *International Journal of Retail and Distribution Management* 24, no. 1: 2.

Robinson, William I. 1996. *Promoting Polyarchy: Globalization, U.S. Intervention, and Hegemony*. Cambridge: Cambridge University Press.

Rodrik, Dani. 1997. "Sense and Nonsense in the Globalization Debate." *Foreign Policy* 107: 19–37.

———. 1999. "Governing the Global Economy: Does One Architectural Style Fit All?" *Brookings Trade Forum 1999*, 1: 105–40.

———. 2000. "Institutions for High Quality Growth: What Are They And How To Acquire Them?" *Studies in Comparative International Development* 35, 3: 3–32.

———. 2001. "Trading in Illusions." *Foreign Policy* 123: 54–64.

"Romania: A Tasteless April Fool's Joke." 2000. *Transitions*, April 19.

Rona-Tas, Akos. 1998. "Path-dependence and Capital Theory: Sociology of the Post-Communist Economic Transformation." *East European Politics and Societies* 12, no. 1: 107–25.

Rose, Richard et al. 1998. *Elections in Central and Eastern Europe since 1990*. Glasgow: University of Strathclyde Studies in Public Policy No. 300.

Rosen, Ruth. 1990. "Male Democracies, Female Dissidents." *Tikkun* 5, no. 6: 11–12.

Rosow, Stephen, Naeem Inyatullah and Mark Rupert. Eds. 1994. *The Global Economy as Political Space*, Boulder. CO: Lynne Rienner Publishers.

Rueschemeyer, Marilyn, ed. 1994. *Women in the Politics of Post-Communist Eastern Europe*. First edition. London: M. E. Sharpe Inc.

Rueschmeyer, Marilyn and Sharon L. Wolchik. 1999. "The Return of Left-Oriented Parties in East Germany and the Czech Republic and their Social Policies." In *Left Parties and Social Policy in Post-Communist Europe*. Eds. Linda J. Cook, Mitchell A. Orenstein and Marilyn Rueschmeyer. Boulder, CO: Westview Press.

Rutland, Peter. 1993. "Thatcherism. Czech-style: Transition to Capitalism in the Czech Republic." *Telos* 94: 103–131.

Rychtařiková, Jitka. 1995. "Recent Changes in Families in the Czech Republic." In *Past and Present Trends in Differentiation of Family Patterns in the Czech Republic*. Research Institute of Labour and Social Affairs, Prague, October.

Sachs, Jeffrey. 1989. "My Plan for Poland." *International Economy* 3: 24–29.

———. 1994. *Poland's Jump to a Market Economy*. Cambridge, Mass: MIT Press.

Sachs, Jeffrey and Andrew Warner. 1996. "Economic Reform an the Process of Global Integration." Development Discussion Paper No. 552, September.

Sajo, Andras. 1997. "Universal Rights, Missionaries, Converts And Local Savages." *East European Constitutional Review* 44: 43–9.

Sakamoto, Yoshikazu. 1997. "Civil Society and Democratic World Order." In *Innovation and Transformation in International Studies*. Eds. Stephen Gill and James Mittleman, Cambridge: Cambridge University Press.

Salzmann, Zdenek. 1990. "Portrayal of Gender Relations in Contemporary Czech Mass Media." *East European Quarterly* 23, no. 4: 399–407.

Šamlova, Mary Hrábík. 1996. "Women and the Unofficial Culture and Literature in Czechoslovakia, 1969–1989." Oakland University, Michigan, unpublished typescript.

Sarah, Rachel. 1996. "Regulating the Booming Prostitution Business." *Transitions* 5, March 8–15.

Sassen, Saskia. 1998. *Globalization and its Discontents*. New York: The New Press.

Saxonberg, Steven. 1999. "Václav Klaus: The Rise And Fall And Re-Emergence Of A Charismatic Leader." *East European Politics and Societies* 13, no. 2: 391–419.

———. 2000. "Women in East European Parliaments." *Journal of Democracy* 11, no. 2: 145–158.

Satterwhite, James. 1992. "Marxist Critique and Czechoslovak Reform." In *The Road to Disillusion: From Critical Marxism to Postcommunism in Eastern Europe*. Ed. Raymond Taras. Armonk, New York: M.E. Sharpe.

Schechter, Michael G. 2000. "Globalization and Civil Society." In *The Revival of Civil Society: Global and Comparative Perspectives* Ed. Michael G. Schechter. London: Macmillan.

Scott, Hilda. 1974. *Does Socialism Liberate Women?: Experiences from Eastern Europe*. Boston: Beacon Press.

Scott, Joan Wallach. 1996. *Only Paradoxes to Offer: French Feminists and the Rights of Man*. Cambridge, MA: Harvard University Press.

Scott, W. Richard. 2001. *Institutions and Organizations*. 2nd ed.Thousand Oaks, CA: Sage.

Sedláková, Mária. 1968. "Jaká kritika." *Vlasta* 17, April 24: 14

Sen, Gita. 1996. "Gender, Markets and States: A Selective Review and Research Agenda." *World Development* 24, no. 5: 821–9.

"Sexuální harašení není českým problémem." 1998. *Lidové Noviny*, February 5: 1.

"Sexuální harašení před olomouském soudem." 1999. *Slovo*, April 15: 3.

"Sexuální obtežování se v Čechách nenos." 1998. *Lidové Noviny*, January 1: 1.

Shen, Jun. 1994. "Czech Women Face Gender Gap In Banking." *Journal of Commerce and Commercial Banking*, February 8, 399, no. 28: 8A1.

Shepard, Melanie and Ellen Pence, eds. 1999. *Coordinating Community Responses to Domestic Violence: Lessons from the Duluth Model*. New York: Sage.

Shore, Marci. 1995. "Listen or Obey? Either Way, Women Should Not Take This Lying Down." *The Prague Post*, February.

Shore, Marci. 1998. "Engineering in the Age of Innocence: A Genealogy of Discourse Inside the Czechoslovak Writer's Union, 1949–67." *East European Politics and Societies* 12, no. 3: 397–441.

Šiklová, Jiřina. 1990. "The Grey Zone And The Future Of Dissent In Czechoslovakia." *Social Research* 57, no. 2: 0347–65.

———. 1993. "McDonalds, Terminators, Coca-Cola Ads and Feminism: Imports from the West?" In *Bodies of Bread and Butter: Reconfiguring Women's Lives in the Post-Communist Czech Republic*. Ed. Susannah Trnka with Laura Busheikin. Prague: Prague Gender Studies Center.

———. 1996. "Jiný kraj, jiné ženy: Proč se v Čechách nedaří feminismus." *Respekt* 13, March 25–31: 17.

———. 1997. "Feminism And The Roots Of Apathy In The Czech Republic." *Social Research* 64, no. 2: 258–279.

———. 1998a. "Men and Women United for a Higher Purpose," *Transitions* 7, January: 34–35.

———. 1998b. "Má feminismus v Čechách šanci," *Nová Přítomnost* 1: 8–13.

———. 1998c. "Why We Resist Western-Style Feminism." *Transitions* 7, January: 30–34.

Šiklová, Jiřina and Jana Hrádílková. 1994. "Women and Violence in the Czech Republic." In *Women Against Violence*. Ed. Miranda Davies. London: Zed Books.

Šilhánová, Libuše. 1997. "Nad Chartou 77: Připomínka a za myšlení." In *Charter 77 remembered*. Ed. V. Prečan. Praha.

Šimečká, Milan. 1984. *The Restoration of Order: The Normalization of Czechoslovakia 1969–76*. Trans. A.G. Brain. London: Verso.

Skilling, H. Gordon. 1976. *Czechoslovakia's Interrupted Revolution*. Princeton, NJ: Princeton University Press.

———. 1981. *Charter 77 and Human Rights in Czechoslovakia*. London: George Allen & Unwin.

————. 1989. *Samizdat and an Independent Society in Central and Eastern Europe*. London: Macmillan.

Škvorecký, Josef. 1992a. "Je možné mluvit se ženou bez pohlavního obtežování?: Dobrodružství amerického feminismus." Respekt, 39, no. 28 October, 1992: 13.

————. "Je možné sex bez znásilnení?" 1992b. *Respekt*, 32, no. 10 August: 10.

————. "Je možné mluvit a psát správně bez diskriminace?" 1992c. *Respekt*, 46, no. 16, November: 13.

Slobin, Greta. N. 1997. "Ona: The New Elle-Literacy and the Post-Soviet Woman." In *Writing New Identities: Gender, Nation, and Immigration in Contemporary Europe*. Eds. Gisela Brinker-Gabler and Sidonie Smith. Minneapolis: University of Minnesota Press.

Šmejkalová-Strickland, Jiřina. 1993. "Do Czech Women Need Feminism? Perspectives of feminist theories and practices in the Czech Republic." In *Bodies of Bread and Butter: Reconfiguring Women's Lives in the Post-Communist Czech Republic*. Ed. S. Trnka with L. Busheikin. Prague Gender Studies Centre, Prague.

————. 1995. "Revival? Gender studies in the 'other' Europa." *Signs* 20, no. 4.

————. 1997. "The Open Book and its Enemies." *Transitions* 6, no. 1: 41–44.

Smith, Tony. 1998. "The International Origins of Democracy: The American Occupation of Japan and Germany." In *Democracy, Revolution and History*. Pp. 191–209. Ed. Theda Skocpol. Ithaca: Cornell University Press.

Snitow, Ann. 1983. "Mass-market romance: Pornography for women is different." In *Powers of Desire: The Politics of Sexuality*. Eds. A. Snitow, C. Stansell and S. Thompson. New York: Monthly Review Press.

————. 1994. "Feminist Futures in the Former East Bloc." *Peace and Democracy News*, Spring.

————. 2000. "Cautionary Tales." 93 *American Society of International Law Proceedings* 214: 35–42.

"Soap Operas, Frozen Food and Convertibles: Report from the front lines of a consumer revolution." 1997. *Newsweek*, March 3: 30–1.

Sofres Factum. 1999. *Názory Na Problém Sexuálního Obtežování Žen Na Pracovišti*, Zprava z výzkumu veřejného mínení. Praha: SOFRES FACTUM s.r.o.

Šolcová, Miroslava. 1984. *Postavení ženy v socialistické společnosti*. Praha.

Soros, George. 1995. "Toward Open Societies." *Foreign Policy* 98: 65–75.

————. 1997. "The Capitalist Threat." *The Atlantic Monthly*, February.

————. 1998–9. "Capitalism's Last Chance?" *Foreign Policy* 113: 55–66.

————. 2000. "The Age of Open Society." *Foreign Policy* 119: 52–54.

Specter, Michael. 1998. "Traffickers New Cargo: Naïve Slavic Women." *The New York Times*, January 11: A1.

Sperling, Valerie. 1999. *Organizing Women in Contemporary Russia*. Cambridge: Cambridge University Press.

"Spor O ženu nasi doby." 1968. *Vlasta*, March 6: 6–7.

Standing, Guy. 1998a. "The Babble of Euphemisms: Re-embedding Social Protection in 'Transformed' Labour Markets." Unpublished manuscript. Geneva, ILO.

———. 1998b. "Societal Impoverishment: the challenge for Russian social policy." *Journal of European Social Policy* 8, no. 1: 23–43.

"Stanovisko redakce Vlasty." 1968. *Vlasta* 14, April 3: 2.

Stark, David and Laszlo Bruszt. 1998. *Postsocialist Pathways: Transforming Politics and Property in East Central Europe*. Cambridge: Cambridge University Press.

Štástná, Jaroslava. 1995. "New Opportunities in the Czech Republic." *Transitions* 1, no. 16: 5–8.

Štástná, Kazi. 1999. "Czech Republic: Taxing the Professionals." *Central Europe Review* 1, no. 22, November.

Steans, Jill. 1999. "The Private Is Global: Feminist Politics And Global Political Economy." *New Political Economy* 4, no. 1: 113–128.

Strange, Susan. 1994. *States and Markets, Second Edition*. Oxford: Basil Blackwell.

Strauník, Alexandra. 1997. "Love For Sale." *Prague Business Journal*, August 4–10:1, 10–11.

Stroehlein, Andrew. 1999. "The Convenience Revolution: Consumerism in Central and Eastern Europe." *Central Europe Review* 8, no. 9 August, http://www.ce-review.org/99/8/theissue8.html.

"Survey of the Czech Republic." 1996. The Financial Times, December 6.

Sykorá, L. 1996. "The Czech Republic." In *Housing Policy in Europe*. Ed. P. Balchin. London: Routledge.

Szalai, Julia. 1997. "Two Studies on Changing Gender Relations in Post-1989 Hungary." Discussion Paper No. 30, Collegium Budapest/Institute for Advanced Study. Budapest, Hungary.

Szucs, Jenos. 1988. Three Historical Regions of Europe: An Outline. In *Civil Society and the State: New European Perspectives*. Ed. John Keane. London: Verso.

Szymanowski, Maciej. 1997. "Při půlnočním polibku: Jak vypadá svět očima českých ženských časopisů." *Respekt* 28, July 7–13.

Tarkowski, Elsbieta and Jacek Tarkowski. 1991. "Social Disintegration in Poland: Civil Society or Amoral Familism." *Telos* 5, no. 7: 103–09.

Tavernise, Sabrina. 2002. "A Russian Rights Crusader, Made by Mary Kay." *The New York Times*, April 20: A4.

Teichova, Alena. 1988. *The Czechoslovak Economy, 1918–1980*. London and New York: Routledge.

Thomas, Daniel. 1999. "The Helsinki Accords and Political Change in Eastern Europe." In *The Power of Human Rights: International Norms and Domestic Change*. Eds. Thomas Risse, Stephen C. Ropp and Kathryn Sikkink. Cambridge: Cambridge University Press.

Tickner, J. Ann. 1992. "On the Fringes of the Global Economy." In *The New International Political Economy*. Eds. Roger Tooze and Craig Murphy. Boulder, CO: Lynne Rienner.

―――. 1997. "You Just Don't Understand: Troubled Engagements Between Feminists and International Relations Theorists." *International Studies Quarterly* 41, no. 4: 611–32.

―――. 2001. *Gendering World Politics*. New York: Columbia University Press.

Torstar Corporation. 1997. *Annual Report 1997*. Toronto.

"Trafficking in Women: In the Shadows." 2000. *The Economist*, August 26: 38.

True, Jacqui. 1999. "Antipodean Feminisms." In *Émigré Feminism: Transnational Perspectives*. Ed. Alena Heitlinger. Toronto: University of Toronto Press.

―――. 1999. "Expanding Markets and Marketing Gender: The Integration of the Post-Socialist Czech Republic." *Review of International Political Economy* 6, no. 3: 360–89.

True, Jacqueline, Marci Shore and Eva Vešínová eds. 1998. Special Issue: Gender and Historical Memory. *Jedním Okém/One Eye Open* 6, (Prague).

Uhl, Petr. 1985. "The Alternative Community as Revolutionary Avant-Garde." In *The Power of the Powerless, Against the State in Central Eastern Europe*. Ed. John Keane and trans. Paul Wilson. Armonk, NY: M.E Sharpe Inc.

"Uloha Českého svazu žen ve společností se mení." 1997. *Prestižní Žena*, November: 1–2.

United Nations Children's Foundation. 1999. *Women in Transition: Regional Monitoring Report No. 6*. Florence.

United Nations Childrens Programme. 2001. Transmonee 2001 Database. Florence: Innocenti Research Centre, UNICEF.

United Nations Development Program. 1996–8. *The Czech Republic Human Development Report*. New York: Oxford University Press.

―――. 1999. *The Human Development Report 1999*. New York: Oxford University Press.

―――. 2000. *Human Development Report 2000*. New York: Oxford University Press.

United States Agency for International Development. 1999. *Addressing Gender Concerns: The Success of the USAID Gender Plan of Action and USAID Country Programs*. Washington DC.

Vajnerová, Ivana. 1998. "Reklama oblíbená neetická, pobuřující . . ." *Strategie* 9, no. 1: 46–7

Van der Pijl. Kees. 1993. "Soviet Socialism and Passive Revolution." In *Gramsci, Historical Materialism and International Relations*. Ed. Stephen Gill. Cambridge: Cambridge University Press.

―――. 1998. *Transnational Classes and International Relations*. New York: Routledge.

Večerník, Jiři. "Ztračene; sny o střední třide: Co přineslo české společnosti osm let kapitalism?" *Mláda Fronta Dnes*, 2–8 February.

Večerník, Jiři, Joseph Hraba and Allen L. McCutcheon. 1997. "Životni šance mužů a žen v odobí transformace: Srovnáni České a Slovenské republiky." *Sociologický časopis* 33, no. 4: 405–421.

Večerník, Jiří and Petr Matejů. 1999. *Ten years of rebuilding capitalism: Czech society after 1989*. Praha: Academia.

Večerník, Jiří. 1995. "Household Incomes and Social Policies: The Czech Republic in the Period 1989–1995." *SOCO Project Paper No. 25*: Vienna, April.

Večerník, Jiří and Petr Matejů. 1999. *Ten years of rebuilding capitalism: Czech society after 1989*. Praha: Academia.

Verdery, Katherine.1996. *What Was Socialism and Why Did it Fail?* Princeton, NJ: Princeton University Press.

Věšínová, Eva. 1996. "Nejen o čarodejnických kosťátech/Not only about witches broomsticks." *Jedním Okem/One Eye Open* 4: 65–70.

Vizdal, František. 1998. "Miloštným vztahum se na pročavisti dobre dari." *Mláda Fronta Dnes*, September 5.

"Vláda žen spatřila svetlo světa." 2000. *Lidové Noviny*, February 5: 1–2.

Vodrážka, Mírek. 1994. "Before the Great Exodus: The Root of Czech Antifeminism." Trans. Pavla Slaba and Anne Petrov. Lecture delivered at the University of California-Berkeley and Stanford University.

———. 1996. *Feministické rozhovory o "tajných službách."* Praha: Černá Kočka.

Večernik, Jiři. "Ztračene; sny o střední třide: Co přineslo české společnosti osm let kapitalism?" Mláda Fronta Dnes, 2–8 February.

Vrba, T. 1998. "The Trade-offs of a Cozy Life: Corruption in the Czech Republic." *The New Presence*, April.

Wade, Robert. 2001a. "Global Inequality: Winners and Losers." *The Economist*, April 28: 79–81.

———. 2001b. "Globalization And World Income Distribution: Trends, Cases, Consequences And Public Policy." Unpublished manuscript, July.

Wagnerová, Alena. 1996. "Emancipation and Ownership." *Czech Sociological Review* 4, no. 1: 101–108.

———. 1999. "České ženy na ceste od reálného socialismu k reálnému kapitalismu." In *Nové čtení sveta feminismus devadesátých let český ma očima*. Ed. Marie Chřibková, Josef Chuchma and Eva Klimentová. Praha: Marie Chřibková.

Watson, Peggy. 1993. "The Rise of Masculinism in Eastern Europe." *New Left Review* 198.

———. 1995. "Explaining Rising Mortality Among Men in Eastern Europe." *Social Science and Medicine* 41, no. 7: 923–30.

———. 1997. "Civil Society and the Politics of Difference in Eastern Europe." In

Joan W. Scott, Cora Kaplan, and Debra Keates, eds. *Transitions, Environments, Translations: Feminisms in International Politics*. New York: Routledge, pp. 21–29.

———. 2000. "Re-thinking transition." *International Feminist Journal of Politics* 2, no. 2: 185-213.

Waxman, Sharon. 1993. "The Newest Profession: They Left Eastern Europe With Capitalist Dreams. Now They're on the Market." *The Washington Post*, September 8: D1, 4.

Waylen, Georgina. 1994. "Women and Democratisation: Conceptualising Gender Relations in Transition Politics." *World Politics* 46: 327–54.

Wedel, Janine. 1998. *Collision and Collusion: The Strange Case of Western Aid to Eastern Europe 1989–1998*. New York: St. Martins Press.

Weldes, Jutta, Mark Laffey, Hugh Gusterson and Raymond Duvall, Eds. 1999. *Cultures of Insecurity: States, Communities, and the Production of Danger*. Minneapolis: University of Minnesota.

Werbowski, Michael. 1998. "Phare mess a taste of EU." *The Prague Post*, July 22–29.

Weschler, Lawrence. 1992. "The Velvet Purge: The Trials of Jan Kavan." *The New Yorker*, October 19: 66–96.

Wieniecki, Jan. 1996. "Letter to the Editor: Professors Kabaj and Kowalik Versus the Facts." *Transition Newsletter*, 3, November/December.

Williams, Brackette, Ed. 1996. *Women Out of Place: The Gender of Agency and the Race of Nationality*. New York: Routledge.

Williams, Kieran. 1997. *The Prague Spring and its Aftermath: Czechoslovak Politics 1968–70*. Cambridge: Cambridge University Press.

Williamson, John, Ed. 1994. *The Political Economy of Policy Reform*. Washington DC: Institute for International Economics.

Williamson, Judith. 1986. "Woman as an island: Femininity and colonisation." In *Studies in Entertainment: Critical Approaches to Mass Culture*. Ed. Tanya Modelski. Bloomington: Indiana University Press.

Williamson, Oliver. 1985. *The Economic Institutions of Capitalism*. New York: Free Press.

Wheatly, Keith. 1992. "Overpaid, Oversexed, and All-Over Prague." *The Times* (London), April 11.

White Paper on Czechoslovakia. 1977. (Paris: International Committee for the Support of Charter 77 in Czechoslovakia).

Whitley, Richard. 1999. *Divergent Capitalisms; The Social Structuring and Change of Business Systems*. Oxford: Oxford University Press.

Whitworth, Sandra. 1994. *Feminism and International Relations: Towards a Political Economy of Gender in Interstate and Non-Governmental Institutions*. London: Macmillan.

———. 2000. "Theory as Exclusion: Gender and International Political Economy."

In *Political Economy and a Changing Global Order.* Second Edition. Eds. Richard Stubbs and Geoffrey R.D Underhill. London: Macmillan.

Wolchik, Sharon. L. 1981. "The Status of Women in a Socialist Order: The case of Czechoslovakia." *Slavic Review* 38, no. 4: 583–602

———. 1981. "Elite Strategies toward Women in Czechoslovakia: Liberalization or mobilization?" *Studies in Comparative Communism* 19, nos. 2–3: 123–42

———. 1994. "Women and the Politics of Transition in the Czech and Slovak Republics." In *Women in the Politics of Post-communist Eastern Europe.* Ed. Marilyn Rueschemeyer. London: M.E Sharpe Inc.

Wolchik, Sharon L. and Alfred G. Meyer. Eds. 1985. *Women, State and Party in Eastern Europe.* Durham: Duke University Press.

Woodward, Alison E. 2001. "Gender Mainstreaming in European Policy: Innovation or Deception?" Paper presented at the Annual Meeting of the American Political Science Association, San Francisco, September.

World Bank. 1996. *From Plan to Market: 1996 World Development Report.* Washington DC: International Bank for Reconstruction and Development/World Bank.

———.2000a. *World Development Indicators CD Rom.* Washington DC: IBRD/ World Bank.

———. 2000b. *Making the Transition Work for Everyone: Poverty and Inequality in Europe and Central Asia.* Prague: World Bank.

———. 2001. *2001 World Development Report.* Washington DC: IRBD/World Bank.

Yeznikian, Oliver. 1981. "Consommation et controle du citoyen: Observations en Tchecoslovaquie." *Espirit* 2: 157–161.

Young, Brigitte. 1999. *The Triumph of the Fatherland: German Unification and the Marginalization of Women.* Ann Arbor: University of Michigan Press.

Zachvalová, Kateřina. 1999. "He cannot get pregnant." *Transitions* 8, no. 7.

Zahálková, Vera. 1968. "Mapa politických práv žen," *Vlasta* 19, May 8: 16–17.

Zelený Krůh. 1996. *Růže Mezi Trním: Ženy v Politikém životů,* (Hands between thorns: Women in Political Life) Praha: Report from the Seminar Women and Politics, 3–5 May.

"Zelezný se omluvil Buzkově." 1996. *Lidové Noviny,* May 20: 3.

"Zeman prý nenašel ženu, která by mohla sedet ve vládů." *Lidové Noviny,* February 12: 2.

Zemplínerová, Alena. 1997. "The Role of Foreign Enterprises in the Privatization and Restructuring of the Czech Economy" WIW Research Report No. 238, The Vienna Institue for Comparative Economic Studies.

"Ženám chýbí společna činnost, ale už na to přísly." 1996. *Prestiž* 2: 3.

"Ženská Otázka." 1998. *The Prague Tribune,* March.

"Ženy mohou dát politice jiný rozmer." 1996. *Lidové Noviny,* May 20: 2.

"Ženy patři k plotne, muži zase ke strojum." 1998. *Mláda Fronta Dnes*, September
    5: 1.
"Ženy v České Republice berou stale o čtvrtinu méne penéz než muži." 1998. *Lidové
    Noviny*, April 14: 1.
Žižek, Slavoj. 1992. "Eastern European Liberalism and its Discontents." *New German Critique* 57: 25–49.

Index